LITERARY/CULTURAL THEORY

POSTSECULAR THEORY

Literary/Cultural Theory provides concise and lucid introductions to a range of key concepts and theorists in contemporary literary and cultural theory. Original and contemporary in presentation, and eschewing jargon, each book in the series presents students of humanities and social sciences exhaustive overviews of theories and theorists, while also introducing them to the mechanics of reading literary/cultural texts using critical tools. Each book also carries glossaries of key terms and ideas, and pointers for further reading and research. Written by scholar-teachers who have taught critical theory for years, and vetted by some of the foremost experts in the field, the series Literary/Cultural Theory is indispensable to students and teachers.

Series Editors

Allen Hibbard
Middle Tennessee State University

Andrew Slade
University of Dayton

Herman Rapaport
Wake Forest University

Imre Szeman
University of Alberta

Krishna Sen
University of Calcutta

Scott Slovic
University of Idaho

Sumit Chakrabarti
Presidency University, Kolkata

Also in the series

Psychoanalytic Theory and Criticism
Feminisms
Jacques Lacan
Dalit Literature and Criticism
Ecocriticism
Postcolonialism Now
Periyar
Marxist Literary and Cultural Theory
Nations and Nationalisms
Mikhail Bakhtin
Popular Culture
Queer Studies
Frantz Fanon

LITERARY/CULTURAL THEORY

POSTSECULAR THEORY

TEXTS AND CONTEXTS

SHUHITA BHATTACHARJEE
IIT Hyderabad

Edited by
SUMIT CHAKRABARTI
Presidency University, Kolkata

Orient BlackSwan

All rights reserved. No part of this book may be modified, reproduced or utilised in any form, or by any means, electronic or mechanical, including photocopying, recording or by any information storage and retrieval system, in any form of binding or cover other than in which it is published, without permission in writing from the publisher.

POSTSECULAR THEORY: TEXTS AND CONTEXTS

ORIENT BLACKSWAN PRIVATE LIMITED

Registered Office
3-6-752 Himayatnagar, Hyderabad 500 029, Telangana, India
Email: centraloffice@orientblackswan.com

Other Offices
Bengaluru, Chennai, Guwahati, Hyderabad, Kolkata, Mumbai, New Delhi, Noida, Patna, Visakhapatnam

© Orient Blackswan Private Limited 2023
First published 2023

ISBN 978 93 5442 140 2

Typeset in Aldine 401 BT 10.5/13 *by*
Akhil Offset Printers
Hyderabad 500 020

Printed at
Navya Printers, Hyderabad 500 013

Published by
Orient Blackswan Private Limited
3-6-752, Himayatnagar,
Hyderabad 500 029, Telangana, India
Email: info@orientblackswan.com

034106

Contents

Editor's Preface   *vii*
Author's Preface   *xi*
Acknowledgements   *xiii*

1. The Problem of Faith and the Postsecular   1
2. Surveying the Field   21
3. The Critique of Postsecular Studies   67
4. The 'Secular Turn' of the Enlightenment   91
   The Historical Context and the Case of Matthew Lewis's The Monk
5. Nineteenth-Century Anxieties and Modern Perspectives   108
6. The New Woman of Faith and Fears in Cholmondeley's *Red Pottage*   118
7. The British 'Crisis of Faith' in Fin-de-Siècle Novels of Colonial India   150
8. Romancing Religious Hybridity   183
   Science, Religion, and the Tensions of the 'Secular' in Corelli's A Romance of Two Worlds
9. The Perils of 'Home' and Paradoxes of the Hijab   212
   Revisiting Rebellion and Liberal Agency in Satrapi's Persepolis

Editor's Preface

For an academic within the discipline of the humanities the question of representation has always been a fraught one. Agency is the entry point, and thereafter tributaries multiply depending on ideological fit or political manoeuvres. The site of play vacillates between body and mind, geopolitical cartographies, landscapes of dissent defined according to synchronic or diachronic tropes of engagement, radical alterity meant to subvert discursive certainties, and the list is endless. Sophisticated, all of them, trained in terminology and jargon, deft methodologies that prise open shibboleths. We do not, or rarely, talk about religion though. Relegated mostly to roundtables or television debates, newspaper editorials or magazine cover stories, help books and high philosophy—the space of theoretical engagement stands out as a site of silence. The silence is often a well-intentioned strategy to avert the 'the risk of getting hijacked for right-wing agendas' (6), as the author of this volume says. But is it not through the interstices of such theoretical silence, such apparent incomprehension, or deliberate historical amnesia of what would constitute religion or religiosity, that easy narratives of essentialisms and appropriations claim legitimacy? As Bhattacharjee notes, '[a]llowing the very idea of faith to be appropriated by a resurgent right amounts to surrendering ownership of a fundamental element of human experience that impacts our lived political, sociocultural and economic realities in powerful ways' (6). In the face of a general, and perhaps deliberate silence, this volume attempts a theoretical intervention into the secular and the religious, to say what is always felt but left unsaid. However, the author also remarks that talking about the meaning or value of faith in our contemporary world is challenging because 'right-wing parties use religion-based rhetoric to victoriously claim the political destinies' of countries, or 'deeply divisive [religious] ideologies are employed to deny basic human rights' (4). Both the history and the geography of the world bear ample testimony to the massacres that are 'enacted by political factions in the name of religion ... shatter[ing] the limits of our comprehension, tolerance and humanity' (6). Given this context, the volume also discusses the substantial body of critique that has grown around the domain of postsecular theory and that questions postsecular theory's 'perilous scholarly practice of moral relativism and the problematic overturning of the fabric of democratic liberalism that this involves' (80). Therefore, in the same breath that we talk about the postmodern or the postcolonial, it is time that we initiate a discussion on the postsecular in all of its complexity. This volume is one of the very few in the subcontinent to be taking up the question of the postsecular. I have always felt that this series needed this particular volume.

In his essay 'Religious Experience as Event and Interpretation', the philosopher Aldo Gargani issues a necessary caveat against 'the metaphysics of presence of theological objects' (114) that would relegate God to being an idealised anthropomorphic entity, beyond the empirical, and within a different ontological realm. It is the way of religious discourse, argues Gargani, to situate the question of the religious beyond the hermeneutic, and therefore away from the secular. The question of the secular has a performative immediacy, and this needs to be iterated within theoretical discourse. This is not to cancel out the speculative, nor to delegitimise the metaphysical intent of the mysterious in God. This is the necessary clearing of space for the hermeneutic, for a journey from transcendence to immanence, for the historicity of religious intention to be studied through the lens of theory. In his argument Gargani creates a postsecular space without naming it, by insisting on divesting the metaphysical charge from religious traditions, thereby opening it up towards interpretative perspectives. In a similar vein, in his essay 'Faith and Knowledge: The Two Sources of "Religion" at the Limits of Reason Alone', Derrida talks about the evil of radical abstraction that is intrinsically linked to the idea of religion (2). He posits the question of religiosity within the Kantian regime of 'reason' by arguing how religion is also a 'political event' that belongs to the 'history of democracy' (8). In the same vein, Maurizio Ferraris argues, in his essay 'The Meaning of Being as a Determinate Ontic Trace', that the idea of *kenosis* at the heart of most religions (in this case Christianity) legitimises the foregrounding of the miraculous over the moral. As a challenge to such a conception, Ferraris too brings in the

Kantian dialectic of reason and argues that the idea of 'secularization may want to hang on to a moral theology and a political theology' (172). It is this sense of the religious as an *event* within the space of the secular, its possibility of creating interpretive communities, that demystify or deconstruct the metaphysical within a secular space. Although, however, the postsecular will not be a reductive space that transforms the metaphysical to the taxonomic, the definitional or the theoretical. It merely initiates a space for conflict and heterogeneity where one can place and discuss religion as a problematic.

The secular, therefore, creates the necessary political space for the interpretive possibilities of religion and religiosity. The philosopher Arindam Chakrabarti brings in the idea of 'sanskara' as an intuitive marker within this space of the political. How does one read the conception of sanskara? One does not fail to notice the already problematised space created by the very act of trying to define sanskara: one the one hand it means reformation or renovation; on the other, it means faith or belief. It is within this apparent ambiguity, this necessary equivocation that the narrative of the secular within the religious must play itself out. Chakrabarti refers to Lord Krishna of the Gita who claims he is sanskara himself and asks everyone to relinquish religion (73). This is the part of faith or belief. On the other hand, Chakrabarti argues that if one were to let go of traditional knowledge of religions and, in the name of sanskara or reformation, wants to build a multistoried conglomeration of all religions in place of the Taj Mahal (75), that becomes political intent. For him, therefore, the space of the political needs to be a nuanced site for the playing out of the secular. The contours of the secular are also too many, and equally fraught.

One cannot overemphasise the need for such a volume on postsecularism in the context of both history and culture, and within the domain of the theoretical. Shuhita Bhattacharjee has taken her time to write this volume, and has unpacked all the complicated strands of the debate from the nineteenth through the twentieth century to the present. As a scholar of literature she has stuck to her specialisation and located the debate within the literary space. I hope this volume will initiate necessary debate and discussion and, in its wake, inspire essays and collections on the postsecular from other disciplinary perspectives. This is an important contribution to the series.

REFERENCES

Chakrabarti, Arindam. *Dharma ekhon jorakranto. Mononer Modhu.* Gaangchil, 2014. 71–81.

Derrida, Jacques. 'Faith and Knowledge: The Two Sources of "Religion" at the Limits of Reason Alone'. *Religion.* Ed. Jacques Derrida and Gianni Vattimo. Stanford UP, 1998. 1–78.

Ferraris, Maurizio. 'The Meaning of Being as a Determinate Ontic Trace'. *Religion.* Ed. Jacques Derrida and Gianni Vattimo. Stanford UP, 1998. 170–99.

Gargani, Aldo. 'Religious Experience as Event and Interpretation'. *Religion.* Ed. Jacques Derrida and Gianni Vattimo. Stanford UP, 1998. 111–35.

Author's Preface

As I meandered through my writing of this monograph, the world erupted with violence along religious lines. Even as this book heads to the press, news has arrived that Salman Rushdie was stabbed on a New York stage, Umar Khalid continues to be held in an Indian prison for political dissent, and Roe v. Wade has been overturned by vociferous political stratagem. At the same time, two apparently unremarkable episodes of conversation from the past have stayed with me. The first took place at a weeklong graduate seminar on 'Religion and the Postsecular' at a North American university that I attended along with several devout Catholic, Methodist and Buddhist friends. On one of our more flippant breaks, as we sat around discussing the best ways to eat right, one among our cohort who happened to be a practising Catholic weighed in. With a kind smile she confessed that her approach was to treat the body like a temple and to desist from thrusting upon it anything that we would not carry into one. For a few moments our circle of budding academics sat in silence grappling with her unusual response. The other incident was from a few weeks ago when I was stunned by one of my students who, hijab-clad and hence naturally intimidated by the recent furore against certain forms of religious clothing in Karnataka schools, asked my permission to drape her headscarf while attending my lecture. My consternation on both occasions draws me to a closer examination of the subject at hand. Beyond the shadow of a doubt, the promise of faith as well as the threat of its militant inverse occupies our current sociopolitical landscape. This convulsive religion-based violence throws a field such as Postsecular Studies into polemical relevance.

The first segment of this volume—consisting of three chapters—is a detailed literature review that aims to fill a gap in the national academic scene where this field of critical inquiry has not been discussed at length and in the international market where it is far from being mainstreamed. Anthologies of literary and critical theory that carry sections on New Criticism, New Historicism (or Cultural Materialism), cultural studies, or gender, postcolonial, Marxist, queer and psychoanalytic theory do not gesture towards the populous field of postsecular theory. Thus, in this first segment, I chart the basic premises and sustained scholarship of this field, privileging panoramic coverage and critical summation over authorial interpretation and focused analysis. In the last four chapters, I approach this field as a scholar of literature. The conversation in the field of postsecular theory can take place at the interface of several disciplines—religious studies, sociology, philosophy and literature being the most significant. So in this second half of the book, I perform a postsecular analysis of literary texts to model what a praxis of postsecular theory may look like in the field of literature.

Writing about a topic such as this is both onerous and daunting. Danièle Hervieu-Léger notes a key conundrum about choosing religion as a subject of sociological analysis: 'How come that the critical detachment characteristic of a scientific attitude in the social sciences is thought to be more difficult, if not impossible, to attain when the subject matter is religion?' (*Religion as a Chain of Memory* 13). This applies not just to the field of sociology but to the larger tradition of rationalist academic writing in other disciplines where scholarly rumination on religion is typically received with a suspicion of authorial subjectivity/complicity. Being not only disengaged from institutionalised forms of religious practice but also actively resistant to its many discriminatory facets that are instrumentalised to spur/legitimise violence, I brave this perception while admitting to having retained a faith in scholarship's ability to delineate, debate and revivify a text's religious impulses. As such my work will attempt to trace the development of postsecular theory, its exposition of the politics underlying the 'religious-secular' binary, its opposition to both 'religious' and 'secular' fundamentalisms, the problematic implications of some postsecular approaches, and the new directions in literary analysis that emerge from a postsecular perspective.

Acknowledgements

This work has been a long time coming, as I have straddled multiple continents, jobs, life lessons and laptops. I must begin by thanking my place of work, Indian Institute of Technology Hyderabad, that provided me a warm snuggly office and a warmer department where I cradled my project and watched it grow. I feel privileged to acknowledge the deep debt I owe to my friends and mentors at the University of Iowa: Lori Branch who helped me nurture my work with unflinching support, Florence Boos who was my pillar with every personal and academic hurdle, and Teresa Mangum who was a saviour with every unarticulated professional quandary I faced. My thanks to Jeff Cox who was such an incredible force to have behind me, and to Joy Dixon whose support has been unparalleled. I am deeply grateful to Joshua King at Baylor University for his generous friendship that has helped me sift through my ideas. My endless love to my lifelong friends, Shanta Dutta and Purna Banerjee, who have scolded me out of several inelegant misadventures and held my hand through dark times. My thanks to Anupama Mohan for bringing new horizons of friendship and opportunities into my life.

I must thank the University of Iowa for awarding me the Marcus Bach Fellowship and the Stanley Award for International Research. I also wish to express my gratitude to the University of Chicago for the generous support of the Robert L. Platzman Memorial Fellowship. I am deeply thankful to the Lumen Christi Institute in Chicago for the many compelling discussions that it enabled on the role of religion in our academic lives. I cannot but remember fondly those in administrative positions for helping me sustain my academic sanity. Among them are Cherie Hansen-Rieskamp and Erin Hackathorn at the University of Iowa, who made my everyday academic life bearable and even pleasurable in their superhuman ways. I must also thank the extremely helpful librarians at the British Library who helped me over several scholarly puddles with a lot of patience. I am also indebted to

Presidency University for administratively supporting me in every possible way in the past years and to Jadavpur University for inciting the scholar in me in my untrained days. Supriya Chaudhuri, Amlan Das Gupta and Paromita Chakravarti at Jadavpur University loom large on my horizon of admirable brilliance and kind pedagogy. My sincere thanks to Bikram and Sreenath at Orient Blackswan who nudged my work along during its glacial phases and contributed their thoughtful insight. And my loving gratitude to my editor and good friend, Sumit Chakrabarti, whose polite insistence and quiet friendship got me through this project. Without his sturdy support, the intellectual joy would have lost out to logistical nightmares. My deepest thanks, of course, are owed to my colleagues and students for inspiring me.

My labour of love owes its life to my mother for raising me with her characteristic conviction and prayer, my father for his gift of unrelenting madness, and my grandparents who taught me to be brave yet kind. I hold a debt of love to my partner-in-life, Sovini, for infusing meaning in everything. My gratitude extends to my old friends who stood by my work undeterred when challenges were overwhelming. My love to my talented friend, Kinjal, for loaning me a meaningful book cover from his treasure trove. And thanks above all to my several productive airport layovers, my quiet corners in busy libraries, and my pocket-friendly brownies in countless cafeterias. Through my cherished solitude, canopied with resolute friends and fur-babies, my work was born.

Cover Photo by Kinjal Bhattacharyya: A civil engineer and researcher by profession, Kinjal leaves such inanities aside to take the best shots—of places, at people, and in pubs. He loves to travel galore and teases passing moments into framed memories. He captured this image at St Michael's Church, Munich.

Chapter One

The Problem of Faith and the Postsecular

The perception of knowledge and faith as incompatible at best and antagonistic at worst is ubiquitous in our culture today, typically portrayed as a relationship between 'enlightened' ways of thinking and religious proclivities, or between liberal–democratic educational templates and religious codes of behaviour. We can, for instance, see the same polarity at play across the otherwise conflicting responses to the 2017 exhibition *Living with Gods* at the British Museum. Commenting on the exhibition in a *Financial Times* article, Christopher de Bellaigue observes that in the modern world 'a psychologist working on loneliness or a prison governor dealing with radicalisation' would agree that 'a settled faith can give inward succour in a way that quinoa and Zumba classes cannot.' In stark contrast, in his review in *The Guardian*, Jonathan Jones fumes that a few minutes into the exhibition 'his skin started to sizzle' and his 'blood [began] to boil' as he 'truly felt branded inside, marked out as a reprobate' because the premise of the event was 'that belief in God(s) is such a universal human trait that if you lack it, you may not be human.' The knowledge–faith binary is crystallised in a recent image widely circulating on social media that shows a horde of people, ostensibly women, in stifling headscarves knotted around their bodies and walking in the same direction as though their collective movement is unthinking or preprogrammed. Contrast is provided by a single woman who, book in hand and stripped of the hijab, walks defiantly against the tide. Emerging at the opposite end of the battalion of visibly blinded followers, she approaches the viewer while deeply engrossed in reading. The image both assumes and emphasises a need to surrender the hijab in order to learn from the book, to which the woman has clearly been freshly introduced.

No one captures this polarity between faith and learning better than the figure of Malala Yousafzai, a young Pakistani activist who was shot by the Taliban for championing girls' education. After attracting global attention as the winner of the Nobel Peace Prize, she emerged at the centre of Western discourses as the prototypical Muslim girl who protested religious fundamentalism in order to secure access to knowledge. Malala's own words endorse these common conceptual categories: 'The extremists have shown what frightens them most—A girl with a book', she once tweeted (@Malala). In the case of this brave girl, always dressed in her hijab and sometimes caught delicately rearranging it in public view, the enigmatic headdress acquires a far more ingestible charge for the Western onlooker because of the way she privileges 'knowledge'/ education over what is mistakenly but widely perceived as an expression of 'faith'—Islamist fundamentalism. In his *New York Times* opinion piece titled 'Before Malala', William Dalrymple's incisive comments are equally revealing. Observing the simplistic and problematic way in which the whole of the Pashtun region is represented as 'ultraconservative and super-patriarchal' in contemporary cultural and scholarly narratives, Dalrymple focuses on the portrayal of the religious (hijab-clad) woman, and suggests that there is 'something disturbing about the outpouring of praise' for Malala. His column helps us identify the implicit narratives brought into play through the euphoric and unambiguous Western endorsement of Malala—a figure who translates easily into the palatable Western archetype of the religious (veiled) woman seeking knowledge and condemning (excessive) religious faith. Dalrymple drives this point home by offsetting the popular response Malala receives against the mainstream invisibility of Malalai of Maiwand, after whom Malala is named. For most Pashtuns, he notes, the name Malala 'conjures up not a brave teenage supporter of education, but an equally brave teenage heroine who turned the tide of a crucial battle during the second Anglo-Afghan war.' The fiery opposer of Western domination 'does not appear in any British account of the

Battle of Maiwand.' Yet according to Afghan sources her actions brought about 'the British Empire's greatest defeat in a pitched battle in the course of the nineteenth century.' While the emotional charge of Malala Yousafzayi's veil is neutralised by her insistence on an education that is implicitly Western and by her subsequent enrolment at (and graduation from) Oxford University, Pashtun oral tradition records Malalai taking to the battlefield to defeat the British army. Grabbing 'a fallen flag—or in some versions her veil', Dalrymple notes, Malalai recites an inspiring verse to shake her fiancé out of a state of fear-induced paralysis in battle. Having defied the widely accepted hierarchy of knowledge over faith, the far less ingestible figure of Malalai is therefore relegated into invisibility, away from mainstream geopolitics and culture.

Of course, this polarity between knowledge and faith does not go unchallenged in creative and scholarly works of literature and culture. It implodes, for instance, in Mohsin Hamid's *The Reluctant Fundamentalist* (a work that I will study in detail in chapter two), when the protagonist, Changez, realises that American commerce is fundamentally premised on an inhumane, unthinking and arrogant pursuit of profit beyond all other values or considerations, and is therefore no different from the religious fundamentalism that is so universally singled out as the evil germ of all global crises. With this realisation, Hamid dismantles the knowledge–faith binary, and the false dichotomy of Western progress and (Islamist) religious fundamentalism.

Despite these insights and interventions, overwhelming cultural forces make it impossible to see beyond predominant Western-centric hierarchies. Contentious debates and controversies centre on the *relevance* of faith in an age of global commercialism, or even the *desirability* of faith given its potential for distortion into fundamentalist violence. In this perplexing and perilous historical moment, it has become increasingly challenging to speak of religion without experiencing self-imposed shame or resorting to socially-imposed categories. As Mark C. Taylor observes in *About Religion*, 'To God we have become unaccustomed; of God we have become unaccustomed to speak, even to think, especially to write. If we slip and find ourselves thinking, speaking, even writing of God, it seems embarrassing, horribly embarrassing—even when our inquiry is critical. All of this God stuff was supposed to have been over a long time ago' (30).

Postsecular theory takes up this onerous task from various disciplinary perspectives. The two chapters which follow review key works of postsecular theory along with the substantial body of critical literature that emerged in response. Any discussion of postsecularism should first acknowledge that it is a difficult time to have this conversation, and that effective discussion can only take place in an insulated environment with a select audience. Engaging with this field is challenging because it requires us to talk about the meaning or value of faith; doing so is problematic in a world where right-wing parties use religion-based rhetoric to victoriously claim the political destinies of vibrant democracies and less secure polities alike, whether in India, the United States or Brazil.

Based on self-proclaimed religious justifications, deeply divisive ideologies are employed to deny basic human rights to select portions of the population, particularly minorities. Examples of this behaviour are countless and horrifying. In parts of the United States and the world, for instance, expectant mothers are denied the right to abort while the LGBTQ community is denied the right to marry. In India, women's legal right to worship in the Sabarimala Temple is still fervently opposed in the popular domain, members of the 'lower' castes are criminally violated in the name of Hinduism, and pogroms against religious minorities are launched under the garb of citizenship regulations and immigration control. Within the Catholic Church, institutionalised immunity is often extended to priests embroiled in cases of child sexual abuse.[1] In other cases, religious vocabularies are used as an instrument to stage mass slaughter or indiscriminate genocide: the executions carried out by the Islamic State (ISIS) in Syria in the name of the Caliphate, the Godhra riots orchestrated by the state through politicised Hindutva armies, or the 2019 mobilisation of violent mobs against Muslim communities in India under the pretext of the Citizenship Amendment Act all come to mind, among countless other examples.[2] In *Religion and the City in India*, Supriya Chaudhuri delineates the perils of contemporary Indian votebank politics observing how the race for 'majoritarian support' has ensured that 'religious prejudice constitutes political capital' and those in power instrumentalise 'the spatial contiguities of urban living to provoke communal conflicts' (5). Patches of land lacerated by wars, riots and terrorist attacks, along with the resultant human rights violations—all staged in the borrowed name of religion—are swelling in size at a frightening pace and can be demarcated on maps with disturbing ease as zones of conflict.

Conflict between human rights and religious institutions/practices remains a visible reality for all and a problem for postsecular thought. When the celebrated Indian poet-lyricist and voice of the educated social conscience, Javed Akhtar, is honoured with the Richard Dawkins Award[3] after decades of holding religious dogma up to scrutiny and protesting the suppression of human rights, and when a nation raw and reeling from religion-based violence revels in the glory and recognition of his work, it seems both logical and admirable.[4] This perceived clash between religion and human rights is the epicentre of dramatic action in Marius von Mayenbur's *Martyr*, which highlights the violent exclusions associated with a literal and conservative interpretation of the scripture. The protagonist, Benjamin, in dogged and thoughtless pursuit of what he considers to be religion, uses biblical quotations to argue against women wearing bikinis, female teachers instructing men and any free expression of sexuality (particularly, gay sexuality). Yet, at the same time, he strategically draws upon established human rights discourses to falsely accuse his teacher of sexually abusing him.

The perils and hypocrisies of such a fundamentalist stance, which denies human rights in the name of (a literally and narrowly interpreted) religion, are also highlighted in the American television series on the lives of staffers in the White House, *The West Wing*. In the third episode of season two, US President Josiah Bartlet encounters Dr Jenna Jacobs. Jacobs remains seated when he walks into the room, insulting the American convention of rising for the president. In a fit of controlled anger, he lambasts the right-wing radio talkshow host for her regressive interpretation of scripture and the way she popularises it on her show by castigating homosexuals. The president begins by sarcastically insinuating that he likes her show for how she announces on live radio that homosexuality is 'an abomination'. When she retaliates by saying that it is the Bible that sees homosexuality as an abomination, he verbally spars with her. He quotes verses from the Bible which seem to condemn modern everyday living—from forbidding the touching of a dead pig's skin (which is what is used to make a football), to punishing one's mother with immolation for wearing garments made from different threads. He reminds her of the ways in which the literal prescriptions of the Bible often offend our modern rights and sensibilities, and how we have culturally outgrown and politically overcome the most archaic, regressive and discriminatory injunctions of the Bible. The conversation is notable in part for its thrilling and dramatic rendering of a point often recorded in insightful scholarship, and in part because it indicates the popular acceptability of the view voiced by the President.

In reality, rampant violence is ubiquitous within faith-based politics and institutionalised religious patriarchy. Across the globe, injustices and massacres enacted by political factions in the name of religion have shattered the limits of our comprehension, tolerance and humanity. Scholars intuit the ways in which any writing about faith at this historical moment runs the risk of getting hijacked for right-wing agendas. In the course of discussing their work, numerous scholars who engage with postsecular studies have encountered legitimate fears surrounding this possibility in dissertation defences, at conferences and on interview panels. Yet such scholars would point out that faith, whether at the level of textual reading or institutional observance, is a reality in the lives of billions. Even while admitting the violent ideological appropriation and instrumentalisation of religion in present-day India, Supriya Chaudhuri indicates the centrality of religious meaning and practice within Indian cityscapes, noting how these urban religious manifestations—whether as multiple permanent/semi-permanent 'small consecrations' or more ephemeral 'large public performances of religious faith'—create 'sacred space within the dead surfaces of everyday urban existence' (5). Allowing the very idea of faith to be appropriated by a resurgent right wing amounts to surrendering ownership of a constitutive element of human experience that impacts our lived political, sociocultural and economic realities in powerful ways.

Religion is also personal in its allegiances and disavowals. As Graham Ward notes in 'The Future of Religion', countless arguments on the subject of 'true religion' are sufficient indication that the study of religion is 'a field of tense passions and convictions in which friends are sought and enemies identified' (180). But given that we inhabit a modernity where religion is tuned into a rhetorical tool for discrimination and violence, both at an individual level and as part of organised state machinery, we need to keep reminding ourselves that this is not the only template for understanding or experiencing faith. Our scholarly duty likewise demands that we consider a diverse and proliferating set of theoretical works, which have overlapping arguments despite widely different contexts and purposes, nestled under the late-twentieth-century term 'postsecular'. Whether from a position of concurrence or criticism, we are obligated to scrutinise this set of observations and interventions into religious practices and beliefs.

What postsecular theory understands as 'religion' or 'religious faith' will gradually become clearer. However, this monograph does not call upon the reader to identify or declare a specific denominational allegiance or sectarian affiliation. It also does not attempt to justify religious practices that offend sensibilities or deny human rights. Instead, it reviews the substantial body of postsecular scholarship emerging from the fields of anthropology, historiography and literary criticism. This scholarship understands faith to be inherent to human experience, to the desire for meaning and to the structures of our sociopolitical thought. Postsecular philosopher John Caputo remarks that even though 'the great religions of the world are important and without them we would quickly lose sight of religious categories and practices', religion should *not* be narrowly understood as 'something confessional or sectarian, like being a Muslim or a Hindu, a Catholic or a Protestant' (*On Religion* 9). As a useful starting point for a much longer and more complicated explanation drawn from several postsecular critics, I find Caputo's idea of faith particularly productive. He understands the religious not by 'distinguishing "religious people," . . . who go to church on

Sunday morning, from non-religious people who stay home and read *The Sunday New York Times.*' Instead, he speaks 'of the religious *in* people, *in* all of us' (9; emphasis added). Taking religion to mean the ways that human beings are religious, he puts it 'on a par with being political or being artistic', in other words, being religious refers to 'a basic structure of human experience and even . . . the very thing that most constitutes human experience as experience' (9).

While this might appear to be a simplistic generalisation, it is actually a critical sociological axiom that builds on a philosophical insight. Christian Smith observes that while sociology criticises essentialism and purports to be objective, it is itself built on a set of presumptions. According to Smith, each and every sociological claim 'assume[s] some account of human motivations' that we typically fail to acknowledge in our sociological works (4). This includes the notion that our modern age is 'atheistic' or 'secular'[5] (which I later refer to as the 'secularisation thesis'). Departing from this tendency, Smith declares at the outset that he will be operating with the manifestly essentialist presumption that 'the animals we call human beings share an identifiable and peculiar set of capacities and proclivities', an 'underlying structure of human personhood' (3). This set of shared characteristics 'distinguishes . . . [human beings] significantly from other animals on this planet' (3) because they are 'moral, believing animals' (7). From this philosophical assumption, Smith arrives at a sociological explanation for 'our persistent practice of sacralizing physical and mental objects' (56). In other words, open acceptance of the philosophical premise that human beings are 'moral, believing animals' allows Smith to productively arrive at a sociological understanding of why and how human communities across history impute qualities of holiness or sacredness to things or ideas (7).

Grounded in such premises, postsecular readings dislodge the confidence of narratives that declare religions obsolete within the modern era or reduce beliefs to violent fundamentalism— narratives that make faith inadmissible at the level of vocabulary and experience alike. Graham Ward observes that in the current moment 'the major cultural wars are between faith communities and the remnants of the "secular," liberal worldview' (*True Religion* ix). This book will demonstrate how postsecular scholars and literary works suggest that fundamentalism is not limited to the use of religious concepts as instruments. The Western politico-cultural template of democratic liberalism, with its roots in hierarchies of exploitation, also needs to be recognised for the essentially fundamentalist ways in which it invalidates the meaning of certain types of experiences and suppresses other states of being. For instance, in *Seven Types of Atheism*, bestselling contemporary atheist John Gray (peer of Richard Dawkins, Daniel Dennett and Sam Harris) details how historical crimes and human rights violations were carried out in the name of science as often as in the name of religion. As Magdalena Maczynska explains, unlike fundamentalism of both these kinds ('religious' and 'secular'), the 'postsecular engagement with religion is the opposite of fundamentalism, valuing messiness over order and ambiguity over certainty' (81).

Unlike 'religious' and 'secular' fundamentalism, postsecular scholarship concentrates on the acute cultural impoverishment that results from denying the significance and meaning of faith. This scholarship does not participate in the project of attributing blame to either religious or 'secular' fundamentalism. Instead, it aims to reveal how geopolitical dynamics leave us with desiccated Western definitions of 'liberty' that discredit whole realms of meaningful action in our lives—actions that revolve around sacrifice, pain and suffering. This interpretive approach is shaped by a view of religious faith described most insightfully by Caputo: that at the heart of the truly religious experience lies an openness to the prospect of dwelling in uncertainty, and a surrender to the 'possibility of the impossible' (*On Religion* 67). Caputo writes: 'the mark of a religious sensibility' is the 'movement of living on the limit of the possible, in hope for and expectation of the impossible, a reality beyond the real' (67). This view lies at the heart of most postsecular theory as I understand it and undergirds my analysis of literary texts in later chapters. The field that emerges from it carries a 'postcritical and postsecular posture' that 'accommodates th[is] passion for the impossible' and harnesses it in literary-cultural analyses (67).

Before committing to this view of religious sensibility and experience as the overarching rubric for postsecular criticism, it is important to briefly recount the problem that arises when one attempts to define religion and adopt it as an object of academic study. As an academic concept, religion has been defined most exhaustively and consistently within the disciplines of sociology and philosophy. According to French sociologist Danièle Hervieu-Léger, the sociology of religion aims to understand the 'structures and the dynamics of modern religious belief' not only by looking at 'beliefs, which are the supreme objects of individual and collective convictions', but also at 'the body of practices, behaviour and institutions in which these beliefs find expression' (3). Debate over the most appropriate designation for this project ('religious sociology, sociology of religion, [or] sociology of religions') emphasises the 'problem of the definition of religion' (9). A sociological approach to religion derives from the academic choice to treat religion 'as a *social phenomenon*' explaining it 'in terms of other social phenomena' and excluding the supernatural as subject matter (9, emphasis added). Gabriel Le Bras likewise wrote about the difficulty of even defining a 'sociology of religion' in the singular, given the plurality of religions. He concludes that a common aim and subject matter for this branch of sociology can only be identified if what is examined is 'the structure and nature of organized groups for whom the sacred provides both the principle and the purpose' (qtd. in Hervieu-Léger 11). In other words, sociology must 'restrict its scope to the community and refrain from exploring "the mysteries of the supernatural"' (11). Thus, the sociology of religion struggles to even arrive at a basic designation for the subject matter, and ultimately limits its jurisdiction to the 'observation of social groups' over engagement with the 'sacred' (11).

When it comes to the discipline of philosophy, efforts to define a philosophy of religion confront very similar (albeit less self-reflexive) dilemmas over the object of study. Even a cursory look reveals contradictions inherent in the very founding assumptions of the field called 'philosophy of religion'. Brian Davies notes that as a distinct branch of philosophy, it is 'an essentially Western phenomenon'; although philosophers have discussed religious topics throughout history, the very notion that there could be such a branch first clearly emerged in the work of German philosopher Georg Wilhelm Friedrich Hegel (2). In their anthology *Philosophy of Religion*, editors Peterson, Hasker, Reichenbach and Basinger note the fundamental opposition between the fields of philosophy and religion, observing that 'philosophy of religion' is 'clearly a branch of philosophy' and 'should not be confused with religion itself or even theology' (Peterson et al. 1). Philosophy aims to 'analyze and critically evaluate', which means the philosophy of religion 'critical[ly] examin[es] . . . basic religious concepts and beliefs'. But religion itself is 'notoriously difficult to define' and therefore intrinsically at odds with the philosophical impulse to be 'as objective and intellectually rigorous as possible' (1). Twentieth-century 'philosophy of religion' has mostly taken an 'analytic' approach, focusing on the 'meaning, consistency, coherence, reasonableness, justification, and truth of our beliefs' (2). Most work was invested in exposing the mendacity of religious claims wherever detectable, but the last quarter of the century saw a dramatic change as the 'positivistic principle of verifiability' was deemed 'inadequate even for science, let alone religion' (2). This latter impulse signalled a shift associated with the postsecular moment itself, yet as a discipline, philosophy has stumbled against the same barriers that greeted sociology when it took up religion as a topic of academic study. Despite these challenges, both sociology and philosophy have continued to engage analytically with this vast area of human experience and thought.

The other scholarly outlet through which religion has received serious treatment is literary criticism. This critical enterprise has traditionally involved exercises such as identifying religious themes and motifs in literary works, or interpreting literary-cultural compositions in light of religious intonations found in historical settings or authorial biographies. This book focuses on postsecular literary criticism, which is a deeper project that requires a major shift in disciplinary emphasis. As Kathryn Ludwig explains, the postsecular 'indicates a shift in the status of the religious within scholarly inquiry' and is ultimately 'a reworking of the story we tell about ourselves' (512). It dismantles an ideological formulation of the religious and the 'secular' as binary, which is common in both popular and scholarly perception, and explores the possibility of envisioning the 'miraculous'—a notion that the 'secularist' regime of post-Enlightenment modernity has excluded from consideration.

The miraculous is ostensibly impossible. In Caputo's formulation, the 'impossible is a defining religious category' for 'with God, everything is possible, even *the* impossible', given that the impossible 'is all part of a divine day's work for God, part of God's job description' (*On Religion* 10). Caputo's emphasis on the 'impossible', or what Mary Gordon calls 'the ungraspable, the incomprehensible', is far from simplistic (3). In fact, it is critical to grasping the heart of religious sensibility. Simone Weil describes this religious state as one in which 'our thought . . . [is] empty, waiting, not seeking anything, but ready to receive in its naked truth the object that is to penetrate it' (49).

In his extended ruminations on messianism, French philosopher Jacques Derrida likewise proposes the incomprehensibility of the religious experience and the open-ended wait for the arrival of the divine. Noting the significance of uncertainty as an element of religious sensibility in *The Gift of Death*, Derrida remarks that history is tied to 'religious faith through a form of involvement with the other that is a venture into absolute risk, beyond knowledge and certainty' (5). The 'essence of the religious'—engagement with an absolute 'other' located beyond the reach of comprehension, and the waiting for its coming—is clearest in his discussions of the messianic, a concept he discovers through Marx (49). Along with contributions from Freud and Nietzsche, Marx's devastating critique of religion is seen as the foundation of 'secular' modernity. But, Derrida nonetheless identifies a 'messianic eschatology' in 'Marxist science or critique', one that is 'messianic without messianism, an idea of justice' underlying the critique itself and deconstruction in particular (*Spectres of Marx* 59). According to Derrida, Marxist critique necessarily carries a messianic eschatology, which also underlies any supposedly 'secular' or atheistic critique of religion. Arguing along these lines, Derrida locates the essence of religion even within a critique that aims to systematically problematise religion.

In *Prayers and Tears*, Caputo further details the idea of the messianic developed by Derrida who uses it to suggest an 'irreducible religious structure' underlying all critique, deconstruction, and religious life (118). Derrida's messianic twist involves distinction between ordinary time and messianic time, which is associated with the religious state of mind. This distinction is drawn from Maurice Blanchot, who differentiates 'ordinary, lived time . . . from an "other" time . . . a time without the present' (*Prayers and Tears* 77). 'Other' time has 'a messianic side, albeit a messianic *sans* any particular messianism' because it involves the 'notion of a future that will never be present' (78). Getting to the heart of Derrida's explanation of the messianic essence of religion, Caputo explains that 'the Messiah never comes' and that 'the very idea of the Messiah would be destroyed were the Messiah, to everyone's embarrassment and consternation, to have the indiscretion to show up and actually become present' (78). For Derrida, the uncertainty and incomprehensibility associated with an open-ended wait for a messiah is essential to the very structure of religious experience. As Caputo succinctly concludes, 'The messianic idea turns on a certain structural openness, undecidability, unaccomplishment, non-occurrence, noneventuality, which sees to it that, in contrast to the way things transpire in ordinary time, things are never finished, that the last word is never spoken' (78).[6] The idea of the coming of a messiah can also be understood as the arrival of justice. It involves the 'waiting or calling for . . . the messianic: the coming of the other, the absolute and unpredictable singularity of the *arrivant as justice*' (Derrida, *Specters of Marx* 28). Caputo explains that messianic time or 'the time to come' is 'the time of the justice to come, that disturbs the present with the call for justice' (*Prayers and Tears* 81). Such a 'messianic' understanding is significant because it suggests that underneath the kind of thought associated with 'unbelief' lies a sort of religiosity. Thus, when Thomas Hardy expatiates on the injustices of life in *Tess of the d'Urbervilles*, in a moment considered representative of the nineteenth-century 'crisis of faith', he recreates what would seem to be the structure of religious sensibility itself. Tess invokes the rampant injustice of our world by telling her younger brother Abraham that some stars are 'splendid and sound' but human beings live on a 'blighted' star (Hardy 31). Voiced against a backdrop of excruciating personal suffering, her lament is not a cynical expression of Victorian doubt but a religious waiting for the messianic arrival of justice.

In light of these opening comments about the meaning of faith and unbelief in our times, the philosophical insights that undergird the field of postsecular studies, and the extensive scholarship surrounding this topic, this book does not aspire to exhaustively list or analyse all the scholarship produced on the subjects of religion, the 'secular' and the 'postsecular'. Needless to say, any such aspiration boasts of ignorance at best and scholarly arrogance at worst. As the book has been produced from the conscious position of an English literary studies scholar, it works within Western cultural and historical frameworks germane to the field. At the same time, it observes the ways in which this field has expanded to acknowledge alternative non-Western paradigms. There are several valuable works on the postsecular that start from a non-Western perspective, drawing upon alternative theorisations of the meaning of religion from non-Western religious contexts (for example, Hindu, Jain, Buddhist, or Islamic) that possess their own sacred texts and lived practices. However, my work does not participate in these alternative approaches. Chapters two, three and four survey some of the landmark works of postsecular scholarship since the inception of this field in the 1990s. To give the reader a sense of the conceptual territory covered by scholars of postsecular theory, historiography and literary criticism, this review is focused rather than exhaustive. I aim to examine the staples and innovations of the field, the insights they offer, and the way these theoretical interventions reshape our reading of literary texts. As the obvious and crucial counterpoint to this review, chapter three delineates the substantial body of criticism that has emerged in response to the claims of postsecular theory—works that challenge the premises, validity and gradual ascendency of the field. These rebuttals not only insist on the significance of reason and a 'secular' public sphere, but also explain the problems with the postsecular tendency to filter all global debates (surrounding issues such as immigration or terrorism) through the religious–secular binary. Later chapters examine several works from the nineteenth to the twenty-first century in order to demonstrate what it means to perform a postsecular reading of a literary text. How can one identify and analyse the debates surrounding postsecularism in literary texts that are consciously holding these polemics up to the reader? By modelling how literary criticism can unfold in this field, I aim to uncover what Lori Branch calls 'the strangeness and particularity of the acts of beliefs and disavowals of belief in the text' (9). Some of the later chapters include works from the nineteenth century, an era associated with a watershed moment of 'secularisation' in both contemporary and modern accounts.[7] A study of these texts uncovers a commentary on the gendered, colonial and racialised construction of the 'secular' and the religious during a time of high imperialism. My approach is a cautious and historically-conscious application of a postsecular-reading technique, admittedly more open-ended than others, to textual products of an age considered the harbinger of 'secular' modernity. These texts illustrate a nineteenth-century transition—the construction of the 'secular' from within the religious—recognised by both postsecular critics and their opponents. The book's final chapter examines a twentieth-century work, Marjane Satrapi's *Persepolis*, that consciously positions itself along the fault lines of the debate on postsecularism by representing both sides of the question—critiquing the value assigned to secularism by Western culture in some parts while opposing a postsecular reading in some others. Ultimately, my work will present a historically conscious understanding of the school of postsecular theory, its contribution and its critique. As Vincent P. Pecora observes, postsecular theory is 'a response to real-world events: the failure of communist materialism, the religious revival that swept the Islamic world, the persistence of religious politics in much of the West' and the 'fruit of substantial intellectual currents in the West since the mid-nineteenth century' (4–5). Thus, the interpretive aim of the work that follows is to see postsecular criticism for the historical development that it embodies, the disciplinary shifts it entails, the possibilities for historical revisionism that it inaugurates and the critique it provokes with its insights.

NOTES

1. Many newspaper reports have addressed these issues in recent times. For an overview of sex-abuse scandals and institutional protection within the Roman Catholic Church, see: 'The Catholic Church Finally Begins to Own up to its Own #MeToo Reckoning' (*Los Angeles Times*), 'Abolish the Priesthood' (James Carroll, *The Atlantic*), 'The Vatican's Failure in the Abuse Scandal' (*The New York Times*) or 'How New York's Catholic Church Protected Priest Accused of Abuse' (Paul Abowd, *Al Jazeera*). On other rights incursions relating to abortion and the LGBTQ community, recent articles abound: 'The Gay Marriage Debate Has Been Won' (Jennifer Rubin, *The Washington Post*), 'This is the Time to Move Past the God vs Gays Debate' (Brandon Ambrosino, *Time*), 'A Pastor's Case for the Morality of Abortion' (Emma Green, *The Atlantic*) or 'Yes, Abortion Activists Use Religious Language. But it's Still About Politics' (Daniel Burke, *CNN*). For an introduction to human rights abuses in the name of religion in India, whether on the issue of caste or gender, see: 'India's Eternal Inequality' (Aatish Taseer, *The New York Times*), 'That Thing Called Caste' (Vaishna Roy, *The Hindu*), 'Two Women Enter a Temple. A Country Erupts' (Supriya Nair, *The New York Times*) or 'The Sabarimala Controversy Revives the Debate Over the Brahminisation of Kerala's Famous Deity' (G. Pramod Kumar, *Huffington Post*).

2. Books researching these events abound. For examples, see: M. D. Deshpande's *Gujarat Riots: The True Story, The Truth of the 2002 Riots* and Manoj Mitta's *Modi and Godhra: The Fiction of Fact-Finding*. On the protests and violence stemming from the Indian government's efforts to implement the Citizenship Amendment Act in India in 2019, there was widespread journalistic coverage across leading news outlets (for example, 'Calculated Chaos: The Delhi Riots are Exactly What CAA is About' by Ajay Gudavarthy, *The Wire*).

3. The award named in honour of the British evolutionary biologist Richard Dawkins recognises values of secularism and rationalism. First established by the Atheist Alliance of America in 2003 and presented by the Centre for Inquiry since 2019, the award honours an individual whose contributions raise public awareness of non-theistic philosophy and advocate increased scientific knowledge.

4. In June 2020, several news portals reported the announcement of Javed Akhtar's award, acknowledging his dedication to rationalism and secularism, and his protests against religious bigotry and human rights violations in the name of religion. For example, 'Javed Akhtar Becomes First Indian to Receive Richard Dawkins Award' by Namrata Joshi, published by *The Hindu*.
5. Let me mention here that throughout the book I place terms like 'secular', 'secularisation', and 'secularising' within single quotes as a constant reminder of the postsecular scholarly premises. This is because, as I will explain later, postsecular studies questions the theory of unilinear and inevitable erosion of faith that is implied by the term 'secularisation', and because it contests the notion that religiosity has diminished in our current times—a notion that is inherent in our characterisation of a 'secular' condition.
6. Caputo reminds us of how this template also works out in the Christian narrative, so that in the case of 'Christian messianism', the historical Jesus of Nazareth is proclaimed as the messiah but has to die 'so that we may wait for him to come again' (*Prayers and Tears* 79).
7. Charles Taylor explains the significance of the nineteenth century saying that the primary feature of the 'secular' age—the understanding of faith as an alternative among others—began in the nineteenth century. He notes that 'at least since the mid-nineteenth century' people have undergone the experience of a 'crisis', feeling compelled 'to give it [faith] up even though they mourn[ed] its loss', while for 'many others . . . faith never even seem[ed] an eligible possibility' (*A Secular Age* 3).

REFERENCES

@malala. 'The extremists have shown what frightens them most - a girl with a book. We must rebuild these schools immediately, get the students back into their classrooms and show the world that every girl and boy has the right to learn.' *Twitter*, 3 August 2018, 3:29 p.m., twitter.com/malala/status/1025388223810494466?lang=en.

Abowd, Paul. 'How New York's Catholic Church Protected Priest Accused of Abuse.' *Al Jazeera*, 25 October 2019, https://www.

aljazeera.com/features/2019/10/25/how-new-yorks-catholic-church-protected-priest-accused-of-abuse.

Ambrosino, Brandon. 'This is the Time to Move Past the God vs. Gays Debate.' *Time*, 26 June 2015, https://time.com/3938518/gay-marriage-response/.

Bellaigue, Christopher de. 'The Return of Religion.' *Financial Times*, 30 March 2018, https://www.ft.com/content/82c174fe-31cd-11e8-b5bf-23cb17fd1498.

Branch, Lori. 'The Rituals of Our Re-Secularization: Literature between Faith and Knowledge.' *Religion & Literature*, vol. 46, no. 2/3, 2014, pp. 9–33. *JSTOR*, www.jstor.org/stable/24752897.

Burke, Daniel. 'Yes, Abortion Activists Use Religious Language. But it's Still About Politics.' *CNN*, 23 May 2019, https://edition.cnn.com/2019/05/23/politics/abortion-religion-views-alabama/index.html.

Caputo, John. *On Religion*. Routledge, 2001.

---. *Prayers and Tears of Jacques Derrida: Religion Without Religion*. 1997. Indiana UP, 2006.

Carroll, James. 'Abolish the Priesthood.' *The Atlantic*, June 2019, https://www.theatlantic.com/magazine/archive/2019/06/to-save-the-church-dismantle-the-priesthood/588073/.

Chaudhuri, Supriya, editor. *Religion and the City in India*. Routledge, 2021.

Dalrymple, William. 'Before Malala.' *The New York Times*, 25 October 2013, www.nytimes.com/2013/10/26/opinion/international/malalas-brave-namesake.html?searchResultPosition=1.

Davies, Brian, editor. *Philosophy of Religion: A Guide and Anthology*. Oxford UP, 2000.

Derrida, Jacques. *The Gift of Death*. Translated by David Wills, U of Chicago P, 1995.

---. *Specters of Marx: The State of the Debt, the Work of Mourning, and the New International*. Translated by Peggy Kamuf, Routledge, 1994.

Deshpande, M. D. *Gujarat Riots: The True Story, The Truth of the 2002 Riots*. Partridge, 2014.

Gordon, Mary. *Reading Jesus: A Writer's Encounter with the Gospels*. Pantheon, 2009.

Green, Emma. 'A Pastor's Case for the Morality of Abortion.' *The Atlantic*, 26 May 2019, https://www.theatlantic.com/politics/archive/2019/05/progressive-christians-abortion-jes-kast/590293/.

Gudavarthy, Ajay. 'Calculated Chaos: The Delhi Riots are Exactly What CAA is About.' *The Wire*. 27 February 2020. https://thewire.in/communalism/delhi-riots-caa-pogrom-calculated-violence.

Hardy, Thomas. *Tess of the d'Urbervilles*. Penguin, 2003.

Hervieu-Léger, Danielle. *Religion as a Chain of Memory*. Polity P, 2006.

Jones, Jonathan. 'Living with Gods Review – 40,000 Years of Religious Art, and This is It?' *The Guardian*, 6 November 2017, https://www.theguardian.com/artanddesign/2017/nov/06/living-with-gods-review-art-religion-british-museum.

Kumar, G. Pramod. 'The Sabarimala Controversy Revives the Debate Over the Brahminisation of Kerala's Famous Deity.' *Huffington Post*, 8 November 2018, https://in.news.yahoo.com/opinion-sabarimala-controversy-revives-debate-052100436.html.

Le Bras, Gabriel. *Sociologie religieuse et science des religions*. Archives de Sociologie des Religions, 1, 1956, pp. 3–17.

Ludwig, Kathryn. 'Inside Looking In: Complicity and Critique.' *Christianity and Literature*, vol. 67, no. 3, 2018, pp. 511–15.

Maczynska, Magdalena. 'Toward a Postsecular Literary Criticism: Examining Ritual Gestures in Zadie Smith's *Autobiography Man*.' *Religion and Literature*, vol. 41, no. 3, 2009, pp. 73–82. *JSTOR*, www.jstor.org/stable/pdf/25746544.pdf.

Mitta, Manoj. *Modi and Godhra: The Fiction of Fact-Finding*. HarperCollins, 2014.

Nair, Supriya. 'Two Women Enter a Temple. A Country Erupts.' *The New York Times*, 8 January 2019, https://www.nytimes.com/2019/01/08/opinion/india-women-sabarimala-temple.html.

Pecora, Vincent P. 'The Secular, the Postsecular, and the Literary.' *American Book Review*. vol. 39, no. 5, 2018, pp. 4–5. *Project MUSE*, doi:10.1353/abr.2018.0061.

Peterson, Michael, et al., editors. *Philosophy of Religion: Selected Readings*. Oxford UP, 2001.

Roy, Vaishna. 'That Thing Called Caste.' *The Hindu*, 30 March 2018, https://www.thehindu.com/opinion/columns/vaishna-roy-on-caste-in-society/article23391827.ece.

Rubin, Jennifer. 'The Gay Marriage Debate Has Been Won.' *The Washington Post*, 27 June 2017, https://www.washingtonpost.com/blogs/right-turn/wp/2017/06/27/the-gay-marriage-debate-has-been-won/.

Smith, Christian. *Moral, Believing Animals: Human Personhood and Culture.* Oxford UP, 2003.

Taseer, Aatish. 'India's Eternal Inequality.' *The New York Times*, 12 October 2016, https://www.nytimes.com/2016/10/13/opinion/indias-eternal-inequality.html.

Taylor, Charles. *A Secular Age.* Harvard UP, 2007.

Taylor, Mark C. *About Religion.* 1999. U of Chicago P, 2007.

'The Catholic Church Finally Begins to Own up to its #MeToo Reckoning.' *Los Angeles Times*, 21 February 2019, https://www.latimes.com/opinion/editorials/la-ed-catholics-abuse-20190221-story.html.

'The Vatican's Failure in the Abuse Scandal.' *The New York Times*, 7 July 2017, https://www.nytimes.com/2017/07/07/opinion/pope-francis-catholic-church-sexual-abuse.html.

Ward, Graham. *True Religion.* Blackwell Publishing, 2003.

---. 'The Future of Religion.' *Journal of the American Academy of Religion*, vol. 74, no. 1, 2006, pp. 179–86. *JSTOR*, www.jstor.org/stable/pdf/4094088.pdf.

Weil, Simone. *The Simone Weil Reader.* David McKay Co., 1977.

Chapter Two

Surveying the Field

DEFINING POSTSECULAR THEORY: THE BASICS

We encounter the overwhelming surge of a 'return-of-religion' narrative in the meticulous consideration of scholars who study religious attendance at places of worship; the astute observations of social commentators who note rising 'fanaticism' among televangelists and neo-Nazis and; the frenzied global political conversations about the post-9/11 world. Graham Ward observes that at the end of the twentieth and the beginning of the twenty-first centuries '[r]eligion is, once more, haunting the imagination of the West' (*True Religion* vii). According to Caputo, the 'impossible has recently become possible again' having 'survived the secularizing and reductionistic critiques that have been directed against religion for the better part of the last two centuries' (*On Religion* 67). Slavoj Žižek notes 'the return of the religious dimension in all its different guises', from 'Christian and other fundamentalisms, through the multitude of New Age spiritualisms, up to the emerging religious sensitivity within deconstruction itself' (*The Fragile Absolute* xxix). Gregg Lambert similarly detects signs of this 'return [of religion] ... everywhere' and 'not only in the Islamic world, but in the former West as well—the return of fundamentalisms, ethnocentrisms, "integrisms" of culture and race, religious wars, even a war to end all positive religions' (38). However, all such conversations about return are premised on a primary assumption that we are (or until recently were) a 'secular' society. In sociological terms, this is explained through what is called the 'secularisation thesis'—a sociocultural axiom and academic staple that assumes the arrival of modernity will inevitably be accompanied by religious decline. Since its rise in the 1990s, postsecular studies is the field of humanities scholarship that has attempted to fracture this axiom's sense of closure and non-negotiability. The term 'postsecular' has been used in a variety of ways, but the one that concerns us here is postsecular studies as 'a descriptor of humanities and social science scholarship in what has been called the "religious turn"' (Branch, 'Postsecular Studies' 91).[1] Branch observes that this religious turn can be dated to around the mid-1990s in philosophy, though there were parallel developments occuring in other fields (91). The field that preoccupies me in this project is that of literature, that Bradley, Carruthers and Tate, in the introduction to *Spiritual Identities*, say 'constitutes a *privileged space* in which the return of the religious can take place' because '[l]iterature, like religion, has always implied a challenge to strict boundaries—between fantasy and fact, transcendence and immanence, the spiritual and the material' (3).

Postsecular theory contains a strong critique of the 'secularisation thesis' at its core. Alongside the rise of the discipline of sociology and sociologists such as Max Weber and Emile Durkheim, this sociological formulation first emerged and grew predominant in nineteenth-century discourses. Peter van der Veer explains that, until recently, the 'secularisation thesis' was 'the most successful element of any sociological theory of modernisation' (14). This thesis locates the essential shift and irreducible difference between tradition and modernity in the dawn of 'secularisation', and defines this 'all-embracing notion of "secularity"' as a culmination of 'notions of progress, liberty, tolerance, democracy, civil society, and the public sphere' (14). Talal Asad explains in *Formations of the Secular* that modernity is 'a project—or rather, a series of interlinked projects—that certain people in power seek to achieve', and that this project 'aims at institutionalizing a number of (sometimes conflicting, often evolving) principles: constitutionalism, moral autonomy, democracy, human rights, civil equality, industry, consumerism, freedom of the market—and *secularism*' (14; emphasis added). The faulty logic of the 'secularisation thesis' is that 'since all societies modernise and secularisation is an intrinsic part of modernisation, then all societies secularise' (Veer 15). Charles Taylor notes that 'stories of modernity in general, and secularity in particular' explain the rise of modernity/'secularity' as the result of human beings 'having lost, or sloughed off, or liberated themselves from certain earlier, confining horizons, or illusions, or limitations of knowledge' (22). Such theories posit certain 'perennial features of human life' or human nature, which they suggest were impeded in previous ages so that new paradigms found expression in modernity/'secularity' (22). These are the assumptions that postsecular theory aims to debunk by demonstrating that modernisation and modernity 'were by no means tied to secularization as their necessary constituent: or at least that this knot was more complicated than earlier supposed' (Chaudhuri 1).

The everyday equivalent of the 'secularisation thesis' is ubiquitous to the point that it goes unnoticed. One popular cultural manifestation of the 'secularisation thesis' is the much-loved character of Sheldon Cooper in *The Big Bang Theory*, who is a physicist at the California Institute of Technology and a geeky mascot for the stereotypical academic. He is predictably critical of his mother's Christian faith and his Texan upbringing that privileged creationism over Darwinian evolution. Mrs Cooper's faith is often exposed as ludicrous and hypocritical, such as when she derives pleasure from hunting (during a religious cruise that organises hunting activities) or sex (while in a relationship with a man she dates after her husband dies). Sheldon even points out to his mother that her choice of a romantic companion is a departure from the rules of her religion. Sheldon's commitment to science seems likewise self-evident to the viewer. It is only in the portrayal of his childhood in the series spin-off, *Young Sheldon*, that the science-versus-religion debates play out in all their complexity. Several episodes depict young Sheldon attending a Baptist church service with his family, or Sunday School with his sister, and citing scientific axioms to challenge biblical narratives. In the episode titled 'Poker, Faith, and Eggs', he enters into a debate with Pastor Jeff about the rational legitimacy of the pastor's sermon. In his sermon, Pastor Jeff admits that many people ask him how he knows there is a God. According to him, it is a case of mathematics: God either exists or does not exist. He concludes the odds are therefore fifty-fifty, which he finds favourable. At this point, his sermon is interrupted by Sheldon, who claims the pastor is confusing possibility with probability. The two discuss the analogy, and when asked by the pastor what he believes the odds are that God exists, Sheldon denies God's existence. He believes religion is faith while science is facts, and he prefers facts. Evidently, Sheldon debunks religious claims in the face of science, evoking the institutionalised modern binary of faith-versus-knowledge/religion-versus-science. Additionally, he explains that if the reality of God was probable then the odds would be fifty-fifty, but since God does not fall into the realm of probability at all but lies far outside of it in the realm of the impossible, the odds of God's existence are zero. This is an interesting pop cultural moment that registers the otherwise unnoticed ubiquity of modern 'secularist' ideology. Sheldon makes the crucial distinction that the odds or chances of a scenario could only be conceivably calculable within the realm of (im)probabilities that can be mathematically calibrated, whereas religion falls within the realm of (im)possibilities that can only be experienced or perceived. Young Sheldon relegates religion to the zone of the impossible without an inkling of doubt, thus reiterating the impossibility of everything that has to do with the religious. This 'secularist' approach is in stark contrast to that of postsecular philosophers and theorists, who emphasise how the religious deals in impossibilities and in the *making possible of these impossibilities*. Insofar as the very kernel of religious experience calls for openness and faith in the possibility of the miraculous or inconceivable, which cannot be mathematically circumscribed, the postsecular approach is inconsonant with predominant 'secularist' approaches.

THE DOMAIN OF THE POSTSECULAR

Scholars have asked whether the postsecular is a constitutive feature of recent texts or whether it is a reading practice that can be applied to texts across different historical periods. For some, as Kathryn Ludwig points out, the postsecular is not a thematic approach that applies only to certain kinds of texts within a defined time frame.

Instead, it is 'a type of criticism, a theoretical perspective from which we may examine works from any time period and genre' (82–83). By this logic, the project of postsecular literary criticism is to 'identify thematic and structural traits that are distinctly postsecular' across different historical periods (Kauffman 69–70). Yet, contemporary fiction has often been seen as a particularly fertile realm in which postsecular themes can be located with great frequency and intensity—a fact that Ludwig insists we do not overlook (83). Magdalena Mączyńska notes the 'definitional challenges' involved in situating 'postsecularism within literary studies', observing that if the word is to denote 'a new kind of contemporary writing' then one must delineate exactly how '"postsecular" texts' differ from earlier works that dealt with religious questions (75). But if the term stands for a new type of critical perspective, then one must distinguish it from both 'the already existing practice of studying the relationship between religious and literary discourses' and 'religiously-inflected approaches to reading literature' (Mączyńska 75). We are therefore left with the following question articulated by Bradley, Carruthers and Tate: 'How does it [the postsecular] challenge received understandings of the relationship between literature and religion and make possible new lines of enquiry?' (3). The answer to this will emerge as I work through examples that appear later in this chapter.

THE STORY OFT HEARD: THE 'SECULARISATION' NARRATIVE

Among the countless scholarly accounts of modern 'secularisation' that presume the 'secularisation thesis', some of the most significant are Bernard M. G. Reardon's *Religious Thought in the Victorian Age*, A. N. Wilson's *God's Funeral* and Owen Chadwick's *The Secularization of the European Mind in the Nineteenth Century*. All three provide succinct and widely accepted summaries of the trajectory of 'secularisation'—an idea that continues to preoccupy scholars and masses alike. As Wilson says, 'The GOD-QUESTION does not go away' (ix). According to an ever so popular narrative in reiterative scholarly accounts that I will not repeat here in any great detail, 'secularisation' begins in the early modern period with Galileo, and then reaches its definitive historical moment with '[e]ighteenth-century skeptical philosophers'—Hume, in particular—and nineteenth-century 'geologists' (Wilson x). The nineteenth century witnessed geological discoveries, evolutionary advances and developments in biblical scholarship and historical studies that all seemed to challenge conventional religious narratives. The rise of comparative religion as an academic discipline destabilised confidence in Christian superiority. German scholarship that engaged in the speculative treatment of history, especially from the Protestant school of Tübingen (headed by D. F. Strauss and F. C. Baur), further debunked staple Christian claims. Landmarks in this trajectory included the publication of *On the Origin of Species* in 1859, the launch of *Essays and Reviews* in 1860 and the rise of the Bishop Colenso debates in the 1860s.

Though this familiar 'secularisation' story does not bear repeating, the accompanying conceptual shift that determined the conditions of belief and unbelief is crucial. This shift was investigated by philosophers such as Charles Taylor, who explains the dawning of the 'secular age' as the emergence of an 'immanent frame' that denies or problematises 'any form of interpenetration between the things of Nature' and 'the supernatural', whether understood in terms of 'the one transcendent God, or of Gods or spirits, or magic forces' (16). Taylor remarks: 'The great invention of the West was that of an immanent order in Nature, whose working could be systematically understood and explained on its own terms, leaving open the question whether this whole order had a deeper significance, and whether, if it did, we should infer a transcendent Creator beyond it' (15–16).

Unlike in the pre-modern age, where 'people recognize[d] something beyond or transcendent to their lives', the emerging 'secular age' brought with it the immanent frame and a new form of subjectivity where 'the source of fullness is seen/lived as within *or without*' (Taylor 16; emphasis added). For the first time, it became possible to imagine a source of 'fulfilment' or 'human flourishing' as residing *entirely within oneself*—a purely immanent basis for human fulfilment (17–18). Drawing on Weber's characterisation of the pre-modern and modern eras as 'enchanted' and 'disenchanted' worlds, Charles Taylor observes that the rise of the disenchanted world and its immanent frame saw the pre-modern 'porous self' replaced with 'the buffered self' (300). The new 'buffered self' began to find 'the idea of [the supernatural, the otherworldly,] spirits, moral forces, causal powers with a purposive bent, close to incomprehensible' (539). This movement was further accompanied by a process of 'interiorization'—the development of an 'Inner/Outer distinction', 'a rich vocabulary of interiority' and the notion that 'an inner realm of thought and feeling [was available for] . . . explor[ation]'(539)— along with the valorisation of 'instrumental rationality' (542).

Ward similarly traces the trajectory of 'secularisation' and the gradual obliteration of the idea of transcendence that this involved. Showing how religion and religious sentiment is a 'social product', Ward demonstrates 'the social production of the religious' over time that included crucial attempts 'to expunge the transcendent' (*True Religion* vii). He analyses the 'various attempts to exorcise [religion's] . . . presence—from Feuerbach's anthropology to Freudian psychology, from the atheism of the logical atomists to the quarantining policies of liberalism' (vii). Throughout history, Western Christianity attempted to find the core of religion, or 'true religion', by stripping religion of what it considered 'unimportant particulars' like rituals and sacraments (Patuleanu 110). Ioana Patuleanu explains that the 'pursuer' became 'more [and more] alienated . . . from his object', and paradoxically, 'interventions meant to purify and spiritualize religion in the quest of an abstract absolute ultimately secularized it' (110). This left us with many different formats for Christianity down the ages (such as 'a set of rational and moral laws, a pantheistic philosophical and artistic understanding of the universe and its infinity, and eventually mere kitsch and special effects'), but none that offered a 'glimpse of any kind of transcendence' (110).

To better understand how postsecular theory fractures this sometimes insightful (as in the cases of Taylor or Ward) but mostly hackneyed narrative of 'secularisation', we need to examine some of the key propositions within the field. With this in mind, the next segment will cover what I have distilled as the three fundamental tenets of postsecular theory that work together to problematise the 'secularisation' narrative.

THE SALIENT FEATURES OF POSTSECULAR THEORY

A Challenge to the 'Crisis' Story and the Binary Principle

Postsecular theory challenges the unilinear narrative of inevitable religious decline that lies at the heart of the 'secularisation thesis', but without recourse to some supersessionary narrative about a 'return of religion'. Postsecular studies finds this 'return' narrative as problematic as the 'decline' narrative churned out by post-Enlightenment modernity. Kaufmann explains how in attempting to debunk the 'secularisation thesis', the postsecular theoretical project resists *any* master narrative —'whether it be a supersessionary narrative of secularization' or 'a triumphal narrative of the return of religion' (68). This problematisation of the religious–'secular' binary brings the appropriateness of the prefix 'post' (in postsecularism) into question. The prefix is premised on the assumption that there once existed a religion-free 'secular' age that was then supplanted by a postsecular one—the latter suggestively a time of the 'return of religion'. However, as postsecular scholarship dismantles the religious–'secular' binary, the connotation implied by this prefix does not hold up. Mączyńska asks whether 'the postsecular' is a 'period designation' indicating that which 'comes *after* "the secular"' or a 'corrective force *within* the momentum of secularism' (73). She then raises the possibility that the term may not signify a temporal designation but a 'critical or interpretative *perspective*' (73). Ludwig likewise explains that the postsecular is not about 'a return to religion' because, when it comes to postsecular moments identified in contemporary texts featuring 'religious themes, journeys of the soul, and engagements with religions tradition', 'the religious is not reaffirmed so much as it is engaged' (83). Postsecular theory thus aims to complicate our understanding of 'the *relationships* between the religious and the secular by moving beyond any model that posits too stark a binary opposition'; instead, it emphasises 'co-existence and co-creation' between these two categories (Kaufmann 68–69). Caputo similarly attempts 'to waylay the usual distinction between religious and secular' by resorting to 'the post-secular' or a 'religion without religion' (*On Religion* 2). By examining how and why certain beliefs or practices came to be classified as religious and 'secular', which ultimately reveals the 'particular [historical and cultural] tradition' anchoring the meanings associated with these terms, postsecular literary criticism effectively overturns the calcified religious–'secular' binary (Kaufmann 71).[2]

In the later chapters of this book, I will uncover and analyse the construction and reification of this binary. In chapters six to eight I will demonstrate how nineteenth-century texts, typically supposed to be about a 'crisis-of-faith' experience or fears of 'secularisation', actually reflect deeper wellsprings of religious ruminations and spiritual self-surrender that counteract the narrative consolidation of a colonial 'secularist' modernity. In chapter nine I will study how Satrapi's twenty-first-century work challenges the way the West uses global discourses that perpetuate the religious– 'secular' binary to claim for itself a superior rationalistic humanity.

Recognition of the Problem of Religious Experience and 'Secular' Rhetoric

Postsecular theory ruminates at length about how modernity has rendered the realm of the religious inaccessible. Scholars explain that the dawn of Enlightenment modernity, in full bloom by the end of the nineteenth century, made the religious incomprehensible except through the realm of the 'secular'. Talal Asad explores this at length, tracing the provenance of the idea of the 'secular'. He begins by noting that in Medieval Europe, the word *saeculum* referred to the period of time between the fall of man and the last day in Christian history. In early modern Europe, however, the 'secular' became a space beside the religious ('Comments on Conversion' 267). During the Enlightenment, the word *saeculum* came to mean the domain of 'purely natural' human action (as opposed to a domain of 'supernatural' belief) (267). Eventually, as a direct result of this Enlightenment paradigm, 'the concept of the social be[came] rooted in "the secular" as the space of human action pure and simple', and '"the religious" be[came] subsumed by it as a social phenomenon to be characterised in terms of that ontological space' (267).

Asad concludes by saying that acting 'in that space is now the condition of being human, regardless of whether one's beliefs and motives are "religious" or not' (267). Based on this understanding of history, postsecular writing necessarily assumes that religiosity cannot be evaluated (or even really acknowledged) within our modern 'secular' society due to the frameworks for discourse set in place by the Enlightenment. Within this pre-existing 'secularist' structure, the only conceivable and acceptable yardsticks for evaluating religiosity are quantifiable parameters, that is, statistical indicators such as attendance at places of worship. And, as postsecular scholars argue, the 'secularisation' narrative rests exclusively on the testimony of such data, citing declining church attendance as evidence.

Even if the evidentiary validity of such numerical indicators is accepted, the weaknesses of the 'secularisation' narrative remain. Peter van der Veer notes how data varies widely across Western societies—as the cases of the United States, the Netherlands and Catholicism are all exceptions to this theory of decline— to conclude that a generalised 'secularisation' story does not appear tenable (5–14). He goes on to address the other aspects of this theory that cite industrialisation and rationalism as factors contributing to 'secularisation'. He shows how contemporary research has problematised these claims. Firstly, during the Industrial Revolution in England there is more evidence of religious expansion than 'secularisation'. Secondly, there is now a consensus that the impact of scientific discoveries such as Darwin's on the decline of religion had previously been overly exaggerated. John Barbour similarly contests the narrative of Western 'secularisation' by reminding us that although scholars often speak of a Victorian 'crisis of faith', there were 'many different crises, each reflecting a particular constellation of religious doubts and expressed in a distinctive way' within the West (54). Further challenges lie in the way social scientists universalise this 'ill-founded story about the West *to include the rest*' (Veer 15; emphasis added). Veer argues that the 'secularisation thesis' is not only unfaithful to Western reality, but is also less applicable to the history of Islam, Hinduism, Buddhism and most other religions. Charles Taylor invests some legitimacy in this 'secularisation' narrative by noting that it applies mainly to 'the "we" who live in the West, or perhaps Northwest, or otherwise put, the North Atlantic world' (1). Yet he also endorses Veer's distinction between a modern Western world to which the conventional narrative partially applies, and other geographical or historical reference frames to which it does not in the least. Taylor concludes by saying that the idea of Western 'secularisation' clearly emerges as accurate if we compare these Western societies with 'anything else in human history'—that is, on the one hand, with 'almost all other contemporary societies (e.g., Islamic countries, India, Africa),' and on the other hand, with 'the rest of human history, Atlantic or otherwise' (1).

The very foundation of the 'secularisation thesis' can be demolished by questioning the legitimacy of corresponding statistical data, therefore disqualifying them as rightful indicators of this historical process. Callum G. Brown explains how confusion about data is an inherent disciplinary failing resulting from the fact that 'secularisation theory' is based on the 'social-scientific study of religion', which is 'one of the great projects of Enlightenment modernity' (11). Based on the work of sociologists such as Max Weber and Emile Durkheim, this nineteenth-century thesis gained currency in sociology in the mid–twentieth century as an account of the declining importance of religious institutions in modernity. What is noteworthy is that social science—an outcome of the Enlightenment project—was itself born in the nineteenth century, and was not only a 'discursive constituent of the secularization debate' (Brown 13) but the very foundation for the 'secularisation thesis.' Therefore, as postsecular scholars conclude, this renders the social-scientific indicators ineligible as a measure of what is purported to be our level of 'secularisation'. As Brad Gregory notes, Christianity and Jesus cannot be 'intellectually apprehended': 'central Christian claims about God—the reality of his providence, the fact of his grace, the compatibility of his will and power with those of each human being—are unavoidably and irreducibly mysterious. Attempts to fathom them will run up against conceptual and linguistic limits derived from the incomprehensibility of a reality that by definition is outside space and time' (Gregory 34–35).

Awareness of the Biases of 'Secular' Liberalism and Democracy

A final motive for postsecular theory is the dismantling of global assumptions surrounding religious fundamentalism (understood as originating in the Global South) and liberal democracy (seen as exclusively enshrined in the modern 'secular' West).

Mączyńska explains that proponents of postsecularism 'position themselves firmly in opposition to fundamentalist models of religiosity' and go beyond *both* kinds of fundamentalism—'the compromised structures of traditional religious belief and the limiting binary language [that is, the knowledge–faith binary] of modern secularism' (81). In doing so, they expose the fundamentalism underlying the Western capitalistic 'secular' enterprise, lush with the promise of modern democracy and liberalism. Žižek, for example, engages in an extended critique of Western capitalism and its disavowed and repressed 'other', to which I will refer in chapter eight. Debunking the Western myth of democratic 'secular' liberalism, Ward provides a historical account of liberalism, explaining how it was not simply 'demystified Christianity' but a 'Protestant Christian project with *imperial inspirations*' (*True Religion* 63; emphasis added). The rational religion or 'reasoned truth' upheld by liberalism, with its ideals of tolerance and religious pluralism, was not just transparently 'Christian in orientation'; it was also 'white, Western European, male' and heteronormative (63). Behind human 'reason', supposed to be capable of uncovering the truth, lay certain assumptions about 'what constituted the "normal" reasoner,' which in turn was defined by a 'consensus concerning what . . . constitutes the "normal" and the "man"' (63). Ward cites Daniel Defoe's *Robinson Crusoe*—a work which inaugurated the novelistic genre that enshrined modern 'secularisation', commercialism, individualism and rationalism—to demonstrate how the imperialist regime institutionalised the 'secular' liberalist ethic while enabling a paradoxical Christianisation. Ward demonstrates how this process involved an instrumentalisation of Christianity through the wielding of the name of God, while the actual presence of God in the world was attenuated.[3] In the end, he rightly concludes that there is 'a politics involved' in this attenuating of the presence of God in modernity. The hand of God 'is only rendered visible when it is necessary, or even "useful", to calm the fears and insecurities that continually arise in the secular space'—fears that are opened up by the 'remoteness of the divine and the free reign given to homo *economicus* to extend his dominion' (*True Religion* 71).

Today, we continue to inhabit this all-too-familiar paradigm wherein the actual presence of God is reduced even as the hand of God is made visible through blanket and facile catchwords. Various slogans invoke the name of 'Ram' in Hindutva-dominated India, 'Allah' in Islamist-controlled terrains, or 'Jesus' at Trump rallies, not so much to 'calm the fears and insecurities' of people in the 'secular' sphere or to reinstate religiosity in the realm but to actively disrupt peace and civil administration for the purposes of vote-bank politics and geopolitical dominion. In short, they instrumentalise the idea or the name of God while simultaneously ensuring God disappears from the 'secular' realm (71).

Nowhere is this better illustrated than in Deepa Mehta's *Leila*, a 2019 Netflix original web series loosely based on Prayaag Akbar's 2017 novel by the same name. The show presents the dystopian spectre of a state structured by religio-cultural fundamentalism and undergirded by the principle of purity, and the resulting horrors of fanatical segregation. Behind the loud rhetoric of oppressive religion, the show reveals the real source of programmed violence: the profit-driven market economy. In other words, efforts to establish monopolistic and profitable control over diminishing natural resources (for example, water) lead the state into ritualising violence through totalitarian mechanisms. Unfolding in the year 2047, a notable one hundred years after India's independence, a supreme leader (Mr Joshi) runs the dystopian social structure of the state of Aryavarta. On the whole, the show seems to suggest that Aryavarta is the culmination of present right-wing governments that are taking on near dictatorial forms and increasingly dominating the global landscape. The state is both a social and ecological dystopia where climate disaster has produced extreme water scarcity. Economic oppression of impoverished classes, the most obvious and immediate fallout of this kind of social structure, is enacted in the name of religion. In Aryavarta, people are separated by sky-high walls that protect individual control over dwindling water resources—a privilege they can purchase. At the heart of the plot lie Shalini, Riz and Leila. Shalini is the protagonist, Riz is her husband, and Leila is their daughter. The show begins by portraying their life of affluence as they luxuriate in a swimming pool. Their use of water for recreation is an obvious and embarrassing mark of their privilege in Aryavarta, where people are dying to secure access to it. This opening picture of opulence and joy is interrupted when fundamentalist goons scale the towering walls of Shalini's house, kill her husband and kidnap her daughter. Shalini is shoved into a purity camp that straitjackets women into a permissible model of femininity based on ritualised religious discourses they are forced to internalise, chant and obey. In the world Shalini now encounters, life is defined by service to the fundamentalist state and people live in ghettos that are demarcated by their specific place in a discriminatory, totalitarian order. One swears allegiance to the state—a sort of 'Hindu *rashtra*' (or polity) symbolising the principle of religious and caste purity—through incantations designed to work almost hypnotically. Shalini's (religious) 'corruption' and consequent punishment is shown to result from the fact that she married a Muslim man, and it is because of this that her mixed-blood daughter—a member of the 'Mishrit' (mixed) category and the corrupt product of cross-religious union—is taken away from her. The narrative that unfolds across the remaining episodes involves Shalini desperately searching for her lost daughter, who accidentally lands in a privileged space among the political elite after a chance overlooking of her status as a 'Mishrit'. In contrast, the worst kind of existence in Aryavarta is abject poverty and institutionalised social discrimination—a fate reserved for the largest part of the citizenry who are called the 'Doosh'. Clearly an imaginative extension of the condition of the 'lower castes' in India today,[4] this is the constituency with whom Shalini now interacts for the first time, seeking their help in order to trace her abducted daughter.

All of this is uncannily similar to both the militant nationalist rhetoric in contemporary India and the totalitarian or fascist regimes elsewhere across the globe. The sky-high walls in the show undoubtedly read as an allusion to violent and exclusionary borders (such as Trump's rhetoric surrounding the Mexico wall), while the caste-, gender- and religion-based pogrom is a resounding echo of contemporary Hindutva violence.[5] Intermarriage among castes or religions is prohibited, and women are whipped into feminine ideality through chants. With a logo reminiscent of a swastika alongside the gassing of aberrant women, both of which replay the horrors of Nazi gas chambers, the entire system of Aryavarta is a strategic throwback to a fascist concentration camp. But what is most interesting is that although violation of the principle of religious purity seems to have landed Shalini and her daughter in this dangerous predicament, the narrative surreptitiously reminds us that the actual reason for her punishment—the real motivations fuelling the fundamentalist state—have nothing to do with religiosity at all.

Audiences are dispelled of assumptions about violent religious agendas when it is later revealed that Shalini's Muslim brother-in-law, Naz, was involved with the Hindu goons who killed Riz. The real motives underlying this seemingly religious crime, and the totalitarian state itself, are of course very different. As Naz reminds Shalini, 'Water is the cause of all this, who told you to fill up your . . . pool with all the water?' Clearly, it is the wealth enjoyed by Shalini and her family, along with access to a large share of an otherwise scant resource, that attracts the attention of the greedy and profit-driven state. The state then secures control over this private wealth by attacking her family. If viewers were left with any doubts over the centrality of commerce, or the irrelevance of actual religious faith to the objectives of this totalitarian state, they are banished entirely in one of the climactic revelations of the first season. The leader of the goons who raided her home, killed Riz and abducted her daughter in the opening scene, and who the audience believed was impelled by his allegiance to a religious creed all along (like every other worker in Aryavarta), is revealed to be Dr Rakesh. Interested only in profiteering, the unscrupulous doctor runs a huge racket in the form of in-vitro fertilisation clinics which sell 'Mishrit' children such as Leila to childless parents. Thus, underlying the rhetoric of religious (and caste) purity is this mammoth capitalistic venture that commercially fuels the economy and propels its most powerful entrepreneurs who remain disguised as religious workers. At the heart of the series is the quiet revelation that despite the institutionalisation of what seem to be faith-based ideals and various kinds of religious fundamentalism, the state mechanism is actually powered by and directed towards a *commercial* fundamentalism. This latter sort is aimed exclusively at production and profit, and rationalised entirely by the financial gains that the structure generates—much like how Hitler's regime, beneath the race-, ethnicity- and religion-based notions of purity, was ultimately a profit-driven mass-production enterprise founded on genocide.[6]

One of the most polemical contemporary texts preoccupied with exposing this kind of commercial fundamentalism, and defusing the inflammable rhetoric of religious fundamentalism, is Mohsin Hamid's *The Reluctant Fundamentalist*.[7] The Pakistani–American author's work exposes the shaky ground on which the Western 'War on Terror' and allegations against religious 'fundamentalism' rest. Raising questions that blur the lines between global heroes and villains, Hamid engages in a philosophical introspection about what 'fundamentalism' even means. The novel tells an intriguing first-person tale of foggy moralities in which Changez, a Pakistani university professor, delivers a monologue to an unidentified and silent American at a Lahore café. He recounts his own American dream and resulting success on Wall Street, followed by a complete disenchantment with this heartless Western commercialism, and his subsequent return to Pakistan.

Over the course of his monologue, Changez divulges everything about his life in America to the silent American: he was at the top of his class at Princeton; despite cut-throat competition among the very brightest, he was hired by Jim, the boss at Underwood Samson, a top-ranking valuation firm on Wall Street; he fell hopelessly in love with Erica (and entered a doomed relationship with her); he was valued and successful at his company, though he was also identified as the cultural and class 'other' by Jim (who himself was an outsider to the privileged American class whom he had contended against and won); he experienced doubts over his misplaced loyalties in a post–9/11 world of racial discrimination; he heartbreakingly learned that he was furthering American (Western) neo-colonialism against the interests of his nation while it continued to be in the throes of poverty and war with India; and he finally returned home to Pakistan to teach in a university. The novel ends with an atmosphere of indistinct fear, lingering doubt and impending violence, and there is no clear sense of the moral allegiances or hidden motivations of either speaker or listener.

The novel initially portrays Underwood Samson as an unproblematic meritocracy where employees are exhorted to 'Focus on the fundamentals' (Hamid 98)—a phrase intended to implicitly remind them of the company's business basics as much as the American ethic of commercial ruthlessness. This world of seeming justice, where a racial-outsider like Changez and a class-outsider like Jim are provided with equal opportunity to succeed, contrasts with the global spectre of so-called Islamic fundamentalism represented in uncomfortably familiar rhetoric. But the novel is alive with an ironic undercurrent from the very start so that, amidst the general atmosphere of unpredictability, suspense, distrust and fear, one is unable both to align Changez with Islamic fundamentalism and to condemn this religio-political force as the source of all evil. Instead, Changez's monologue gradually leads the reader to realise that the commercial fundamentalism underlying America's inhumane, unthinking and arrogant pursuit of profit beyond all other values and concerns is no different from the religious fundamentalism blamed for all global violence. In fact, Mira Nair, who directs the film based on this novel, writes of how she used Underwood Samson 'to explore the concept of economic fundamentalism alongside that of political fundamentalism' (57).

The novel specifically points to how terms such as 'terrorism' or 'fundamentalism' are instrumentalised by the West, operating as 'slippery and dangerous trope[s] in the hands of dominant geopolitical forces, military leaders, formations of counter-terrorism, and the mainstream western media,' while ignoring Western economic fundamentalism or the 'terror and violence of new forms of [Western] imperial sovereignty' (Morton 247). Changez eventually realises that West-dominated global developments have institutionalised 'the advancement of a small coterie's concept of American interests in the guise of the fight against terrorism' (Hamid 178). The illusion of a just and democratic American meritocracy crumbles in the aftermath of 9/11, as the nation begins to manifest prejudicial violence: '[E]ven at Underwood Samson I could not entirely escape the growing importance of *tribe*', Changez notes (117). Awakened by the quiet reflection of Juan-Bautista, who is at the helm of the final company Changez evaluates on behalf of Underwood Samson, he comes to see himself as a 'modern-day janissary' (152). Yet the novel also leaves the reader with many uncomfortable questions that lead us to ponder the possibility of human weakness and cruelty. How does one resist the temptation to resort to violence against an arrogant enemy? Or, when confronted with intolerance, what are the limits of one's tolerance? We encounter tense moments that could be indicative of alleged religious fundamentalism, such as when Changez relishes televised images of the twin towers crashing, or when, at several points, he seems to threaten his American listener with violence in retaliation for what he perceives to be America's covert preparation for attack, or when he stands unflinchingly on the precipice of physical violence after being accosted with a racial slur in a parking lot in the aftermath of 9/11. On this latter occasion, he yells back and grabs a 'tire iron' from his car, and 'for a few murderous seconds' he feels ready 'to shatter the bones of [the offender's] skull' (118).

Ultimately, however, the novel dwells in an intense and recurrent atmosphere of suspicion and conspiracy with no clear heroes or villains at an individual level (neither the Pakistani speaker nor the American interlocutor are openly vilified) or in a collective sense (neither Pakistan/the Global South nor America emerge as irredeemably devious). As Hamid explains, the novel's mystifying form and content is preoccupied with 'the tension which comes from a sense of mutual suspicion between America and the Muslim world' (qtd. in Yaqin 46). No moral endorsement favouring one side of this binary, and certainly no outright condemnation of Pakistani fundamentalism is given by the author. Instead, the novel projects its postsecular commentary by highlighting the exploitative, predatory, commercial and rapacious nature of the American marketplace that includes both academia and the workplace. Changez uses the metaphor of a prostitute to emphasise the crass commercialism of American academia, saying, 'Princeton raised her skirt for the corporate recruiters who came onto campus and . . . showed them some skin . . . I was a perfect breast . . . tan, succulent, seemingly defiant of gravity' (5). In Mira Nair's adaptation, Changez also implies the militaristic ruthlessness of American commerce by constantly referring to himself at Underwood Samson as the 'Navy Seal of finance'. Though Changez in the novel is portrayed as unpredictable and potentially violent, the text emphasises the suggestively sly, perilous and insidious nature of the American interlocutor—a narrative strategy meant to plant suspicions about larger Western claims to moral superiority that circulate the globe unquestioned. Lacking an overt moral motivation for his menacing presence in Lahore, the American figure in the novel acquires an ethically suspect bearing even for the reader. The man is (arguably) less than forthright or noble, pretending to be a common civilian even as Changez intuits and suggests that he is an army-man or a spy (possibly a CIA agent) on a covert mission. His fidgety and cautious demeanour—in which he texts instead of calling a contact (2), reaches under his jacket for what he says is a wallet but which Changez is sure is a gun (30), and displays nervous (5) or invasive predatory behaviour (31)—repeatedly arouses the reader's moral suspicions as Changez keeps alerting us to it. Furthermore, defying typical reader expectations, the visibly uninvited and ominous Western figure looming on the Lahore skyline is characterised as implicitly lascivious. When Changez imparts how the American man lecherously ogles women with an 'intensity of . . . gaze' and by getting 'distracted' (16), including one particular student from the nearby National College of Arts who 'ca[tches] [his] eye,' the depiction recalls a typical representation of Islamic conservatism and prurience (22). He thus highlights how claims to morality employed by both the East and the West are more audibly and powerfully instrumentalised by the West as a rationale for global hegemony and how these claims are ultimately questionable. Obfuscating the moral positionality of both sides, the text as a whole powerfully convolutes Western definitions of liberal humaneness and foreign fundamentalism.

DEFINITIONS AND READING APPROACHES

Pondering the basis and implication of the assertion that we live in a 'secular' age, Charles Taylor observes two common assumptions. Firstly, most people recognise that '[r]eligion or its absence is largely a private matter' for us today, and therefore 'political society is seen as that of believers (of all stripes) and non-believers alike' (1). Secondly, most agree that 'religious belief and practice' has diminished, church attendance has dwindled, and 'people [are] turning away from God' in Western European countries (2). However, Taylor remarks that the best summation of our 'secular' age is provided by a third set of explanations that 'focus on the conditions of belief' (3). According to this interpretative approach, we have 'move[d] from a society where belief in God is unchallenged and indeed, unproblematic, to one in which it is understood to be one option among others, and frequently not the easiest to embrace' (3).[8] So we have gone from a society in which it was 'virtually impossible not to believe in God', even for those who discussed atheism, to a society in which 'faith, even for the staunchest believer, is one human possibility among others' (3). Our 'earlier "naïve" framework' has shifted to a modern "reflective" one' (14), from an 'engaged' standpoint to a 'disengaged' one (12).

Set against this context, my use of the words 'religion' or 'spirituality' does not refer to a theological or denominational category that evolved at a point in time. Instead, it alludes to two different scholarly understandings of these terms. On the one hand, I allude to the conceptual category implied by these terms and what it came to represent in a post-Enlightenment (Western industrialised) modernity ruled by this idea of 'secularity'. More accurately, this is an idea of 'secularised religiosity'—the notion of religion as a social-scientific category measurable by empirical data such as churchgoing statistics. On the other hand, I also imply alternative definitions proposed by postsecular scholars such as Caputo and Derrida—definitions I have discussed earlier where faith is seen as an experience of love for the 'other', an openness to dwelling in complete uncertainty, a trust in the possibility of the impossible, and a willingness to wait open-endedly for the arrival of the absolute 'other' who also signifies justice. As Charles Taylor sums up, faith is a state of fullness and a place of power that we all experience, whether believer or unbeliever.[9] Thus, though readers and postsecular critics approach religion from different historical and cultural contexts, and the primary texts examined in this book also evoke various religious/denominational allegiances, each with its unique understanding of specific theological concepts, it is still possible to draw upon what Ward suggests is a common Western legacy as we converse about the postsecular intervention in literary studies. Ward observes that what is common is 'a history in which Christendom came to an end' but 'different cultural and national histories . . . [continued to] live out that Christian legacy', 'a legacy that dramatically change[d] with the advent of Protestantism and the rise of nonconformism and evangelism' and that was further influenced by the rise of a 'new plurality linked to colonization and various patterns of migration through which that Christian legacy is [still] being culturally and politically negotiated' and that finally culminated in 'the dissemination of secular values, the rise of the scientific worldview, and instrumental rationality' ('The Future of Religion' 181).

Postsecular studies as a whole, and this monograph in particular, concentrates on literature as an area of critical exercise. The reason for this focus, as noted by Bradley, Carruthers and Tate, is that literature 'constitutes a *privileged space* in which the return of the religious can take place' (3).[10] That a review of postsecular theory would concentrate on literature seems like an organic and necessary step. Detweiler and Jasper, editors of *Religion and Literature: A Reader,* explain that 'human speculation on the self and the universe' developed at the start of history—long before 'the development of abstract, critical, and methodological thought' (xi). It was always expressed naturally through the literary medium, such as in 'myths, stories, and poetry' (xi). In 'The Rituals of Our Re-Secularization', Branch further reminds literary scholars that 'literary theory, not to mention the inexhaustible well of meanings unearthed in criticism and teaching, tells us that literature and religion do converge at the site of belief and meaning-making' (10). Examining several contemporary works in reference to questions asked by Douglas Coupland in his collection *Life after God*, Bradley, Carruthers and Tate conclude that 'the "cracks" into which religious impulses flow in a world without religion' are actually the 'space of literature' (5). Literature itself offers neither an alternative to nor a substitute for religion, but instead provides a space in which the *'religious experience can happen'* (5; emphasis added). Several significant works of postsecular scholarship harness this space for energy and change promised by literature, suggesting through close readings how literary texts function as organic media where religious meanings are created and spiritual experiences are facilitated. This process simultaneously allows for what Mark Knight calls an 'open[ing] up [of] the meaning of literary texts'— an interpretative goal whose significance for scholars of literature must not be underestimated (4). Drawing on this interpretive strategy, the following chapters of the book engage in a historically grounded reading of nineteenth- and twentieth-century literary texts to understand the kinds of religious enactments and 'secular' constructions that populate these topical documents, avoiding what Branch calls 'a habitual flattening of or deafness to religious discourses' ('Postsecular Studies' 93).

A crucial aspect of postsecular theory is its philosophical engagement with the deconstructive nature of faith. Derrida's infamous 'theological turn' in French phenomenology, embodied in his 1994–95 essay, 'Faith and Knowledge', lies at the heart of this development. In this essay and in 'Force of Law', Derrida's central critical move was to debunk the faith–knowledge binary undergirding Enlightenment thought.[11] As such, several theorists have demonstrated how, upon closer inspection, the faith–knowledge binary breaks down and we begin to realise that faith underlies our existence (and sense of knowledge). Both faith and knowledge, or 'religion' and 'science' as Michael Naas calls them, 'share a common source' (189). He explains that '[f]or science, like religion, requires faith, trust, credit, and so on, an originary faith that is anterior to every science and is the quasi-transcendental condition of all knowledge' (189). Ultimately, we all inhabit a space of non-knowing or uncertainty—a space of openness to the truly 'other' and the clearly impossible. That is, '[n]on-knowing is the inescapable element in which decisions are reached', and all of our decisions 'are covered by a thin film, a quiet and uneasy sense, of unknowing' (Caputo, *On Religion* 19).

This claim draws upon a detailed and complex discussion of the faith–knowledge binary in Derrida's work. In his essay titled 'Faith and Knowledge' in *Acts of Religion*, Derrida observes that while configured as opposites in the Enlightenment, faith and knowledge are actually 'bound to each other by the bands of their opposition' (43). Throughout his work, Derrida suggests two different perspectives on how faith constitutes the basic structure of our life and language. Firstly, faith underlies religion, which requires faith in God or the miraculous/impossible. Similarly, in *On Religion*, Caputo ruminates at length about how religion requires faith in the impossible. Secondly, according to Derrida, deconstructive reading or thinking itself calls for a faith-based openness to the 'truly other' (*'tout autre'*). The 'truly other' lies in the realm of the different (*'hyper'*)—that which lies outside the realm of similarity and possibility—and therefore in the realm of the impossible. And faith thus openly awaits this absolute 'other'. Caputo explains in *The Prayers and Tears of Jacques Derrida* that '[d]econstruction desires . . . [and feels a] passion . . . for the impossible' (3). Caputo points out that what fascinates Derrida is 'the "experience of the impossible," the possibility of this impossibility, by the absolute heterogeneity that the *hyper* introduces into the order of the same, interrupting the complacent regime of the possible' within which we ensconce ourselves for comfort (2). Thus, deconstruction 'sees itself as a pact with the *tout autre*, with the promise of the different, an *alliance* with the advent, the event, of the invention of alterity' (15), and— reaching the heart of the matter—'in theology the *tout autre* goes (and comes) under the name of God' (4).

The sociopolitical significance of Derrida's ruminations cannot be overstated. Derrida contends that we are all inhabited by the desire and consumed by the passion for the impossible, the *tout autre* or the wholly 'other'. This contention allows for the possibility of relating to an 'other' that is distinct from one's self. Furthermore, religion and deconstruction are bound by their faith in the impossible, in the wholly other, and therefore *in God*, and this not only underlies our language and life, but also forms the significant sociopolitical foundation for our relation across difference. Interestingly, therefore, faith premised in deconstruction, and deconstruction undergirded by faith, represents for many postsecular scholars the philosophical possibility of understanding and loving the social, racial, cultural or political 'others' who are radically different from (and even antagonistic to) us in their opinions, preferences and desires.

Postsecular theory has also provided many experts of religion and postcolonialism with both the impetus and medium to challenge the assumption of universality surrounding the Western idea of 'religion'. Scholars have repeatedly emphasised the historical and ideological complexity underlying the notion of religion, noting the Western cultural imperialism that its use implies as well as the inapplicability of this term in non-Western contexts. Graham Ward observes that the use of the term is 'enmeshed in ideologies' and charged with certain 'cultural politics', and is therefore no 'objective, scientific label' ('The Future of Religion' 180). In fact, he points out, some scholars of Islam, Hinduism or Buddhism avoid the term because it has no cognate translation in the languages of the countries where these religions have peaked in popularity and practice. Along with many others, Wilfred Cantwell Smith, Peter Harrison and Richard King reiterate that the idea of religion is in itself a Western construct derived from the Romans, predominated by Christianity and filtered through Enlightenment modernity. Talal Asad notes that the Christian Church has historically occupied itself with 'identifying, cultivating, and testing belief as a verbalizable inner condition of true religion' (*Genealogies of Religion* 48), and that in post-Enlightenment Europe, religion was reduced to 'the right to individual belief' (45). The development of this 'modern' sense of religion can be seen as a move away from an earlier understanding premised on an integral connection between ritual, doctrine and (embodied) belief. This earlier understanding was lost in the intellectualisation that came with high medieval scholasticism and the Reformation that followed. For the Reformers, in particular, belief became about intellectual (and heartfelt) assent to propositions, so that they lost, to varying degrees, the connection between an intellectualised, interiorised 'faith' and external works and rituals. Jo Carruthers notes the usual way that the 'secularisation' of Protestant Christianity is understood—as a reduction of religion to a moral system that is devoid of any theological essence, as outlined by Max Weber (5).[12] Geoffrey A. Oddie observes that this latter modern understanding of religion developed in medieval Europe, and found reflection 'in accusations of heresy and in the debates of the Reformation' that 'persisted in Christian thinking throughout the colonial period' (14). Asad describes this modern shift as one in which religion went 'from being a concrete set of practical rules attached to specific processes of power and knowledge, . . . [to becoming] abstracted and universalized' (*Genealogies of Religion* 42). It became, as Oddie remarks, 'something expressed objectively in written creeds, doctrine or stated belief' (13). In *Politics of Piety*, Saba Mahmood notes that this view of religion (a 'secularized conception of religiosity') 'commands particular weight in the development of non-Protestant religious traditions—particularly non-Western traditions' (xiv). Mahmood explains how this understanding of religion has largely transformed non-Western religions from within because the 'inequality of power relations . . . between Western Christendom and its Others, the West and the non-West' sets up 'the history of Protestant Christianity as the entelechy that all other religious traditions must emulate in order to become truly modern' (xiv).

This internalisation of Western conceptual frameworks for understanding religious experience, including the use of the word 'religion' for self-description, took place mainly in the late-seventeenth and eighteenth centuries (Ward, *True Religion* 80). The universalisation of this sense of religion, which was 'formed by and through the universalisation of Christianity', began to be used for other ends (80–81). As I discussed earlier with respect to Defoe's *Robinson Crusoe*, for instance, it was used to justify and facilitate imperialist expansion; it was also internalised by those on the receiving end of the process of colonisation. In sum, according to Kaufmann, the invisible hand of Protestant Christianity has always controlled most of our assumptions about what counts as religious or 'secular' (71).

This can be remedied by paying attention to other religious traditions that provide a counter-context for many of these assumptions. I attempt to do this in my reading of nineteenth-century Anglo-Indian novels in chapter seven and Satrapi's *Persepolis* in chapter nine. Gauri Viswanathan explains that in drawing on the Protestant and imperialist understanding of religiosity, along with its concomitant definitions of the 'secular' sphere, we have arrived at the modern historical moment across democracies in the Global North and South. In this moment, national identity, now equated with the 'secular', is considered primary, while the religious is reduced to only a mode of social organisation and is associated with what is considered relatively 'primitive' (Viswanathan xii). Viswanathan observes that this 'shading of religious identity into the artificial fabrication of a *secular*' (xi) national identity has created a kind of modern 'secular' national order where, when the 'beliefs actually held . . . [are] expressed, [they] are so far outside the identifiable, accepted categories that their nonrecognizability makes them appear [like the] dangerous, threatening, "other,"'—'fanatical, militant, or cultish'— making other customary laws seem 'separatist and antinational' (xiii).

Saba Mahmood counters this perception of public religiosity through a case study of the Egyptian mosque movement, offering alternative ways to reinterpret the meanings of agency or freedom. To briefly summarise and anticipate what I will return to in the final chapter of this book, Mahmood's aim is to challenge 'secular' Western feminist premises by drawing on her ethnographic study of the norms of 'piety' followed by the women of the Egyptian mosque movement. Challenging the meaning of the term agency in reference to these women, Mahmood suggests we need to 'detach the notion of agency from the goals of progressive politics' in order to understand what their actions mean to them (14). In the context of this grassroots-level ethnographic study of women conducted in the mosques of Cairo, she reminds us of the futility of trying to recuperate 'latent liberatory potentials' from within a movement widely perceived as illiberal. Instead, Mahmood identifies very different templates for agency and subjectivity that emerge as we study the forms of religious conduct manifested in this movement. Drawing from the interventions of poststructuralist feminist scholarship, Mahmood observes how 'agency' is imagined within 'secular' liberal formats only in terms of the 'binary model of subordination and subversion'—a model that assumes that any liberatory choice representing agency can only come from the act of resisting the norm (14). Yet the model for agency proffered by this group of Egyptian women derives not from an act of resisting norms but from *inhabiting* norms—a notion alien to our secular-liberal political sensibilities (23). As such, these women destabilise normative politics and dislodge existing gender hierarchies by consciously choosing to participate in this moral-reform movement. This participation requires docile and submissive social conduct on their part, and reworks the definition of agency and choice on which our political system rests. This critical postcolonial context of postsecularism provides the backdrop for the textual readings that will follow later in the book.

OUR CRISIS AS ACADEMICS: THE UNIVERSITY AS A 'SECULAR' SPACE

Douglas Jacobsen and Rhonda Hustedt observe that 'higher education was about public knowledge' and that public knowledge has always been 'defined in purely secular terms' (10). As Charles Taylor reminds us, the 'presumption of unbelief has become dominant in more and more ... milieu' and has 'achieved hegemony ... in the academic and intellectual life ... whence it can more easily extend itself to others' (13). In examining the 'secular' associations of academia, it would be interesting to begin by discussing the 1962 film *Night of the Eagle* (known to American audiences as *Burn, Witch, Burn!*), in which a juxtaposition of two shots evocatively captures the situation. In the first shot, which appears near the opening of the film, a university professor energetically writes the words 'I DO NOT BELIEVE' on a blackboard. In the second shot, shown at the very conclusion of the film, the professor, now in tatters, leaves the room with the words on the blackboard reading 'I DO BELIEVE'. Suggestive of a bildungsroman trajectory from scepticism to belief, this journey is enacted within the space of the university classroom and in the life of a college professor. The film opens in Hempnell Medical College, with Norman Taylor, a sociology professor addressing the class by scribbling on the blackboard in big bold letters: 'I DO NOT BELIEVE.' This statement of unbelief, he says, include the 'four words needed to fight the supernatural, witchcraft, superstition, psychic, et cetera, et cetera,' all of which represent to him a 'morbid desire to escape from reality'. Emphatically stressing the 'not' in the imperative, the professor proceeds to explain that these elements of the supernatural 'can only exist in an atmosphere of belief'. Speaking of science, which is perceived to be the obvious rival of the supernatural, he says that '[e]ach day science founded on years of research and truth, emerges with feats which put our old-fashioned magicians to shame.' But the argument is undercut by the analogy he uses to describe these scientific accomplishments: 'Aladdin rubbed a lamp and the genie appeared; today we press a button and the whole of mankind is obliterated.' Interestingly, the genie metaphor highlights the *magically* destructive potential of science, suggesting that the scientific accomplishments are so enormous in their (destructive) impact that the feats themselves become defined by an aspect of wonder and inexplicability rather than the element of rigorous research. Moreover, these scientific achievements are not merely celebratory. Instead, they are capable of destroying humanity and are therefore evil within a world that believes in peace and love. Norman's college lecture strings magic and science together into not only the same sentence, but also the same historical continuum, implying that popular belief and magic are far more innocent than science which, though located on the same axis, leads to a more destructive end by ruthlessly conjuring the means to eliminate humanity both figuratively and literally. Ironically, this hints at the amount of faith required from practitioners of a discipline as destructive as science in order to realise such visibly heinous feats. It is crucial, of course, that the debate is worked out in the institutional space and language of the discipline (sociology) that birthed, housed and popularised the 'secularisation thesis'. The film spans the period of a single day, during which the professor goes from vehemently refusing the possibility of the supernatural to gradually accepting and realising its power. The latter occurs when the wife (Flora Carr) of his colleague (Lindsay Carr), jealous of his advancement within the department, tries to spoil his chances for promotion by practicing a West African spiritual-healing magic called 'Obeah'. Flora attempts a kind of auditory hypnotism on Norman's wife, Tansy Taylor, by sending Norman a magical cassette tape that, when played, paralyses the listener with fear and disables their capacity for self-defence. Though the tape plays when both Tansy and Norman are present, Tansy is shown to be more vulnerable to its workings—most likely because she too inhabits this realm of belief (as she is earlier shown working a spell to protect Norman, before he stops her in a fit of indignant rationalism). The eerie climax of the film shows Tansy's room catching fire after Flora casts her magic spell. Stone eagles come to life from the Gothic architecture of the college and attack Norman as he runs, with the spell-inducing tape playing loudly over the public announcement system. Unable to shake off the effect of this spell and falling into an almost trance-like state, a visibly agitated, terrified and confused Norman runs wildly to escape the attack. The next morning, Norman is shown looking weary and shattered as he picks himself up in the classroom in which he had taken refuge when the stone eagles attacked him. As he musters his strength and walks out, the camera pans to the blackboard to show that his accidental collapse against it had erased the operative word 'not' from the declarative sentence he himself had written the day before. The viewer is left staring at the board that now reads 'I DO BELIEVE'. The narrative ends on this image, with the triumphant erasure of disbelief from the board and, implicitly, from Norman's academic mind as well.

Cultural depictions have always shown the university classroom as a fraught place, and the university professor as an enigmatic figure circling the issues that lie at the very heart of the debate on faith. At the peak of the 'secularisation' debate in the nineteenth century, the figure of a university professor, Van Helsing in Bram Stoker's *Dracula*, enlightened us about the presence of the supernatural. The famous exhortation, which Van Helsing delivers to Jonathan Harker, alludes to the limitations of Western science alongside the growth of alternative faiths and the increasing boldness of occult claims. Condensing the implications of the entire nineteenth-century debate into one brief paragraph, Van Helsing obfuscates the boundaries associated with the disciplines of science:

> Do you not think that there are things which you cannot understand, and yet which are, that some people see things that others cannot? . . . Ah, it is the fault of our science that it wants to explain all, and if it explain not, then it says there is nothing to explain. But yet we see around us every day the growth of new beliefs, which think themselves new, and which are yet but the old, which pretend to be young, like the fine ladies at the opera. I suppose now you do not believe in corporeal transference. No? Nor in materialization. No? Nor in astral bodies. No? Nor in the reading of thought. No? Nor in hypnotism. . . . (Stoker 204)

This figure of the researcher–scientist, the academician who pursues scholarship, also comes up against similar dilemmas in other nineteenth-century texts such as *Dr Jekyll and Mr Hyde* or *The Island of Dr Moreau*. What is interesting is the common characterisation of the academic space (the university classroom in particular)— as rationalistic and devoid of the spiritual. In focusing on this dominant characterisation and eventually on the wellsprings of faith behind it, I am setting aside the recent interpenetration of campuses with the rhetoric of the religious right—a violent reality that has been covered within my larger discussion of the political right's recent resurgences with its accompanying social conservatism. The longest and culturally dominant understanding of the university as a 'secular' space, however, is deeply reminiscent of a history that is far from 'secular' and pedagogical experiences that are not in the least rationalistic. In her discussion of the literature classroom, Lori Branch notes how its tenor is determined by the fact that a significant portion of the current literature professoriate was 'trained after 1970 in critical methodologies that assumed the truth of the secularization thesis' and 'in fact desired that outcome as a presumed route to various forms of liberalism' ('Postsecular Studies' 93). In his chapter 'Why Faculty Find It Difficult to Talk about Religion', Mark U. Edwards Jr discusses why academics feel reticent to talk about their religious leanings and explains that this difficulty is largely due to the turn taken by academia over the past few centuries. Today's 'modern professional disciplinary communities' only value 'modern rational and empirically verifiable means of finding truth', he writes. Since they aim to 'explain the world as it is and as it had come to be without recourse to either mystery or miracle', God becomes 'methodologically and interpretively unnecessary' (83). Edwards observes that natural sciences were the first to follow in this direction, followed by social sciences and humanities. This has now led to a point where, even in a literature classroom, religion is a suspect intruder. As Tracy Fessenden summarises in her essay, '"The Secular" as Opposed to What?', the 'legitimating narrative of literary scholarship' works on certain related assumptions. It assumes that literature 'once was religious, became less and less so (with the march of "knowledge") and is now decidedly secular' (632). It also assumes that the professional study of literature exists and has existed not to be religious but 'as the replacement for religion as a failing enterprise', and that literature was 'birthed by, for, and as the secular, from which the traces of religion . . . must continually be expunged' (632).

Branch elaborates on the institutionalised scepticism that holds us back, remarking that we are 'self-constrained [by our] . . . reliance on critical reason and our 150-year-old imperative to legitimate the disciplinary study of literature as a production of knowledge within the research university' ('The Rituals of Our Re-Secularization' 10). The emergence of the modern research university with its own ideological framework of knowledge production—one that categorises knowledge, knowledge-production mechanisms and the classroom as 'secular'—has a complex history of its own. This history has been surveyed by a vast body of secondary scholarship, and even a cursory review is useful for understanding the context of its birth, the cultural currents through which it develops and the debates from which it draws substance over several centuries.

Douglas Gordon Jacobsen and Rhonda Hustedt Jacobsen note in 'Postsecular America' that the twentieth century marked a strange intertwining of the historical processes of 'secularisation' and the ideology of 'secularism' that determined the nature of American and, by extension, all Western institutions of higher education. A 'careful and critical investigation of the ordinary "secular" world is not the same as secularist education', but the 'forces of secularization and secularism intertwined' in the twentieth century, reshaping higher education and making it 'secularist' in nature (9). David John Frank and Jay Gabler recount the conventional story about the impact of 'secularisation' on scholarly inquiry in *Reconstructing the University,* observing how the 'divine and diabolical forces' of the pre-modern era had 'randomized reality so as to flout analysis' (23). An 'altered cosmology' that set in with the 'decline of religion' then replaced this ethos with 'systematic and law-like forces, which rendered reality as predictable and amenable to inquiry' (23)—thus making possible the academic template of the modern university.

In stark contrast to the religious ethos that carries a sense of both unpredictability and indecipherability, the university classroom is an unproblematically 'secular' space where the rational and definable prevail over the mysterious and incomprehensible. As Jacobsen and Jacobsen observe, 'universities have almost always located themselves on the secular, skeptical, and speculative side of society' (8). The rise of the university is therefore linked with the tides of modern 'rationalization and secularization' that dawned gradually and climaxed in the post-Enlightenment period, a development that 'opened more and more territories of nature and society to reasoned scientific examination, boosting the relevance and stature of universities tremendously' (23).

In 'The Religious Convictions of College and University Professors', Neil Gross and Solon Simmons outline a similar trajectory for 'the history of American higher education'. They identify the 'closing decades of the nineteenth century' as a period of 'academic revolution' wherein professors, particularly those at elite institutions, 'began thinking of themselves as scientists and scholars whose major task was to seek out the truth, not to propagate religious dogma' (19). Jacobsen and Jacobsen trace the trajectory of this 'revolution', which was visible in twentieth-century American universities and culminated in the late 1970s when 'religion as a matter of living faith and practice had essentially been bleached from the goals and purposes of higher education at the nation's major universities' (10).

Secondary scholarship offers two different perspectives on the problems posed by these accounts of the modern university's transparent and obvious 'secularism'. The first perspective is present in the work of Neil Gross and Solon Simmons, who follow the critical direction of the current historical moment, that is, 'reassessing secularization theory in general', and apply it to a reconsideration of 'the secularization of American higher education' (20). Through their reading, they show how the contemporary American university is far from 'secular', even (and especially if) we examine the personal beliefs of the professors themselves. The second perspective is that of Brad Gregory's in *The Unintended Reformation*, where he debunks the prevalent idea that a scientific revolution led to 'secularisation'. He revises both the logic and the timing of the 'secularising' shift, demonstrating how it originated at a time long predating the scientific revolution and from *within* religious traditions rather than outside of them. Gregory argues that it was actually 'doctrinal controversy in the Reformation era [that, centuries before the emergence of modern science,] unintentionally marginalized theological discourse about God and the natural world' (22). He clarifies that these underlying assumptions about the 'incompatibility of science and religion' derive 'not from science but in the first instance from a seemingly arcane metaphysical presupposition of some medieval scholastic thinkers' (33). Lori Branch similarly contests the notion that a scientific revolution precipitated a 'crisis of faith', noting that 'secularisation' was not so much 'a political process or part of scientific method' but 'in a [more] profound sense the result of a rationalizing process which . . . was active in Puritanism, Dissent, and beyond' and 'which had been taking place at the heart of western Christianity at least since high Scholasticism and certainly long before the Restoration' (*Rituals of Spontaneity* 25). It is this ancient trajectory of the rise of 'secularisation' from *within* faith that Gregory delineates in detail, ultimately connecting it to the rise of the university as a modern and 'secular' institution. He explains that '[f]ew things are as difficult as keeping clear about the distinction between God and creation as understood in traditional Christianity' (3). Despite their formal grammatical similarity, statements such as 'the book is on the table' and 'God is in heaven' are not comparable in traditional Christian metaphysics (33). However, such statements began to be made comparable in discourse about God beginning in the fourteenth and fifteenth centuries. Soon the 'appropriation of certain ancient philosophical ideas [that were] revived in the Renaissance and [in] the upheavals within Christianity during the Reformation era' (33) attempted to craft the same narrative and conceptual manoeuvers. Between the third and seventh centuries, Patristic authors drew on the philosophical framework of neo-Platonism. So too did medieval monastic authors. After the twelfth century, theologians in Latin Christendom drew on a combination of Aristotelianism and Neoplatonism, reshaping the very form of theology and examining the truth-claims of Christianity to show their coherence and compatibility with what is known and knowable by rational means (34–35).

These are the intellectual currents that led to the dawn and widespread acceptance of a new metaphysics—one that proclaimed 'the mutual exclusivity of natural causality and transcendent, divine presence' (33–34). Eventually, the notion came to crucially undergird modern science. Gregory ends his work with an extended discussion about 'the later institutionalization of these assumptions in modern universities'—assumptions that underlie 'the common conviction today that knowledge and reason—in contrast to faith and feelings—are and must be secular' (34).

In the following review of several eminent scholars in the field, I briefly recount the rise of the modern 'secular' university from within faith-traditions for the purpose of understanding its complex inheritance and pivotal position in the debates surrounding religion. By reading these historians, I show how discourses about faith constructed the idea of knowledge from within religion itself in a way that birthed both the faith–knowledge binary and cemented assumptions of 'secularity' underlying the 'knowledge'-seeking university.

Monika Asztalos, in 'The Faculty of Theology', details the shift from early medieval monasticism to late medieval scholasticism, when philosophy and speculative reason entered discussions of faith. This shift to scholasticism drew on the philosophy of antiquity and changed the very form of medieval theology, triggering developments that resulted in theological disputations and departments of theology across medieval universities. Asztalos studies the impact of works preceeding the late medieval scholastic era (such as those of Saint Augustine and Boethius) on figures from the eleventh and twelfth centuries (beginning with Gerbert of Aurillac) to observe how this influence opened the way for the entry of philosophy and speculative reason into discourses of faith. This manifested in the works of Anselm of Canterbury, in cathedral schools with teachers like Anselm of Laon, and in commentaries called *Glossa ordinaria*—a genre that elevated contemporary masters to *auctoritates* or authorities and introduced an orderly theological discussion of different topics,[13] culminating in Peter Lombard's *Sentences*. Asztalos notes that it is these shifts heralding scholasticism that 'applied philosophical notions of necessity and impossibility to God's power, thereby restricting God's omnipotence' (410). Developments such as these distilled the central issue that later became the predominant subject of debate for theological faculties in medieval universities—'the reconcilability of the articles of faith, such as God's omnipotence, with reason' (410).

Rüegg explains how, following the scholastic emphasis on logic and reason, the university then led the way towards a kind of intellectualism. In *A History of the University in Europe (Vol 1)*, he draws from the work of Makdisi, the American Islamicist, to summarise how the university was a 'product of the Christian West of the twelfth century' (qtd. in Rüegg 8). First, medieval popes attempted to consolidate their religious and political authority by supporting the university. Seven values were iterated to legitimise the *amor sciendi* (love of knowledge) in religious terms—and its institutional form, the university. Despite the religious context for their origin, universities served a practical purpose by producing professionals. Most significantly, they also functioned according to the ultimate parameter of objectivity as they were bound by a foundational mandate to engage in the pure search for truth. The university therefore followed scholasticism by heralding this kind of institutionalised intellectualism, founded in an adherence to reason and the imperative of truth and objectivity. Significantly, the university paired this rationalistic intellectualism with a fundamental understanding of itself as religious.[14]

In 'Relations with Authority', Notker Hammerstein describes how universities gradually shrank during the late Middle Ages from institutions intended to represent all of Christendom to much narrower political units associated with the nation state and 'a growing sense of patriotic ("national") self-determination' (114). 'Secular' or political powers had also grown more intimately connected with the maintenance of universities, despite not being able to fully control their workings. Hammerstein observes that with the rise of humanism, 'the continuing high evaluation of learning and of universities as places of learning was given additional decisive support' (115). Instruction in more practical matters, such as the natural sciences, economics and philology, was encouraged. Theology—which until the early Middle Ages had been the monarch of all university faculties—now 'held only an inferior position, although it remained within the system of university disciplines' (123). This shifting emphasis in university education and its wider relevance became increasingly clear in the seventeenth century. In *The Industrious Revolution*, Jan de Vries recounts how a process of 'confessionalization' took place within Christianity at this time. Different confessions (for example, 'Calvinists, Lutherans, Catholics') came to place a very high premium on the university, making it their aim 'to penetrate to the broad base of society with programs of education, institutionalization, and, of course, conversion of souls' (56). In the section '*Sacra Facultas* and the Coming of German Modernity' from *Protestant Theology and the Making of the Modern German University*, Thomas Albert Howard explains that the late seventeenth and eighteenth century witnessed a decline of the older universities in Germany, alongside a major shift that involved the expansion of the philosophical faculty, which challenged and diminished the importance of the theological faculty. Howard follows a trajectory that begins in the late medieval period with a notion of knowledge (*scientia*) distinct from the post-Enlightenment practice of *Wissenschaft*, and with the undebated primacy of theology over logic among the university faculties. But by the eighteenth century, philosophy had emerged as the predominant faculty in the

Surveying the Field 57

university. This same period was marked by both rampant criticism that accused universities of backwardness and widespread attempts at university reform. Such efforts were captured in the premier reform universities of Göttingen and Halle, and in the ascent of the philosophy faculty starting around 1740. Howard notes that '[w]hile the theological faculty was still symbolically regarded as the first of the higher faculties, its traditional primacy was greatly attenuated' and 'the confessional rationale for the university gave way here ... to purely secular and statist justifications' (104). Critics of the university from this time onwards repeatedly insisted on the need to fundamentally restructure the relationship between the various university faculties, with philosophy assuming (as it had begun to at Göttingen and Halle) a 'more extensive and independent role within the university and one partially imitative of the type of learning associated with scientific academies and societies' (121).[15]

In the sections 'Theologia between Science and the State' and 'Conclusion: Janus Gazing' in *Protestant Theology and the Making of the Modern German University*, Howard describes 'the theological faculty's steady diminution as a component of the overall university system' (270) in nineteenth-century Germany (and eventually in the Western world), even as the features of the new German Protestant theology acquired renown internationally. Tracing the 'dominant intellectual, political, and social trends of the mid and late nineteenth century,' Howard observes how the ideal of *Wissenschaft*, as the defining principle governing all faculties, was extended beyond a few innovative universities (such as Berlin) to include nearly all German universities (270). He then discusses the 'continuing ascendency and expansion of the philosophical faculty—both in its humanistic, historical, philological aspects and its positivistic, natural scientific ones'—that affected university theology (270). Thus, led by Germany, nineteenth-century Protestant theology in modern German universities represented a watershed for Christianity *and* university education in that it marked the institutional demotion of theology in relation to faculties founded in ideas of reason and science.

From this historical process, which positioned the university at the heart of debates on religion and tied it to popular perceptions of 'secularism', emerged the modern university with its fraught lineage and polemical belongings. One literary work in particular, Marius von Mayenburg's *Martyr* (2015), brings the divergence of the academic and religious into creative focus and pushes us to the edge of the persistent debate about borders. The play revolves around Benjamin, a student who tries to militantly change his school's practices and policies in order to bring them in line with what he considers to be appropriately religious, based on the most conservative and discriminatory reading of the Bible. The proponent of uncompromising science, who stands in opposition to Benjamin, is his science teacher, Erica White. Benjamin opposes White's position as his teacher, protesting the right of 'a woman to teach or to have authority over a man' because the Bible ordains men with supremacy over women in all situations (Mayenburg Chapter 10). He also protests the wearing of bikinis by female students during swimming sessions, claiming that their doing so offends the Biblical norms of modesty. Instead, he seems to favour a situation where, 'the whole school swims in a religious fashion' (Chapter 7) in 'high-necked swimsuits' (Chapter 4). The school principal, Belford, summons Benjamin to learn more about his complaints and discipline him. In the end, however, Belford ends up supporting Benjamin's arguments in front of the rest of his staff. He justifies Benjamin's religiously charged position by specifically invoking the *pedagogical* nature of the situation, explaining to White the inappropriateness of wearing bikinis in school by saying, 'After all, you don't teach in your bra either' (Chapter 4). Another powerful representation of the commonly perceived antagonism between the academic and the religious can be seen in the disruptions that take place in Erica White's 'Sex Education' classroom. During these lessons, Benjamin condemns the classroom exercise of putting condoms on bananas as he considers the academic instruction on sexuality irreligious. This extreme polarisation of the scholarly (scientific) and the religious ultimately shows not only how Benjamin's delimiting and regressive scriptural interpretation denies the validity of pedagogical realities, but also the futility of academic templates that struggle to engage with the religious. Still, the play ends on a hopeful note with academia reaching out to the religious. White transitions from her earlier furious denial—'I don't care what the Bible says'—to a frantic and unrelenting study of the Bible dedicated to revealing the many possible scriptural interpretations beyond the merely regressive ones cited by Benjamin (Chapter 10). Spurred on by her newfound insights, White jubilantly declares that Jesus is gay by citing a Biblical passage that details how one of the disciples leant 'on Jesus' bosom' and how Jesus 'loved' him (Chapter 15). White then adopts a Christ-like posture of martyrdom in the climactic scene, nailing her feet to the floor of the classroom to assert her right to be there as she awaits a fresh batch of students. On one level, she manifestly denies belief in God by implying that her lessons for all future batches of students will teach the premise that wondrous creation, such as that of human anatomy, is the unfolding of a scientific principle 'without God'. She imagines that as she demonstrates in her class the 'bone structure, upright walking, heart, circulation, the senses, brain' on the skeleton, they will watch with 'wide-open faces wondering if it's real', and she will explain how each of these is 'a miracle, every single one, even without God'. Based on this claim, she asserts her right to the 'secular' academic space: 'I belong here. I'm right and you're not' (Chapter 27). But even while polarising faith and science and claiming that only she is 'right,' White continues to unconsciously draw from her fervent and dedicated reading of scripture—an exercise that had led her husband to call her as addicted to scripture as an addict is to cocaine. She speaks and acts in a way that draws upon spiritual language and the religious faith in miracles. She demonstrates a willingness to surrender to the cause of science through a martyr-like crucifixion. She even indirectly induces the element of faith within the pedagogical space by welcoming the workings of religious 'miracles' when as she decides to wait (patiently nailed to the floor) for a miraculous solution to appear (Chapter 27). The university and faith remain irreconcilable in the end, but the text ponders this rift in our contemporary context to suggest that an infusion of meaning across these porous borders may be viable.

NOTES

1. Lori Branch delineates three other senses in which the term has been used since its first appearance in Philip Blond's *Post-Secular Philosophy* (1998): (i) a 'Radical Orthodox' theological orientation such as Blond's, pioneered at Cambridge in the 1990s; (ii) a political designation, as in Jürgen Habermas's 'Notes on a Post-secular Society', describing Europe as no longer homogenously 'secular' and grappling to integrate religious citizens in the public sphere; (iii) a literary–historical designation, originating from John McClure's *Partial Faiths: Postsecular Fiction in the Age of Pynchon and Morrison* (2007), identifying post-WWII literature more occupied with faith than the modernist fiction that preceded it (Branch, 'Postsecular Studies' 91).

2. This resistance to any master narrative, whether of the decline of religion or of its contemporary return, aligns postsecular studies with the postmodern impulse against all 'grand narratives' (Lyotard xxiii). Ludwig, in fact, sees 'the postsecular as emerging from within postmodernism' (83), just as Bradley, Carruthers and Tate note that it is 'from within the very state of postmodernity itself that the return of the religious begins' (2). The editors of the latter work also note John Millbank's thesis about the tactical alliance between Christianity and postmodernity 'in pursuit of the common enemy of Enlightenment reason, empiricism, positivism and science' (qtd. in Bradley et al. 2).

3. Ward argues that the advancement of imperialism in Defoe is inseparable from a 'Christianization in which the role of Jesus Christ is increasingly less "useful"', and the only thing that remains useful are 'the virtues enjoined by Christianity' such as 'tenderness, compassion, generosity, hospitality, courage, temperance, hope, gratitude, benevolence' that help the development of civil government (*True Religion* 71). It is this 'attenuation' of the role of Christ that actually allows for the so-called 'secular' liberalist 'civil government' in the imperialist modernity put forward by the novel (70).

4. Endnote 1 from chapter one provides, among other things, examples of reportage on systemic caste discrimination in India.

5. This contemporary reality has been widely discussed in political, social and cultural forums, and has been investigated through global

journalistic efforts. A few of the innumerable journalistic articles on the topic include: 'The Violent Toll of Hindu Nationalism in India' (Eliza Griswold, *The New Yorker*), 'How Hindu Supremacists Are Tearing India Apart' (Samanth Subramanian, *The Guardian*) and 'Ground Report: In Riot City, Hindutva Mobs Rage with Impunity as Police Watch in Silence' (Ajoy Ashirwad Mahaprashasta, *The Wire*).

6. Among many scholarly works, one of the most intensive accounts is to be found in Jacques R. Pauwels' *Big Business and Hitler*.
7. A portion of this analysis is drawn from my essay, 'Reimagining Reluctance: The South-Asian Diaspora and Global "Homing" in Mira Nair's *The Reluctant Fundamentalist*.'
8. Charles Taylor notes that 'belief is an option, and in some sense an embattled option' in Christian societies like the United States, but is 'not (or not yet) in the Muslim ones' or for the 'vast majority of Indians' (3).
9. Charles Taylor writes: 'Somewhere, in some activity, or condition, lies a fullness, a richness; that is, in that place (activity or condition), life is fuller, richer, deeper, more worth while, more admirable, more what is should be. This is perhaps a place of power: we often experience this as deeply moving, as inspiring' (5).
10. The editors of *Spiritual Identities* note that literature allows this space for the expression of religious sensibilities because '[l]iterature, like religion, has always implied a challenge to strict boundaries—between fantasy and fact, transcendence and immanence, the spiritual and the material' (Bradley et al. 3).
11. This philosophical turn towards the religious has been considered problematic by authors like Gregg Lambert. Lambert argues that the recent shift towards religion that manifests in the works of several continental philosophers ultimately leaves one with an abstracted religiosity that is devoid of actual material religious belief and practice. He thus problematises the 'return of religion' by citing as instance Caputo's 'religion without religion' (to which I referred earlier in this book), or Jean-Luc Nancy's 'deconstruction of Christianity' that cancels out real religion altogether by philosophising it. As Lambert describes it, this return is also the announcement of 'the moment when God finally succumbs to something like a peaceful (albeit not natural) death, at the very

moment when the word "religion" itself loosens its death grip on life, and turns about into a new openness, a new horizon, a new hope for religion without "religion'" (38).

12. I briefly explain the interpretations and implications of Weber's work later in the next chapter.
13. These commentaries led to the introduction of *quaestiones* into the biblical commentaries and manifested most prominently in the work of Peter Abelard and in the theological collecting of *sententiae*—the origin of theological *summae*—in which different topics were presented in a systematic order.
14. Even at this time though, the 'arid intellectualism' promoted by '[c]ontemporary theologians' and, as Rüegg noted, adopted to a large degree by the university, was seen as suspect by Erasmus, the humanist who emphasised 'virtuous living' and 'blamed scholasticism for promoting the notion that theology was a contemplative discipline, divorced from piety and ministry' (Furey 1).
15. This is also emphasised by Kant, who stressed the need to prioritise philosophy over theology because, unlike the higher faculties like theology that were bound by 'external legislators', philosophy 'had no master but "the free play of reason"' and thus functioned autonomously as the free 'dispenser of liberal, rational enquiry within the university' in 'the interests of science *(Wissenschaft)*', where 'reason . . . is authorized to speak out publicly' in the name of truth (Howard 125–26). This laid the basis of the university system, governed by philosophy instead of theology.

REFERENCES

Asad, Talal. 'Comments on Conversion.' *Conversion to Modernities: The Globalization of Christianity*, edited by Peter van der Veer, Routledge, 1996, pp. 263–74.

---. *Formations of the Secular: Christianity, Islam, Modernity*. Stanford UP, 2003.

---. *Genealogies of Religion: Discipline and Reasons of Power in Christianity and Islam*. Johns Hopkins UP, 1993.

Asztalos, Monika. 'The Faculty of Theology.' *A History of the University in Europe, Volume 1: Universities in the Middle Ages*, edited by Hilde de Ridder-Symoens, general editor Walter Rüegg, Cambridge UP, 1991, pp. 409–41.

Barbour, John D. *Versions of Deconversion: Autobiography and the Loss of Faith*. UP of Virginia, 1994.

Bradley, Arthur, et al. 'Introduction: Writing Post-Secularity.' *Spiritual Identities: Literature and the Post-Secular Imagination*, edited by Jo Carruthers and Andrew Tate, Peter Lang, 2010, pp. 1–8.

Branch, Lori. 'Postsecular Studies.' *The Routledge Companion to Literature and Religion*, edited by Mark Knight, Routledge, 2016, pp. 91–102.

---. 'The Rituals of Our Re-Secularization: Literature between Faith and Knowledge.' *Religion & Literature*, vol. 46, no. 2/3, 2014, pp. 9–33. *JSTOR*, www.jstor.org/stable/24752897.

---. *Rituals of Spontaneity: Sentiment and Secularism from Free Prayer to Wordsworth*. Baylor UP, 2006.

Brown, Callum G. *The Death of Christian Britain: Understanding Secularization, 1800–2000*. 2nd ed., Routledge, 2009.

Caputo, John. *On Religion*. Routledge, 2001.

---. *Prayers and Tears of Jacques Derrida: Religion Without Religion*. Indiana UP, 2006.

Carruthers, Jo. *England's Secular Scripture: Islamophobia and the Protestant Aesthetic*. Continuum, 2011.

Chaudhuri, Supriya, editor. *Religion and the City in India*. Routledge, 2021.

Derrida, Jacques. *Acts of Religion*. Edited by Gil Anidjar, Routledge, 2002.

Detweiler, Robert, and David Jasper, editors. *Religion and Literature: A Reader*. Westminster John Knox P, 2000.

Edwards Jr., Mark U. 'Why Faculty Find It Difficult to Talk about Religion.' *The American University in a Postsecular Age: Religion and the Academy*, edited by Douglas Gordon Jacobsen and Rhonda Hustedt Jacobsen, Oxford UP, 2008, pp. 81–98.

Frank, David John, and Jay Gabler. *Reconstructing the University*. Stanford UP, 2006.

Furey, Constance M. *Erasmus, Contarini, and the Religious Republic of Letters*. Cambridge UP, 2006.

Gregory, Brad S. *The Unintended Reformation: How a Religious Revolution Secularized Society*. Belknap P of Harvard UP, 2015.

Griswold, Eliza. 'The Violent Toll of Hindu Nationalism in India.' *The New Yorker*, 5 March 2019, https://www.google.com/amp/s/www.newyorker.com/news/on-religion/the-violent-toll-of-hindu-nationalism-in-india/amp.

Gross, Neil, and Solon Simmons. 'The Religious Convictions of College and University Professors.' *The American University in a Postsecular Age: Religion and the Academy*, edited by Douglas Gordon Jacobsen and Rhonda Hustedt Jacobsen, Oxford UP, 2008, pp. 19–30.

Hamid, Mohsin. *The Reluctant Fundamentalist*. Penguin, 2007.

Hammerstein, Notker. 'Relations with Authority.' *A History of the University in Europe, Volume 2: Universities in Early Modern Europe (1500–1800)*, edited by Hilde de Ridder-Symoens, general editor Water Rüegg, Cambridge UP, 1991, pp. 114–153.

Howard, Thomas Albert. *Protestant Theology and the Making of the Modern German University*. Oxford UP, 2006.

Jacobsen, Douglas Gordon, and Rhonda Hustedt Jacobsen, editors. 'Postsecular America.' *The American University in a Postsecular Age: Religion and the Academy*. Oxford UP, 2008, pp. 3–18.

Kaufmann, Michael. 'Locating the Postsecular.' *Religion & Literature*, vol. 41, no. 3, 2009, pp. 68–73. *JSTOR*, www.jstor.org/stable/pdf/25746543.pdf.

Knight, Mark. *An Introduction to Religion and Literature*. Continuum, 2009.

Lambert, Gregg. *Return Statements: The Return of Religion in Contemporary Philosophy*. Edinburgh UP, 2016.

Leila. Directed by Deepa Mehta, performances by Huma Qureshi, Siddharth, Seema Biswas, Rahul Khanna, Sanjay Suri, Arif Zakaria, Ashwath Bhatt, Anupam Bhattacharya, Netflix, 2019.

Ludwig, Kathryn. 'Don DeLillo's *Underworld* and the Postsecular in Contemporary Fiction.' *Religion & Literature*, vol. 41, no. 3, 2009, pp. 82–91. *JSTOR*, www.jstor.org/stable/pdf/25746545.pdf.

Lyotard, Jean-François. *The Postmodern Condition: A Report on Knowledge*. 1979. Translated by Geoff Bennington and Brian Massumi, U of Minnesota P, 1984.

Mączyńska, Magdalena. 'Toward a Postsecular Literary Criticism: Examining Ritual Gestures in Zadie Smith's *Autograph Man.*' *Religion & Literature*, vol. 41, no. 3, 2009, pp. 73–82. *JSTOR*, www.jstor.org/stable/pdf/25746544.pdf.

Mahaprashasta, Ajoy Ashirwad. 'Ground Report: In Riot City, Hindutva Mobs Rage with Impunity as Police Watch in Silence.' *The Wire*, 26 February 2020, https://www.google.com/amp/s/m.thewire.in/article/communalism/delhi-riots-jai-shri-ram-hindutva-bjp/amp.

Mahmood, Saba. *Politics of Piety: The Islamic Revival and the Feminist Subject.* Princeton UP, 2012.

Makdisi, George. *The Rise of Colleges: Institutions of Learning in Islam and the West.* Edinburgh UP, 1984.

Mayenburg, Marius von. *Martyr.* Translated by Maja Zade, Kindle ed., Oberon Books, 2015.

Morton, Stephen. 'Introduction.' *Journal of Postcolonial Writing*, vol. 46, no. 3–4, 2010, pp. 246–50. doi.org/10.1080/17449855.2010.482404.

Naas, Michael. *Miracle and Machine: Jacques Derrida and the Two Sources of Religion, Science, and the Media.* Fordham UP, 2012.

Nair, Mira. *The Reluctant Fundamentalist: From Book to Film.* Penguin Studio, 2013.

Night of the Eagle. Directed by Sidney Hayers, performances by Peter Wyngarde, Janet Blair and Margaret Johnston, Independent Artists, 1962.

Oddie, Geoffrey A. *Imagined Hinduism: British Protestant Missionary Constructions of Hinduism, 1793–1900.* Sage Publications, 2006.

Patuleanu, Ioana. 'Graham Ward: True Religion.' *Iowa Journal of Cultural Studies*, vol. 7, no. 1, 2005, pp. 109–112.

Rüegg, Walter. 'Themes.' *A History of the University in Europe. Volume 1: Universities in the Middle Ages.* Edited by Hilde de Ridder-Symoens, general editor Walter Rüegg, Cambridge UP, 1991, pp. 3–34.

Stoker, Bram. 'Dracula.' *Project Gutenberg*, 16 August 2013, http://www.gutenberg.org/files/345/345-h/345-h.htm.

Subramanian, Samanth. 'How Hindu Supremacists Are Tearing India Apart.' *The Guardian*, 20 February 2020, https://www.theguardian.com/world/2020/feb/20/hindu-supremacists-nationalism-tearing-india-apart-modi-bjp-rss-jnu-attacks.

Taylor, Charles. *A Secular Age.* Harvard UP, 2007.

Veer, Peter van der. *Imperial Encounters: Religion and Modernity in India and Britain.* Princeton UP, 2001.

Viswanathan, Gauri. *Outside the Fold: Conversion, Modernity, and Belief.* Princeton UP, 1998.

Vries, Jan de. *The Industrious Revolution: Consumer Behavior and the Household Economy, 1650 to the Present.* Cambridge UP, 2008.

Ward, Graham. 'The Future of Religion'. *Journal of the American Academy of Religion*, vol. 74, no. 1, 2006, pp. 179–86. *JSTOR.* www.jstor.org/stable/pdf/4094088.pdf.

---. *True Religion.* Blackwell Publishing, 2003.

Wilson, A. N. *God's Funeral: The Decline of Faith in Western Civilization.* W. W. Norton, 1999.

Yaqin, Amina. 'Mohsin Hamid in Conversation.' *Wasafiri*, vol. 23, no. 2, 2008, pp. 44–49.

Žižek, Slavoj. *The Fragile Absolute: Or, Why is the Christian Legacy Worth Fighting For?* Verso, 2009.

Chapter Three

The Critique of Postsecular Studies

Postsecular criticism has been received with reactions ranging from disorientation and disinterest to cynicism and concern. The scholarly response has been one of honest, invested critique directed at a school of criticism that has been perceived as a threat both to the academic structure and to sociopolitical ways of thought. The conversation around postsecular studies has therefore been substantially enriched by the sustained critique it has generated. Both parties to the debate have weighed in, powerfully and richly, on issues of social and geopolitical interest. In order to better understand how the narrative of postsecularism has contributed to cultural discourse, political assumptions and academic templates, the scholarly critique of postsecular theory needs an extended review of its own.

A common issue for many critics of postsecular studies is the field's use of imprecise definitions for popular terms. Here, a mere two examples will suffice. Firstly, the definition of religion itself is ambiguous as a basis for academic study. Reflecting the disapproving views of many, critics such as Vincent P. Pecora declare that religious belief is 'more or less useless as a category of critical interpretation' because 'religious belief *per se* is so elusive and variable a property of consciousness in the majority of mortals'—for some it is a 'fleeting fantasy', for many an 'unthinking habit', with the 'most pious' often 'filled with terrible doubt' (5). Instead, Pecora suggests a study of the religious aspects of literary-cultural works by shrinking and converting the metaphysical or intangible associations of their religious components into a textual/linguistic exercise. This, in turn, would make the works accessible and translatable within typical academic templates. He notes that we should attend to 'the language of a text, and not some set of putative beliefs' in order to approach religion 'on the same grounds as we would approach, say, class, race, gender, or empire' (5). Secondly, many scholars are similarly confused about the meaning of the term 'postsecular'. For instance, Aamir R. Mufti asks whether the postsecular marks 'a transition in the world at large, in intellectual practices concerned with understanding the world, or some combination of both' (9).

Several critics of postsecular studies identify a key problem in how the field is complicit in several of the systemic assumptions that it critiques. According to Mufti, the notion of the postsecular that 'authoriz[es] this discourse' of postsecular studies is ironically itself 'at bottom positivistic in nature' (7). He points to how postsecular studies challenges the numerical basis of the 'secularisation thesis', for example, with 'the "fact" of the continued, widespread existence of communities of the faithful across the world' (7). Frederick Cooper likewise observes how postsecular studies falls prey to the same structural error it sets out to critique, explaining that 'antisecular critics assume generic, ahistorical versions of secularism and colonialism spread out over four centuries' (407). They thus reduce Europeans to a 'people without history, a tag formerly reserved for the victims of their colonial endeavors' (407).

Discussing other 'secularist' assumptions that postsecular criticism perpetuates, critics like Laura Levitt note how postsecular criticism is also premised on 'a normative Protestantism' that it fails to acknowledge even as it asserts that 'a purely "secular" critical realm [is] already in place' (108).[1] Kathryn Ludwig draws from Levitt to agree that works of postsecular studies are premised on 'the "invisible hand" of Protestantism' and thus continuously participate in the 'reduction of "religion" to "belief"'—a 'secularist' trait that postsecular criticism itself strongly critiques (qtd. in Ludwig 513). According to Ludwig, recognising that they are 'influenced, even unknowingly' by this 'partial definition of religion', critics need to address the inherent dependence on a 'specific Christian worldview' that determines so much of 'what counts as "religion" in scholarly discourse' (513). One solution would be to engage both with those who 'espouse secular worldviews' and others who 'experience religion differently than they do' (513). At the same time, critics should avoid the implicit 'secularist' presumption that reason can uncover and undo error by always remembering that the problem cannot be remedied through merely 'seek[ing] out additional information' in this manner (513–14). Instead, Ludwig suggests postsecular scholars advance what she calls a 'complicity critique', or the recognition that we are always 'both inside and outside the categories under discussion', as an antidote to these structural problems besieging the field (512).

Critics of postsecular studies further highlight the ways in which the field draws on the binary of religion and secularism that it is so invested in debunking. Both Tracy Fessenden and Laura Levitt wonder whether the postsecular critique continues to reinscribe the binary that it purports to undermine (qtd. in Ludwig 512). Ludwig observes the same problem, particularly in the field of literature, where postsecular interventions 'initially appeared as a kind of "turn" or "return"' or a kind of 'heightened concern for the perceived secularity of the field of literary studies and a recognition of an increase in religious themes and forms' in literature (512). Demonstrating yet again how postsecular studies 'remains bound by a religious/secular binary', she argues that postsecular theory often proposes a 'subtraction theory in reverse, allowing a failed secular project to give way to the triumphant return of religion' (512). The traditional 'subtraction theory' of 'secularisation' (implied by many and posited most clearly by Charles Taylor on page 270 of *A Secular Age*) observes a gradual falling away from religion due to 'secular' incursions till religion disappeared completely into the 'secular', resulting in the revelation of 'the truth' or 'the residual kernel of fact underlying the husk of invention or superstition which used to surround it' (513). However, scholars of postsecular studies argue that 'the secular sphere did not emerge with a decline in religion but was constructed by identifying certain values and practices as "religious" and relegating them to the private sphere', leading to the '"subtraction" of religion' from the public sphere (513). This 'reverse subtraction theory' comes with a 'sense that the secular is equivalent to a non-religious, value-free, neutral site' and creates the space for the staging of a 'triumphant return of religion (albeit in new clothes)', once again reinscribing the 'religious–secular' binary (512–13).

Mufti notes that postsecular studies takes, as its 'vaguely formulated object of critique', a version of the 'secularisation thesis' that is a 'vulgarized' and unserious account of secularism (7). This version is 'more Weber than Marx, Nietzsche, or Freud' and essentially 'a straw man' set up for the purpose of this discursive attack (7). Exonerating Max Weber's much-vilified thesis on the intersection of capitalism with Christianity, Mufti explains how the work is misinterpreted in the field of postsecular studies.[2] Weber does not account for the substitution of the religious with the 'secular', he writes, but frees us from the 'religion–secular' binary that congeals around this typical postsecular interpretation. Weber essentially permits a way of understanding a fundamental characteristic of our contemporary world: the *'inescapability* of calculation and instrumental rationality in a capitalist society and thus the fundamental transformation of religious belief and practice in the transition to the modern social order' (Mufti 8).

In his essay 'Is the Postcolonial Also Postsecular?', Bruce Robbins also disrupts the postsecular reinscription of the 'religious–secular' binary by debunking the untempered, simplistic and sweeping blame mechanism that it sets up. He remarks that 'there is really no excuse to give up on the instruments of scholarly discrimination and fold secularism into a generic, undifferentiated "modernity"' (260). Observing that the tendency of postsecular studies is to condemn 'secularism', modernity, nation states and the West for its complicity in a project of systematic erasure, Robbins points out that if one looks at the premodern age of empires that preceded the modern era of nation states dominated by the 'secular' West, then one realises that the 'sole responsibility for the world's preventable suffering cannot be made to fall on either states or empires, either premodern, precapitalist or modern, capitalist social formations' (258). In fact, 'neither the Crusades nor the Muslim conquests were generated by nation-states', and any 'global, non-Eurocentric history' will be replete with 'hundreds of [examples of] large-scale premodern atrocities with which "the West" was not involved' (258). Robbins suggests that there is a politics underlying the way 'antisecularists rehabilitate religion, allowing it to stand for "the rest" against "the West"' (259). In this counternarrative, 'Marxism, liberalism, democracy, gender equality, and so on become so much of a problem that they cannot even be imagined as components of a solution', (259). Repositioning the target of blame, Robbins censures postsecular critics for reducing issues such as the (deeply multifaceted) 'war on terror' or immigration into the 'religion–secularism' binary. Furthermore, he disapproves of what he considers to be the opportunism of postcolonial critics who, having lost the topical relevance of their field of expertise to some extent, draw on the 'religion–secularism' binary to replace the colonial one (262).

Both Robbins and Mufti dismiss the binary nature of postsecular equivalences between the 'secular/religious' and the 'West/non-West'.[3] Robbins recalls the native origins of 'secularism' in postcolonial countries, noting that '[n]ot all impulses toward what would now be called secularism were products, direct or indirect, of colonial rule' ('Is the Postcolonial Also Postsecular?' 259). Similarly, Anuradha Dingwaney Needham and Rajeswari Sunder Rajan write in their introduction to *The Crisis of Secularism in India* about the reserves of '"indigenous" secularism' in India that derive from significant native 'traditions of popular tolerance, rationalism, secular humanism, and attitudes skeptical and ironic about religion' (21). These reserves are 'not [simply] reducible to the forms of elite or cosmopolitan secularism' that are typically attributed to the 'influence of Nehru and/or a deracinated modernity' (21).

In a similar effort to overturn postsecular binary equivalences, Samuli Schielke analyses secular strands emerging from within mainstream Islamic cultures through a case study of Egyptian secularism. What is 'the positive ground on which a non-religious life can be built in a social world that is saturated by religion' (302), he asks, and in a 'society profoundly affected by a religious revival'? (303). Defying conventional understandings of Islamic societies, Schielke notes two prevalent and alternative approaches towards the issue of religion and secularism in Islamic societies, and the common ground and insufficiency of both these perspectives. Schielke observes how 'Muslims in particular have been made to represent the contradictions surrounding the apparent failure of the "secularization thesis"' (302). A predominant Western approach is represented by the 'new atheists'[4] who object to Islam in very 'radical and sweeping ways, declaring Muslims to be essentially incapable of rational reflection and moral action', and the alternative approach, also mainly Western, is 'an emerging critical anthropology of secularism'[5] that is in a more 'sympathetic vein' (302). Though opposed to each other, both of these views depict Western 'approaches to Islam and secularism' that 'share a wider political and intellectual sensibility' reminiscent of the Orientalist construction of the East as the archetypal 'other' of the West— whether 'as a vilified object of hate or as the starting point of a sophisticated academic critique of liberalism' (302). This perceived binary opposition between 'Islam on the one hand and secularism and non-religion on the other' makes us overlook what Schielke considers to be a crucial fact—that 'non-religion and atheism have long had supporters among Muslim peoples, too' (302). With respect to Egyptian 'secularism', Shielke explains, it is important to understand that 'non-religiosity is not necessarily a child of a Christian genealogy of the secular, and definitely not alien to Muslims' (303). This is true 'even if its shape and some of its positive claims are borrowed from notions of Western origin and global currency (most notably, human rights and feminism)' (302). In contrast to an emerging critical anthropology of 'secularism' that considers 'secularism' to be 'a perilous Western import' and that therefore focuses—as do Talal Asad and Saba Mahmood for instance—on 'the formation of the exclusionary secular state and its citizen-subjects', Schielke emphasises not the political or institutional aspect but the moral aspect of indigenous Egyptian 'secularism'. He observes that Egyptian 'secularism' is often 'less about governance and more about conviction, less about subjectivation and more about a subjective search for a sound moral base for life', and that it therefore needs to be understood as 'an intimate *moral* discontent with a prevailing sense of religion' (303–02; emphasis added). Mufti further delineates the split between the same two prevailing approaches of 'new atheists' on the one hand, who function as 'apologists for the geopolitics of the dominant Western powers', and the new anthropologists of Islam on the other hand (11). For Mufti, the problem with these diverging approaches lies in a pair of assumptions common to both. The first assumption is that 'as a spiritual, intellectual, and political culture, Islamism marks a "return" of Islam, either uncontaminated by, or having shaken itself free of, the liberal thought and practice of the modern West'. The other assumption is that this return means 'the loss and attempted recuperation of past social and cultural forms', that is, the recuperation of the 'authentic' past (10–11). Mufti disagrees with how the 'emergent "postsecular" common sense in the humanistic disciplines' employs this rhetoric of 'authenticity'—firstly, to understand Islamist practices 'as an expression of religious consciousness directed against the inroads of secularism' and secondly, to project secularism itself as nothing other than 'an ideological impulse of the ongoing projects of Western imperialism' (11)—assumptions that do not accurately reflect the reality of Islam and Muslim societies. Thus, Mufti declares that he is not a postsecularist because the view of contemporary Islam established through these assumptions is entirely misleading and works to 'close off prematurely the possibility of a materialist and historical understanding of the present in the Islamic world and a critical engagement with it' (11). Mufti notes that in these postsecular anthropological analyses what disappears altogether is the 'overwhelming number of lived forms of Islamic religiosity', especially 'all forms associated in numerous Islamic societies with women's religious lives', leaving only 'the configuration of contemporary political Islam, theologically diverse but nevertheless Salafi-revivalist in its constitutive gestures' (11). On the one hand then, this new ethnography of Islam ignores the regressive oppression that is a reality in the lives of countless women across Islamic countries. And on the other hand, this postsecular ethnography actively agrees with the assumptions of its own object of study, Islamism, embodied by the Salafi-revivalist religiopolitical practices—concurring with Islamism's tendency to think of itself in 'revivalist terms as a return to the true tradition of Islam' and overlooking the fact that no such return to pure authenticity is possible (12). Mufti asserts that this is a baseless claim because Islamist thought and practice 'cannot be understood in any other way than as inflected through the regimes of colonial law' and as products of 'late, postcolonial capitalism', and it therefore cannot sustain its claim of being 'authentic' and 'uncontaminated by the modern imperial process' (12). With these observations, Mufti unsettles the polemical binary equivalences between the 'secular/religious' and the 'West/non-West' that are common to postsecular theory.

A separate set of allegations levelled at postsecularism has to do with what its critics consider to be the problematic and perilous *political* implications generated by this school of criticism. For instance, postsecularism implies a kind of anti-statism that Bruce Robbins finds arbitrary and politically irresponsible. In 'Is the Postcolonial Also Postsecular?', Robbins criticises the degree to which scholars vilify the state and condemn secularism for its association with this structure. He observes how, for Asad, the state is a 'villain' with a 'pre-existing will to power' that it exercises by 'defining the category of religion' and excluding it from the 'putatively neutral public sphere' (260). Asking the reader to ponder 'how much guilt' 'secularism' should take on for 'association with the state', Robbins reminds us that it is not 'secularism' but religion which is guilty of association with and instrumentalisation by the state. The 'antistatist provinciality' of postsecular studies counters the field's claims of political seriousness because practitioners tend to 'think that one's political duties begin and end with declaring the state one's enemy'—the same state that defines our ideal of the welfare state as the provider of public welfare institutions and regulations such as, for example, regulation of multinational corporations, regulations providing for subsidies on staples and for the inspection of clean water and air (261).

In his essay 'Why I am Not a Postsecularist', Vassilis Lambropoulos highlights another problematic political aspect of postsecularism: how it manifests a larger political trend that was born out of 'the postmodern belief that freedom is unattainable and the revolution pointless' (79–80). This is a kind of post-politics that imagines a collective identity 'after political action has been deemed futile', 'expresses a melancholic nostalgia for something irrevocably lost' and does not believe in political action by any other means—whether by 'aesthetic or judicial politics, social or minority movements' (80). Lambropoulos sums up: 'It is about the nonpolitics of belonging and caring, not the politics of governing or rebelling' (80). As such, Lambropoulos's argument suggests that postsecularism arises when one has 'despaired of politics' and no longer finds the ideals of revolution or freedom meaningful, ultimately signaling a kind of indifference towards politics at best and a dismissive condescension towards it at worst (80).

Bruce Robbins foregrounds another political issue with postsecularism in 'Why I am not a Postsecularist', directing our attention towards the problematic 'larger political meaning of . . . locally meaningful practices' that postsecular scholarship valorises (62). These practices conflict with the staples of a liberal democracy, but the postsecularist often 'maneuver[s]' us into ignoring this by creating a postsecular academic template 'in which such issues need not and cannot be raised' (63). Robbins observes the way Saba Mahmood, a 'major spokesperson for postsecularism' who aligns herself with Asad, studies the Egyptian women of the mosque movement and tries 'as hard as possible to credit the vocabulary of religion deployed by the subjects themselves as the privileged means of access to their self-understanding'; in doing so, she makes 'the true meaning of their actions' exclusive to the women's own understanding of their behaviour (62). The approach is problematic for Robbins because it simultaneously 'excludes any exterior judgment on these practices in terms of their comparative meaning or political ends' (62). One could provide a justificatory anthropological account for 'a fascist youth movement' along these lines because, from the perspective of the participants, such a movement or others like it can always be 'positively valued for what it gives them', such as 'a sense of self-discipline, belonging, purposefulness, and collective agency' (62).

Another one of Robbins's sociopolitical objections to the postsecular way of thought derives from what he sees as one of its foundational approaches—a kind of faith in divinity that expects the individual to be 'grateful' because 'things might well have turned out a lot worse, and we should be grateful they didn't' ('Why I am not a Postsecularist' 64).[6] Pointing to systemically oppressed communities (such as the Dalits in India) and historical wrongs against humanity (such as the Holocaust), Robbins censures this approach rendering the ethic of gratitude suspect and meaningless: 'But to what or whom is one supposed to be grateful? . . . Once you start looking into scenes of existence like these, gratitude doesn't seem like the most precisely calibrated response' (65). In her essay 'The Empire Prays Back: Religion, Secularity, and Queer Critique', Nikita Dhawan takes issue with how the sociopolitical move to include religious and anti-Western perspectives often ends up endorsing regressive discriminatory templates. According to Dhawan, postsecular critiques (often postcolonial in motivation and strongly opposed to Western racism) display 'silences on and the lack of critique of homophobia and heterosexism in diasporic and postcolonial contexts, which are explained away as having been caused by, and as a reaction to, Western racism' (192).

For most critics of postsecular studies, a significant point of departure is an argument favouring the continued relevance and uncontested significance of reason, the predominance of which postsecular theory is invested in overturning as part of its opposition to post-Enlightenment 'secularist' modernity. Pecora responds to the field of postsecular studies by declaring that no matter how much he agrees with these 'current efforts to re-think how we understand religion', he has 'no desire to abandon the power of secular reason'—that is, no desire 'to throw out the baby of evidence-based, logically plausible, and this-worldly analysis along with the bath-water of ignorance about religious tradition' (5). In 'Terror: A Speech After 9-11', Spivak similarly argues that reason is not a public virtue to be dispensed or trifled with. 'My point,' she writes, is that 'whatever your politics or your religion, the place of reason in whatever secularism might mean remains implacable' (105). Akeel Bilgrami agrees, and it is worth quoting him in entirety here:

> It seems more and more urgent to declare oneself a secularist (and I hereby do so) in a time when wars are waged by a government dominated by the thinking of the Christian Right, terror is perpetrated in the name of Islam, occupation

of the territories of a continuously displaced population is perpetuated by a state constituted in explicitly Jewish terms, and a beleaguered minority is killed in planned riots by majoritarian mobilizations reviving an imagined past of Hindu glory. (174)

Ryan Gillespie too questions the usual postsecular critique of reason, which alleges that the 'the conditions of modernity', such as the predominance of reason, 'delimit human flourishing' (1–2). Gillespie observes that according to the postsecular view the functioning of 'reason' results in the 'general secularization of public life and intellectual thought' (2). Gillespie recounts the usual attack on reason by the 'strong skeptics'[7] and feminists who point out that reason is not universal or autonomous but desire-based, plural and the outcome of 'social processes', and that therefore what counts as established public reason in a society is determined entirely by the predominant gender, class, sexual and racial hierarchies of that society (6). Opposition to unjust societies has been launched on the premise that reason is subjective and based on desire, and that therefore the preeminence of any one set of reasons is always contestable and unacceptable. But to Gillespie, this postsecular reevaluation is problematic because it 'leav[es] us with a truncated conception of reason as divorced from morality and/or spirituality' (2). While fully acknowledging that the 'Janus faced' nature of reason can be used to both 'emancipate' and 'oppress' (7), he nonetheless disagrees with this postsecularist denunciation of reason in the context of the current discussion about multiculturalism, 'secularism' and religious conflict. '[N]ot all reasons are equally weighty,' he declares, so we also need to be able to 'maintain commitment to *better* reasons' (6). We need to emerge from our 'agonistic democratic politics' of modernity because 'ignoring the possibilities of an emergent *we* from *I* and *you* discontinuities and ideologies lands us back in polarized, insular communities' (6–7). The end result destroys the possibility of a 'public sphere' and 'collective deliberation', which is a crucial component of a democracy that we cannot afford to neglect (6–7). Instead, Gillespie believes reason can take two forms that come into play: normative reason and motivating reason. Both individuals and groups function in accordance to either motivating reason (which asks, 'What can I do?') or normative reason (which asks, 'What ought I/we do?'). The primacy of the latter cannot be sidelined as 'normative reasons, unlike typical motivating reasons, are not strictly subjective and agent based' and 'cut across the religious/secular divide' (8–9). Most importantly, 'public reason aims to be based on and built by normative reasons and owes little to motivating reasons' (8). But 'if [our] conception of a liberal democracy' is one where the 'state should have no influence over competing visions of the good life' and where 'whatever is legal is (morally) permissible', then we ignore our *obligation* to make the *right* [choice]' and to 'act in accordance with normative truths' (8–9). In this analysis, reason emerges across various religious camps and the religious–'secular' divide as the rightful guide for public decisions based on a sound understanding of ethical responsibility (or 'What ought I/we do?').

Another approach, outlined in Spivak's 'Terror: A Speech After 9-11', is uniquely pragmatic. Spivak begins by acknowledging the reality of the contemporary world, noting that '[t]hose sanitized secularists who are hysterical at the mention of religion are quite out of touch with the world's peoples and have buried their heads in the sand' (102). While suspicious of 'any assertion of the "universalism" of reason-based secularism', Spivak emphasises the significance of this tenet as a *mechanism* (107). In order for reason and the 'secular' to function in a meaningful way, Spivak suggests some practical measures. Firstly, as part of our modern Western legacy, the 'prejudice' that governs us is that '[Ju]deo-[C]hristian[ity] is *the* secular religion'—it is typically seen as 'the religion of reason, de-transcendentalized into secularism' (105). And so, '[i]f reason is to be our ally, . . . it cannot be fetishized, . . . laundered [J]udeo-[C]hristianity' (105–06). As Spivak explains later in the essay, '[n]o religion has a special privilege to' secularism (106). Secondly, she advises us to stop thinking that there is 'some enlightened spirit of secularism' for which we must 'initiate new conversion rites' (106). We should instead acknowledge secularism as 'only ever in the letter', an 'idiom rather than ground of belief', and 'train fiercely to protect it as such' (106–11). '[S]ecularism is not an episteme', she clarifies, but 'a faith in reason in itself and for itself, protected by abstract external structures—the flimsiest possible arrangement to reflect the human condition' (106). We should 'think of secularism as an active and persistent practice, an accountability' that is 'as thin as an ID card, not as thick as "identity"' (106). The value of 'secularism' lies in its practical relevance to society, and in the political urgency that surrounds it and makes it indispensable. As 'a mechanism to avoid violence' it should 'be learned as mere reasonableness' (106). We must therefore commit to this 'set of abstract reasonable laws' in order to 'avoid religious violence', and institute immediate training to inculcate this understanding among citizens (107). An important set of views critical of postsecular thought objects to the moral relativism associated with multiculturalism that postsecular readings seem to imply and support. Of key importance is the work of Akeel Bilgrami, who discusses the issues surrounding multiculturalism. While not endorsing 'classical' liberal arguments in favour of 'secularism',[8] he notes the problem that could arise in culturally relativist multicultural societies where 'there are no external reasons' and where 'all we have are reasons and arguments internal to the moral psychologies of agents' (175). Bilgrami begins by asking whether, in such a context, we are 'theoretically obliged to concede a relativism about values' so that ultimately 'secular liberal values have only a relative truth on their side' (175–76). He disagrees with this sidelining of 'secular' liberalism and suggests that within our multicultural framework we focus on not just the present but the *history* of communities that challenge the ethic of 'secular' liberalism nowadays, and find from within their past such traditions that are naturally aligned with this ethic. Vassilis Lambropoulos exhibits a similar distaste for ethical relativism, and further critiques multiculturalist positions that undervalue political 'secular' governance. After declaring that he is not a postsecularist because he is not a 'multiculturalist', Lambropoulos explains how the multiculturalist advocates for a 'polyphonic diversity' and 'cohabitation' among communities that accord '[a]ll positions . . . equal space and time so long as they do not turn against the liberal regime'; this treatment makes 'questions of sovereignty, governance, rule, legitimacy' peripheral, relegating them to 'the realm of democratic theory' (79). This approach, he implies, seems politically ignorant and irresponsible. Mufti too questions the validity of the new postsecularist anthropology of Islam—the kind exemplified by Talal Asad and Saba Mahmood. He contests its component of 'ethnographic philanthropy'—a 'split method' in which the 'cosmopolitanism of the (Western) anthropologist in the postcolonial era' requires her to 'be "a critic at home and a conformist abroad"',[9] condemning certain types of sociopolitical practices in the West while treating the same uncritically when observed in the non-Western world (14–16). Theoretically, the practice of this sort of postsecularist 'ethnographic philanthropy' forces a detachment from one's own society—'from its (ethnocentric) sense that its life is the only true or natural one—in order to defend someone else's attachment to their way of life' (15). But actually the Western critic closes off 'in advance any possibility of . . . *critical involvement* in the postcolonial societies' and reserves self-criticality only for her own context (16). Such a position is based not on principles of benignity or fairness, Mufti clarifies, but on a sense of superior Western rationality. The critic is called upon to believe that her 'own [Western] beliefs and values are rational, coherent, universal' while exempting the object of the ethnographic study from the possibility of any such critical self-evaluation of its own ideological 'premises'. Thus, the new postsecularist anthropology of Islam is founded on a paradox where, in an attempt to be anti-ethnocentric (or value-neutral) when examining the cultural 'other', 'the postcolonial liberal Western subject' ultimately ends up engaging in ethnocentric anthropology (16).

Given the influential nature of Saba Mahmood's contribution to the field of postsecular studies, a fair number of critics have taken up criticism of the views she presents in *Politics of Piety*. Much of this critique remarks on the perilous scholarly practice of moral relativism and the problematic overturning of the fabric of democratic liberalism that this involves. In her essay 'Is Islam Bad for Women? New Interrogations', Nadia Fadil reviews Mahmood alongside other commentators focusing on the gender aspect of the 'Muslim question' that has become so central to all political and cultural debates.[10] In 'The Echo Chamber of Freedom: The Muslim Woman and the Pretext of Agency', Sadia Abbas observes how Muslim women have become 'perhaps the most visible emblems' of the contemporary 'Islamic resurgence'—the oft-discussed politico-cultural 'return of religion' accompanied by the 'academic turn to religion' which is fuelled by the 'postsecularist theoretical machinery' (160). Western policy discussions centre the '"problem" of the veiled woman', producing a range of theoretical responses 'whose fascination lies primarily in their sinuous, creative, usually more *philic* than phobic attempts to deal with the anxiety generated by the veil and by the Islam it is taken to signify' (160). In 'Irony, Embodiment, and the "Critical Attitude": Engaging Saba Mahmood's Critique of Secular Modernity', Matt Waggoner criticises how Mahmood restricts the extent to which critics can engage in cross-cultural ethical analysis. In 'Mahmood, Liberalism, and Agency', Bharat Ranganathan challenges Mahmood's proposition that 'liberalism is merely procedural' and insists that it 'turns on certain substantive norms' (249). For example, liberalism evokes strict 'commitments to[wards] respecting people's basic rights and liberties' and 'educating people to see both themselves and others as autonomous and equal members of moral and political communities' (249). Mahmood's work suggests that agency in general, and women's agency in particular, may derive from the act of 'inhabiting norms', but Ranganathan reminds us that this template ends up including many practices 'decried by liberal and some feminist theorists' (249). This is crucial for Ranganathan because, according to his elaboration of the 'liberal view', 'practices that override one's status in the political community cannot be defended on the grounds that they are necessary for particular forms of human flourishing' (249). He concludes that as Mahmood's argument against liberalism is premised on 'caricaturing it', it therefore 'lacks polemical force' (249). Mahmood's assertion that certain forms of Islamist conduct (ones that are otherwise self-abnegating) can be seen as crucially subversive actually appears to be 'an apologetics for certain forms of religious creativity' that ends up 'reifying an illiberal and unequal status quo' (249). The key issue here, of course, is understanding the meaning of 'consent' in a libertarian society. What are the limits and possibilities of 'consent' in specific situations where one is seen as 'freely choosing' self-victimisation? Demolishing Mahmood's suggestion that liberalism is merely procedural, Ranganathan notes the importance of grasping how it is founded not only on the concept of 'autonomy as an end state' but also on 'autonomy as a side constraint' (250). According to the latter, the 'rights of others determine the constraints upon [one's] actions' in a liberal society, and one cannot, while pursuing one's own goals, 'override another's status in the moral and political communities' (250). So, Ranganathan clarifies, '[c]onsent . . . isn't a necessary or sufficient condition for certain sorts of interactions', (250). There is no legitimate form of 'libertarian contract' between people where one can agree to surrender one's own autonomy by, for example, becoming a slave or agreeing to be cannibalised by another (250–53). This is because, in the act of striking such an agreement, 'one is overriding either one's own or another's basic rights and liberties' (251). While the agreement appears to be based on an individual's 'consent' to self-abnegate, the consent is actually ambiguous and untenable given that tradition and social conditioning can 'corrosive[ly]' affect individuals into learning to make certain so-called 'choices' (251).[11] In her own analysis of Mahmood's *Politics of Piety*, Sadia Abbas problematises the way the word 'agency' has become a 'redemptive term' (187) in discussions surrounding Muslim women or 'religious injustice' (175), to present suffering, 'human pain' and 'worldly injustice' as acceptable (188). Thus, where Mahmood ascribes agency to the women of the Egyptian mosque movement, Ranganathan observes they are not acting 'autonomously' at all (252). They cannot choose to give up their autonomy through bodily actions that require the surrender of liberty because 'one simply can't remove external constraints and obstacles and believe in an agent's ability to honor his or her standing in moral and political communities' (252). Ranganathan's study likewise suspects the kind of 'practices . . . for self-cultivation [that] require one to override one's basic liberties and rights', such as gender-specific, submissive ways of dress or behaviour that the Egyptian mosque movement requires of women (256). Since these practices limit their options for movement, self-expression, or action, they ultimately 'reify paternalistic social and political structures' (Ranganathan 256).

In 'Saba Mahmood and Anthropological Feminism After Virtue', Sindre Bangstad draws on Melinda Cooper[12] and notes that Mahmood's analysis in *Politics of Piety* 'operates in the iterative mode, whereby she herself "repeats and validates the moral norms of her pious interlocutors"' (32). Moreover, Bangstad reminds the reader of the particular anthropological challenge faced when studying Muslims across the world and attempting to conduct fieldwork in and through mosques. The limitations of this ethnographic methodology become evident in the case of Mahmood's work, as neither the researcher nor the reader gets a sense of the 'extent to which moral dispositions cultivated in the ritual sphere are consonant with the actual behaviour of these pious Muslim women in other social fields' (32). We fail to 'learn much about the extent to which the moral dispositions cultivated in the ritual sphere reflect non-conflicted and coherent moral selves which remain so over time (rather than contextual and transient ones)' (32). Most importantly, we do not get to learn about the social status and class positions of the Egyptian women Mahmood studies. Thus, we are unable to uncover the ways status and class may impact their ritual practice—a narrative 'obscuring of class and social relations' that, according to Bangstad, is delimiting and 'symptomatic of the "culturalist turn" of the postcolonial and poststructuralist left, and the "culturalization of politics"'[13] (33). Bangstad's larger criticism of Mahmood for the way she obscures the political dimension in her ethnographic study is furthered when Bangstad observes that no matter how honestly the Muslim women of the Egyptian mosque movement considered themselves to be separate from political power and its exercise in contemporary Egypt, 'the practices they are engaged in also contribute towards the reproduction of certain forms of gendered (patriarchal and social) power relationships in new forms, and toward the crafting of new social and political hegemonies' (33). Drawing from Ortner,[14] Bangstad calls Mahmood's refusal to depict the lives of the Egyptian women in all their complexity 'ethnographic refusal' (34).[15]

All such scholarly attempts that end up legitimising patriarchal regression in trying to support the right to veil are, according to Sadia Abbas, problematic. One example that she analyses at length is Joan Scott who, in her work *The Politics of the Veil*, critiques French racism and treats the veil as a representation of resistance to French colonialism. Abbas points out that in doing so Scott ends up valorising the choices and experiences of a segment of the French-Muslim population that is firmly committed to orthodox Islam and the wearing of the veil. In doing so, Scott grants this demographic unit the privileged position of 'agents who get to represent Islam' (Abbas 162). Abbas further notes how Scott understates the possibility of coercion in the case of young girls who veil, and casts coercion 'as a reworking of tradition, as a cultural therapeutic meant to mitigate the chaos of urban life' (162). This equating of potentially *coercive* measures with *tradition*, and the casting of tradition as implicitly Muslim, creates a problematic political effect. Scott's position later appears untenable when she disavows other practices, such as 'honor killings', as not being sanctioned by Islam (162). This is because Scott's initial line of argument leaves her with no way to argue that a practice that claims to sanction a tradition associated with Islam is not, in fact, authorised by religion (162). Scott then justifies patriarchy in Muslim contexts with frequent claims that it is no worse than in the case of France—a logical manoeuvre that, in Abbas's view, does a grave disservice to the possibility of gender justice. In the end, Abbas wonders whether 'secular or reformist Muslim feminists (located within this context that is dominated by the disciplinary 'metropolitan gaze') are even able to 'talk about patriarchal structures that draw upon Islam' (165). These 'metropolitan intellectuals' labouring under 'postcolonial guilt' ironically 'get to anoint good Muslims and tar bad ones' in a 'neoconservative hierarchy', writes Abbas (165). In the end, the real limitation of the 'postsecularist universe' is that 'there can be no secular or anti-Islamist Muslims or Muslim reformers' in it (Abbas 165). Instead, there is a 'continuous subsumption of most Muslims to the most orthodox kinds' even while the 'plurality of Islamicate cultures' is constantly invoked (Abbas 165).[16]

The field of postsecular studies therefore generates a vortex of debates around itself, creating a conversational matrix that addresses essential contemporary geopolitics, the global 'return of religion' phenomenon, its resonances in the disciplinary methodologies of the humanities and its impact on the interpretive strategies within literary criticism. The chapters that follow will demonstrate the ways in which literary readings can draw on postsecular insights in order to better understand and illuminate literary texts as products of complex historical cross-currents. These currents include, among other sociocultural developments, the construction of the religious and the 'secular' in relation to hierarchies of gender and race. The literary analyses will also explore textual moments of self-conscious reflection on the merits of the postsecular as well as of the counterargument to postsecularism, in a twentieth-century global space. Bearing in mind Spivak's remark that a certain kind of training in shaping a public classroom through pedagogy has 'become the especial burden of an institutionalized faculty of the humanities' (83), my aim will be to understand how this public humanities initiative may be implemented through literary readings in a manner that resolves the tensions between moral relativism and the yearning for faith.

NOTES

1. Levitt cites other critics such as Ann Pellegrini, Janet R. Jakobsen and Tracy Fessenden ('Disappearances: Race, Religion, and the Progress Narrative of U.S. Feminism') who identify the same issue.
2. This refers to Max Weber's fin-de-siècle sociological work, especially 'The Protestant Ethic and the Spirit of Capitalism', which is most commonly understood as providing an explanation for the gradual 'secularisation' in the modern age, and for arguing that this took place through rapid capitalistic progress that ultimately had Protestant roots. Weber's most widely cited and discussed interpretation is that the ideas of ascetic Protestantism held by groups such as the Calvinists (who believed in predestination) played a role in creating the capitalistic spirit by positing for its followers the idea of the worldly 'calling' and suggesting to them that profit (or materialistic success) held religious value because it functioned as a sign of one's status as the elect predestined for salvation.

3. In his essay 'Is the Postcolonial Also Postsecular?', Bruce Robbins explains how the religious–'secular' binary does not work as an accurate account of West/non-West relations because 'the West has never been constitutively secular and the non-West has never been constitutively religious' (259). Aamir Mufti, in 'Why I Am Not a Postsecularist', explains that he is not a postsecularist because 'postsecularism typically maps the secular–religious antagonisms of the history of the West onto postcolonial spaces in general and Muslim societies and communities in particular' (19). This means that familiar Western 'secular'–liberal templates are ultimately restaged in postsecularism so that postsecularist claims of being a new departure or of having rejected older ways of thinking about Islam are not sustainable.

4. This term refers to contemporary atheists such as John Gray, Richard Dawkins, Daniel Dennett, and Sam Harris, whom I mentioned earlier in this chapter. Schielke cites Richard Dawkins in particular, and identifies Michael Onfray and Ibn Warraq as examples of 'new atheists' who take issue with Islam.

5. Schielke uses this phrase (302–03) to refer to: Saba Mahmood's essays, 'Secularism, Hermeneutics, and Empire: The Politics of Islamic Reformation' and 'Religious Reason and Secular Affect: An Incommensurable Divide?'; the volume edited by Talal Asad, Wendy Brown, Judith Butler and Saba Mahmood titled *Is Critique Secular?*; John R. Bowen's *Why the French Don't Like Headscarves: Islam, the State, and Public Space*; Nadia Fadil's 'Managing Affects and Sensibilities: The Case of Not-handshaking and Not-fasting'; Irfan Ahmad's *Islamism and Democracy in India: The Transformation of Jamaat-e-Islami*; and Sindre Bangstad's *Sekularismens Ansikter*.

6. Robbins explains that he is referring here to Connolly's influential work *Why I Am Not a Secularist*, that carries at the heart of its notion of the postsecular, a general 'gratitude for existence' (qtd. in Robbins 'Why I am not a Postsecularist' 64). This is, as Robbins notes, a response to Bertrand Russell's *Why I Am Not a Christian* that stresses the 'absurdity of the idea that everything happens for a purpose' (64).

7. Gillespie uses this term to refer to post-World War II intellectuals such as Foucault, Derrida and Deleuze 'who hold the maxim "De omnibus dubitandum est"', meaning 'everything must be doubted'—the title of a work by Kierkegaard.

8. According to Bilgrami, classical arguments in favour of secularism have assumed there are 'reasons that all rational people should be bound by' and that these reasons always 'justify basic secular and liberal ideals' (175). Indicating that such classical secularism is problematic, Bilgrami clarifies that no such reasons exist; the only reasons that support secular liberalism are those that 'appeal not to something that all rational people will find compelling, just in virtue of their rationality, but rather . . . to substantive value commitments that some may hold but others may not' (175).
9. Mufti quotes Lévi-Strauss's *Tristes Tropiques*, in which Lévi-Strauss speaks of the 'two divergent attitudes of the anthropologist who is a critic at home and a conformist abroad' (386).
10. Fadil examines other works by Edward Said (*Orientalism*), Christian Joppke (*Veil: Mirror of Identity*) and Sindre Bangstad ('Saba Mahmood and Anthropological Feminism After Virtue') to chart the critical narrative.
11. Ranganathan observes that both Nussbaum and Buchanan explain the negative effect of socialisation and tradition on one's actions, beliefs and perceptions of oneself and others (253).
12. Bangstad draws from Melinda Cooper's 'Orientalism in the Mirror: The Sexual Politics of Anti-Westernism' (39).
13. Bangstad here refers to Žižek's *Violence: Six Sideways Reflections*.
14. Bangstad refers to a concept discussed by Sherry B. Ortner in 'Resistance and the Problem of Ethnographic Refusal'.
15. This, according to Sherry B. Ortner and as quoted by Bangstad, is an anthropological stand where the anthropologist refuses 'to know and speak and write of the lived worlds' of those under study (qtd. in Bangstad 34), and is not interested in producing 'richly textured ethnographic accounts and "thick descriptions"' of this set of people (34).
16. Abbas disagrees with Mahmood for the way Mahmood's project 'exceeds the ethnographic specificity, value, or accuracy' of her claims, and contrasts it with what she considers to be the excellent and far more specifically located study of Hezbollah women by Lara Deeb titled *An Enchanted Modern: Gender and Public Piety in Shi'i Lebanon* (Abbas 185).

REFERENCES

Abbas, Sadia. 'The Echo Chamber of Freedom: The Muslim Woman and the Pretext of Agency.' *Boundary 2*. vol. 40, no. 1, 2013, pp. 155–89.

Ahmad, Irfan. *Islamism and Democracy in India: The Transformation of Jamaat-e-Islami*. Princeton UP, 2009.

Bangstad, Sindre. 'Saba Mahmood and Anthropological Feminism After Virtue.' *Theory, Culture and Society*. vol. 28, no. 3, 2011, pp. 28–54. *Sage Journals*, doi:10.1177/0263276410396914.

Bilgrami, Akeel. 'Secularism and Relativism.' *Boundary 2*, vol. 31, no. 2, 2004, pp. 173–96.

Bowen, John R. *Why the French Don't Like Headscarves: Islam, the State, and Public Space*. Princeton UP, 2006.

Connolly, William E. *Why I Am Not a Secularist*. U of Minnesota P, 1999.

Cooper, Frederick. 'Postcolonial Studies and the Study of History.' *Postcolonial Studies and Beyond*, edited by Ania Loomba, Suvir Kaul, Matti Bunzl, Antoinette Burton and Jed Esty. Duke UP, 2005.

Cooper, Melinda. 'Orientalism in the Mirror: The Sexual Politics of Anti-Westernism.' *Theory, Culture & Society*. vol. 25, no. 6, 2008, pp. 25–49. *Sage Journals*, doi:10.1177/0263276408095543.

Deeb, Lara. *An Enchanted Modern: Gender and Public Piety in Shi'i Lebanon*. Princeton UP, 2006.

Dhawan, Nikita. 'The Empire Prays Back: Religion, Secularity, and Queer Critique.' *Boundary 2*, vol. 40, no. 1, 2013, pp. 191–222.

Fadil, Nadia. 'Managing Affects and Sensibilities: The Case of Not-handshaking and Not-fasting.' *Social Anthropology*. vol. 17, no. 4, 2009, pp. 439–54. *Wiley Online Library*, doi:10.1111/j.1469-8676.2009.00080.

Fessenden, Tracy, '"The Secular" as Opposed to What?' *New Literary History*, vol. 38, no. 4, 2007, pp. 631–36. *JSTOR*, www.jstor.org/stable/pdf/20058030.pdf.

Gillespie, Ryan. 'Reason, Religion, and Postsecular Liberal-Democratic Epistemology.' *Philosophy and Rhetoric*, vol. 47, no. 1, 2014, pp. 1–24. *JSTOR*, doi:10.5325/philrhet.47.1.0001.

Joppke, Christian. *Veil: Mirror of Identity*. Polity P, 2009.

Kierkegaard, Søren. *Johannes Climacus; Or, De Omnibus Dubitandum Est, and A Sermon.* A. & C. Black, 1958. https://archive.org/details/johannesclimacus0000kier.

Lambropoulos, Vassilis. 'Why I am Not a Postsecularist' *Boundary 2*, vol. 40, no. 1, 2013, pp. 77–80. *Duke UP*, doi:10.1215/01903659-2072882.

Lévi-Strauss, Claude. *Tristes Tropiques.* 1955. Translated by John Weightman and Doreen Weightman, Penguin, 2012.

Levitt, Laura. 'What is Religion Anyway? Rereading the Postsecular from an American Jewish Perspective.' *Religion and Literature*, vol. 41, no. 3, 2009, pp. 107–18.

Ludwig, Kathryn. 'Inside Looking In: Complicity and Critique.' *Christianity and Literature*, vol. 67, no. 3, 2018, pp. 511–15. *Sage Journals*, doi:10.1177/0148333117731581.

Mahmood, Saba. *Politics of Piety: The Islamic Revival and the Feminist Subject.* Princeton UP, 2012.

---. 'Religious Reason and Secular Affect: An Incommensurable Divide?' *Is Critique Secular? Blasphemy, Injury, and Free Speech* (The Townsend Papers in Humanities, no. 2), edited by Talal Asad, Wendy Brown, Judith Butler, and Saba Mahmood. U of California P, 2009. *Fordham Scholarship Online*, doi: 10.5422/fordham/9780823251681.003.0003.

---. 'Secularism, Hermeneutics, and Empire: The Politics of Islamic Reformation.' *Public Culture.* vol. 18, no. 2, 2006, pp. 323–47.

Mufti, Aamir R. 'Why I Am Not a Postsecularist.' *Boundary 2*, vol. 40, no. 1, 2013, pp. 7–19. *Duke Press*, doi: 10.1215/01903659-2072846.

Needham, Anuradha Dingwaney, and Rajeswari Sunder Rajan. 'Introduction.' *The Crisis of Secularism in India*, edited by Anuradha Dingwaney Needham and Rajeswari Sunder Rajan. Duke UP, 2007.

Ortner, Sherry B. 'Resistance and the Problem of Ethnographic Refusal.' *Comparative Studies in Society and History.* vol. 37, no. 1, 1995, pp. 173–93. *JSTOR*, www.jstor.org/stable/179382.

Pecora, Vincent P. 'The Secular, the Postsecular, and the Literary.' *American Book Review*, vol. 39, no. 5, 2018, pp. 4–5. *Project MUSE*, doi:10.1353/abr.2018.0061.

Ranganathan, Bharat. 'Mahmood, Liberalism, and Agency.' *Soundings: An Interdisciplinary Journal*. vol. 99, no. 3, 2016, pp. 246–66.

Robbins, Bruce. 'Is the Postcolonial Also Postsecular?' *Boundary 2*, vol. 40, no. 1, 2013, pp. 245–62.

---. 'Why I am Not a Postsecularist.' *Boundary 2*, vol. 40, no. 1, 2013, pp. 55–76.

Russell, Bertrand. *Why I Am Not a Christian*. 1957. Routledge, 2004.

Said, Edward W. *Orientalism*. 1978. Random House US, 2014.

Schielke, Samuli. 'Being a Non-Believer in a Time of Islamic Revival: Trajectories of Doubt and Certainty in Contemporary Egypt.' *International Journal of Middle Eastern Studies*, vol. 44, no. 2, 2012, pp. 301–20. *Cambridge Core*, doi:10.1017/S0020743812000062.

Scott, Joan Wallach. *The Politics of the Veil*. Princeton UP, 2007.

Spivak, Gayatri Chakravorty. 'Terror: A Speech After 9-11.' *Boundary 2*, vol. 31, no. 2, 2004, pp. 81–111. *Duke UP*, doi:10.1215/01903659-31-2-81.

Taylor, Charles. *A Secular Age*. Harvard UP, 2007.

Waggoner, Matt. 'Irony, Embodiment, and the "Critical Attitude": Engaging Saba Mahmood's Critique of Secular Modernity.' *Culture and Religion: An Interdisciplinary Journal*. vol. 6, no. 2, 2005, pp. 237–61. *Taylor & Francis Online*, doi:10.1080/01438300500226414.

Weber, Marx. *The Protestant Ethic and the Spirit of Capitalism: and Other Writings*. 1905. Penguin Classics, 2002.

Žižek, Slavoj. *Violence: Six Sideways Reflections*. Profile Books, 2008.

Chapter Four

The 'Secular Turn' of the Enlightenment

THE HISTORICAL CONTEXT AND THE CASE OF MATTHEW LEWIS'S *THE MONK*

THE HISTORICAL CONTEXT

The late seventeenth and eighteenth centuries are consistently described in scholarly accounts as the age of Enlightenment and as central to the 'secularising' shift—as a historical period that marked the defining transition from the premodern experience of religiosity to a precipitous decline in faith and the concurrent rise of reason. Caputo describes this shift dramatically noting how 'in modernity, the question of God is profoundly recast' so that '[i]nstead of beginning on our knees, we are all seated solemnly and with stern faces on the hard benches of the court of Reason as it is called into session'. 'God is brought before the court, like a defendant with his hat in his hand, and required to give an account of himself... if He expects to win the court's approval' (46). This change is seen as having been propelled by the emergence of a profit-driven economy and the new print marketplace directed at mass consumption—developments that instituted empiricism, commercialism and rationalism as the reigning social values and the defining cultural ethic. In *Imperial Encounters*, Peter van der Veer discusses these beginnings, explaining that the idea of 'secularisation' originated in the separation of Church and state—a signal of Enlightenment development. Both Peter van der Veer and Graham Ward note how the relationship between political and ecclesiastical authority emerged as the foundational issue in the aftermath of the religious wars of the sixteenth and seventeenth centuries. Arguing over the question of whether political loyalty to the state was conceivable in the absence of allegiance to the religion of the state, the American and French Revolutions proved path-breaking in establishing that political loyalty could indeed rest on citizenship instead of membership in the state Church. This ideal was effectively achieved in different ways in different nations,[1] but ultimately set the stage for the solidification of the 'secular' public sphere that we tend to take as normative in the democratic political template of our current times. In *True Religion*, Ward explains that in the face of the Thirty Years War, when superstition and idolatry had become perilous, a modern understanding of religion was emerging through the 'rationalization of religion', 'not just as practices of religious piety, but also in terms of articles or "confessions" constituting the faith' (54). Ward cites as central to this process the writings of Edward, Lord Herbert of Cherbury, whose works engendered and reflected the crucial 'changing understanding of "religion"'—religion as shifting away from 'theological accounts of the soul' and questions of denominational religious truth towards a 'philosophical account of the psyche, the mind' which asked the 'philosophical question'— 'what is truth' (53-54). Herbert, tremendously influential both for the seventeenth-century and for later towering figures such as Grotius, Mersenne, Gassendi, Descartes and Locke,[2] made the 'truth' of religion 'universal and self-evident'—self-evident 'to those who rightly use their reason' (54)—and formulated a five-axiom archetype for the form of religion applicable universally across all human cultures, initiating a shift to the modern understanding of religion. The emphasis on reason was crucial in the way it redefined the experience and understanding of religious faith. As Nicholas Adams explains, the period saw the movement from 'minimal rules' to 'maximal reason'—that is, reason increasingly began to govern the relationships between religions, at first for the preservation of religious pluralism, before ultimately intruding upon the *internal* understanding of the religions themselves (10).

In a world recovering from the violent religious strife of the Thirty Years War, Herbert's formulation was designed to locate religion in the subjective sphere, away from the public sphere. His writings effectively established religious beliefs as a private matter (appealing to individual reason), and consequently labeled the public sphere as an 'independent, autonomous, neutral and objective space' (Ward 60)—a foundational Western dualism which was most evocatively expressed by Locke in the following generation,[3] and which, as Gauri Viswanathan observes (chapter two), continues to carry problematic implications for our modern times. Moreover, the Peace of Westphalia (1648) and the Act of Toleration (1689) set the basis for the seventeenth-century rise of liberalism as a thought system and social reality. Based on such an enabling ideological foundation, these developments also led to the systematisation of tolerance, social consensus and religious pluralism around the time. Several concepts began to emerge intellectually in the late seventeenth century—the 'new understanding of human liberty' as something that was valuable and needed safeguarding, and as a 'new understanding of being human' and a 'set of rights' that needed to be extended to all human beings (Ward 60). Charles Taylor explains the 'new vision of moral order' that emerged in the seventeenth century with the rise of 'new theories of Natural Law', most significantly embodied in the works of the theorists Grotius and Locke—a moral order that played a key role in the development of modern Western society (Taylor 159). These theorists emphasised that society grew out of natural laws where human beings possessing equal rights freely consented to being part of a society (159). Liberalism itself, as discussed in chapter two, was a Protestant–Christian and imperialist project. Ward also explains how, following from the imperative of reason and the philosophy of liberalism, the resultant sense of 'religion', as it emerged in modernity, was a 'Protestant Christianity', 'monotheistic and Bible-based', aimed at fostering a 'Protestant culture' (60). These axiomatic foundations provided a basis for religious pluralism and social consensus in the seventeenth century to which eventually religious minorities like the Jewish people could adapt (60). Thus, a modern understanding of religion arose that was based on empiricism and rationalism—

one that reflected the increasingly mercenary economy and invested value in central religious axioms to which individuals were seen as consenting.

In *Rituals of Spontaneity*, Lori Branch observes, quoting Shaun Irlam's *Elations*, that 1650 to 1750 has been identified as the critical transitional period that witnessed the supposed 'end of the theological cosmos and the beginning of the modern era of rational enlightenment, experimental science, historical awareness, and political understanding' (qtd. in Branch 4). Branch, however, questions this straightforward 'secularisation thesis' and its explanation for how 'Restoration and Enlightenment' witnessed the rise of the 'concept of the secular and the ideology of secularism' (5). She remarks that this usual story was 'not so smooth or evenly paced as has been supposed' and 'secularisation' was not, as is imagined, 'a simple decline in religious belief and practice, part and parcel with modern economy and technological advances' (5). Branch questions this narrative by studying the rise of spontaneity as an aesthetic in the late seventeenth and early eighteenth centuries. She studies the contemporary cultural and poetic valuation of 'spontaneous emotional effusion'—a notion connected with the modern dissident/nonconformist idea of 'enthusiasm' as opposed to the pre-modern privileging of ritual, and a notion that 'was taken as *evidence* of the condition of one's heart . . . when that heart came to be conceived of as an object of investigation, appraisal, and exchange like so many others in the given world' (4). Drawing on this, Branch shows that the literatures of this time (free prayer pamphlets, spiritual autobiography, moral sense philosophy, sentimental novels and poetry) 'expound this new value for spontaneous emotional feelings' that significantly resonate with the contemporary 'languages of experimental discovery and with mercantile and emerging consumer discourses of being current and up-to-date' (4). Thus, Branch crucially establishes a connection between two developments in the late seventeenth and early eighteenth centuries—the rise of the religious rhetoric of spontaneity and modern Protestant enthusiasm on the one hand, and the forces of empiricism, rationalism and commercialism that are associated both with the Enlightenment and with the rise of the genre of the novel on the other—ultimately showing that 'secularisation' was a *'rhetorical process*, which takes place first of all *within religious discourse itself*, by which economic and empirical discourses make it harder and harder to speak of the value of *faith*—or of anything—except in terms of certainty and possession' (Branch 5; emphasis added).

I will examine this interpenetration of religious concepts and empirical-commercial metaphors in the next segment with reference to Matthew Lewis's *The Monk* (1796) to show how a 'secularising' shift was taking place from within religious literary discourses—not in a way that endorsed a 'decline of faith' story, much as the 'secularisation thesis' would have us believe, but in a way that reconfigured the experience and meaning of faith from within.

THE ENTANGLEMENTS OF FAITH AND THE 'SECULAR' IN MATTHEW LEWIS'S *THE MONK*

In his landmark work, *The Rise of the Novel*, Ian Watt quotes Eugène-Melchior de Vogüé's views of the novel, concurring with him about the 'atheistic presumption in the novel's exclusion of the non-natural', and remarks: 'it is certain that the novel's usual means—formal realism—tends to exclude whatever is not vouched for by the senses: the jury does not normally allow divine intervention as an explanation of human actions. It is therefore likely that a measure of secularization was an interdisciplinary condition for the rise of the new genre' (Watt 83–84).[4] Examining the novel against the backdrop of its birth in the eighteenth century, a period marked by a new marketplace commercialism and empirical rationalism, Watt implies that the genre is rooted in a historical moment of 'secularisation' and that it delegitimises anything that is extra-sensory or non-empirical/'non-natural'. What is even more striking is the legal language in which Watt explains this, stating that 'the jury' does not allow the supernatural as an explanatory framework (84). On the one hand, this rhetoric connects with Caputo's characterisation of the Enlightenment through courtroom imagery (quoted at the start of this chapter), and on the other hand it connects with Puritan covenant theology of the seventeenth and eighteenth century on which I will soon elaborate. Watt goes on to explain how the novel was born with the shift from the Bunyanesque allegorical narrative to Defoe's realistic writing, which located man at the centre so that human actions came to be valued for their own sake and no longer depended on a religious context for meaning and significance. Arising from this eighteenth-century 'secularising' context of the rise of the novel is the interesting case study of the Gothic to which *The Monk* belongs, a genre that was born towards the end of the century and that was visibly religious in its imagery and topography. The Gothic is generally understood as a literary-cultural mode that subverts eighteenth-century empiricism. Scholars have variously explored it as a genre that expresses the anxiety-ridden, fragmented, frightening and dark underbelly of the Enlightenment project. The repressed irrational of Enlightenment modernity is often understood to be literally and topographically embodied by the typical supernatural horrors, ghosts, corpses and subterranean dungeons of this genre. In an essay called 'Virtue and Terror: *The Monk*', Peter Brooks indicates how Lewis's novel, located in the moment of the eighteenth-century 'secular turn', occupies the fraught space between the religious and the 'secular'. Brooks notes that this novel is 'one of the first and most lucid contextualizations of life in a world where reason has lost its prestige, yet the Godhead has lost its otherness; where the Sacred has been re-acknowledged but atomized, and its ethical imperatives psychologized' (115). Peter Grudin similarly suggests this novel's mediation of the supernatural and the empirical. In '*The Monk*: Matilda and the Rhetoric of Deceit', Grudin reminds us that Todorov discusses Matthew Lewis's *The Monk* as an example of the '*fantastique*' where the reader, who presumes a rationalistic world order, faces a moment of hesitation when confronted with the inexplicably supernatural. This fantastic in Todorov's theorisation is distinct, as Grudin suggests, from 'the explained supernaturalism of Ann Radcliff' or '*l'etrange*' (the uncanny) and 'the accepted supernaturalism of *Melmoth the Wanderer*' or '*le merveilleux* (the marvellous) (Grudin 145). Richard Murphy, in *Theorizing the Avant-Garde* (1999), explains that Todorov's realm of the marvelous is 'an area in which supernatural events may occur and can be accepted as such through the literary convention of the "once-upon-a-time" contract, whereby all "reality-testing" by the reader and the figure alike is suspended' (188)—a realm in which falls *Melmoth the Wanderer*. The realm of the uncanny is one in which 'the function of reality-testing is preserved, so that the apparently supernatural events which occur in the narrative may be rationally explained as deriving for example from the unconscious', as in Freud's idea of the 'uncanny' (188)—a realm in which falls Radcliffe's Gothic novels. Matthew Lewis's *The Monk*, however, is distinct from both and associated with the 'fantastic'—fantasy as the subversive underbelly of realism, characterised by 'an extended hesitation on the part of the reader and an inability to decide whether the unusual events are real or illusionary, naturally or unnaturally caused' (188). Thus, on the whole, scholars situate this novel in the precise historical moment of the 'secular turn' that was conflicted between the religious and the irreligious, and consider it a manifestation of the fantastic that hesitatingly hovers between the realms of the supernatural and the natural/empirical. Summing up this point, Brooks argues that in a world newly marked by '[r]ationalism and desacralization' the Gothic performed a 're-exploration of the numinous' resulting in a 'radical redefinition of the spiritual forces at play in the universe' (250). Caught in this complex historico-cultural moment, and manifestly supernatural in many ways, Lewis's work operates very deeply in the foundational empirical impulse of the novelistic tradition. The intertwining of the 'religious' and the 'secular' at the time of the birth of the secular era becomes evident in Matthew Lewis's *The Monk*, which I will show engaged in the most unabashed supernaturalism while channelling empirical rationality and contractual commercialism underneath its religious/supernatural rhetoric.[5] My analysis will focus on the way Lewis represents the supernatural legend of the 'Bleeding Nun' as caught between history and fiction, and how he portrays the supernatural realm as pervaded by the rhetoric and logic of empirical rationality, commerciality and legality. Ultimately, the text demonstrates how the overarching frameworks of eighteenth-century epistemology simultaneously contain and convey the elements of the supernatural by infusing its very representation and rhetoric with the empirical.

The Monk tells a horrifying story of rape, incest and murder. More specifically, it stages '"Catholic" incest and lust . . . [and] its ambiguous, homoerotic nuances' in a Protestant England that believed in 'the Black Legend of monastic Catholicism'— that 'Catholicism perverted "pure" religion, producing deviant sexual practices originating from "unnatural" vows of chastity' (Blakemore 521). The novel revolves in part around the reputedly virtuous monk, Ambrosio, who engages sexually with a nun in love with him, Matilda, and then over the course of the novel determinedly pursues, rapes and murders the innocent Antonia, despite attempts by her mother (Elvira) to protect her. Antonia's lover, Lorenzo, also fails to save her from Ambrosio's predatory grip, but is able to rescue his sister, Agnes—who was supposed to have been secretly murdered under the instructions of Ambrosio but who ultimately surfaces alive and dungeon-bound at the very end of the narrative. Once saved, Agnes is reunited with her lover, Raymond. The prioress who had imprisoned and tortured Agnes under Ambrosio's orders faces punishment at the close of the novel, as does Ambrosio himself, who has to face the Inquisition and is condemned to burn. What is of paramount importance, however, is a subplot surrounding the ghostly tale of the Bleeding Nun—a gory supernatural legend in which the Bleeding Nun was rumoured to attack the castle of the Baroness. It is in an early episode between Agnes and Raymond that we see this drama enacted when Agnes attempts to escape with Raymond while under the vigilance of the Baroness by dressing up as the Bleeding Nun who they imagined would go unstopped by the guards because the figure was known to be an age-old apparition. Their assumption proves to be accurate, and Raymond does escape with Agnes disguised as the Bleeding Nun, but their carriage crashes on the way and when he regains consciousness, Raymond discovers Agnes is gone. Chillingly, he realises a few months later that it was in fact not Agnes but the actual ghost of the Bleeding Nun that had eloped with him.

Ann Radcliffe describes Lewis's kind of Gothic writing in her essay, 'On the Supernatural in Poetry' (1826), by drawing a distinction between the element of 'terror' that is characteristic of her own texts, and that of 'horror' which is representative of

Lewis's work. She argues that terror is characterised by obscurity or indeterminacy in its treatment of potentially repugnant events, while horror specialises in unambiguous displays of atrocity. This may lead us to interpret terror supernaturalism more easily as a psychological outgrowth of an anxious mind—merely symbolic and cathartic in nature. The far more palpable, immediate, and frighteningly real supernatural in Lewis's horror Gothic makes it impossible to explain away the many outrageous manifestations. *The Monk* offers no empirical/natural explanation for the Bleeding Nun, Elvira's ghost, the Matilda/Devil figure (who strikes a fatal deal with Ambrosio) or Matilda's exchanges with the dead. Crucially, descriptions of these supernatural figures and exchanges in the text are infused with the suggestive language of empirical rationality, commerciality and legality. In this respect, it is useful to begin by examining the episode where, praying at the Statue of St Rosolia, her patroness, Antonia chants the 'Midnight Hymn' and submits herself to the 'protection of heaven' (Lewis 194). The hymn ends with what is a definitive expression of contractual agreement. This notion of the contract is crucial given the idea of the covenant that, according to David Zaret, gained unique centrality in seventeenth-century Puritan theology. In *The Heavenly Contract* (1985), Zaret observes how covenant theology, that became prominent in prerevolutionary Puritan thought, tempered the earlier predestinarian emphases in Calvinism and gave the individual believer more space for personal initiative (where the believers attempted to look at their own lives to identify marks of their heavenly election instead of reinforcing the notion of undecipherable predestination) by introducing notions of contract, exchange and reciprocity into the relations identified between God and the person. Zaret notes in particular how covenant theology derives the idea of the covenant significantly from 'secular precedents established by use of contracts in daily life' and how they used the 'principles and practices associated with the use of worldly contracts' to develop the 'idea of a heavenly contract [that works] as a pastoral guide to the introspective search for evidence of election' (163). *The Monk* draws on this charged and topical image of the contract, applying this economic metaphor rhetorically to the realm of the supernatural/religious. Antonia's hymn ends thus:

> Pleased that my soul has 'scaped the wreck,
> Sighless will I my life resign,
> And yield to God my spirit back,
> As pure as when it first was mine. (Lewis 255)

The idea of signing away or attempting to 're*sign*' one's life, and the associated notions of ownership, commercial answerability and contractual agreement, are evoked in this space of the religious. Antonia later reads a Spanish ballad which again introduces empiricist legality and commerce into the relationship of two lovers who bridge the gap between the mortal and the supernatural. The ballad tells the story of Imogine pledging her love to Alonzo, who is leaving for the war, in distinctly legal terms, where she assures him that he can retrieve and re-'claim' her and charge her a penalty if, upon his return, he detects faithlessness in her:

> If e'er I, by lust or by wealth led aside,
>   Forget my Alonzo the Brave,
> God grant that, to punish my falsehood and pride,
> Your ghost at the marriage may sit by my side,
> May tax me with perjury, claim me as bride,
>   And bear me away to the grave! (Lewis 314)

And when Imogine does in fact forget Alonzo, who is at war in a faraway land, and marries the Baron, she is greeted by exactly this supernatural spectre on her wedding day—an otherworldly figure come back to tally accounts. From its 'Skeleton's head . . . The worms they crept in, and the worms they crept out,/And sported his eyes and his temples about,/While the spectre addressed Imogine' (315). This 'Spectre', from which everyone turns away with a 'terrified shout', seeks vengeance, but in evident legal rhetoric where the spectre forces Imogine to 'suffer the pain of her crime' (244). And this contractual penalty, with its assumption of commerce, comes to now characterise the supernatural realm, thus connecting Imogine's worldly and otherworldly existences as she transitions from her mortal state to the form of a spirit. Despite Imogine's transition into the incorporeal, and therefore suggestively into the transcendental, ethereal and spiritual, there is no new ethical dimension that is introduced into the understanding of Imogine's 'crime', and no change in the terms of the demanded punishment.

Imogine's otherworldly state continues to be governed by prevailing eighteenth-century empiricist ideological frameworks. Imogine now appears in the hall with her 'Skeleton-Knight' and shrieks as he whirls her as penalty. Alonzo similarly inhabits this empiricist continuum between the earthly and the supernatural codes with the 'Knight' and the 'Skeleton' blending seamlessly. And the humans become spectators to this grisly supernatural enactment of worldly legal codes. They even become participants in the execution of this legal drama by sitting and drinking 'out of skulls newly torn from the grave', sipping their 'liquor [which] is blood' and watching the spectres dance around them.

Lewis further inscribes the supernatural within the framework of the empirical by locating the novel strategically in the complex contemporary discursive landscape caught between 'history' and 'romance'. I argue that avoiding both options in the binary between 'naïve empiricism' and 'extreme skepticism' that McKeon discusses, Lewis adopts a narrative stance that can be called 'extreme empiricism', in which the supernatural is circumscribed by and embossed within the outlines of the empirical. Explaining the fraught nature of seventeenth-century 'secularisation', Michael McKeon defines the terms in which the crucial questions of truth and 'historicity'—ideas central to the Restoration and the early eighteenth century—were being debated at this time. McKeon observes that the epistemological terrain on which the genre of the novel coalesced during this period was characterised by a binary between what he calls 'naïve empiricism' and 'extreme skepticism' (21). He notes how, on the one hand, the 'naïve empiricism' of 'true history' opposed the discredited idealism of romance, insisting on the empirical world of the senses and matter as an end in itself instead of as a means to the spirit, while on the other hand, it thereby generated a countervailing, 'extreme skepticism' which in turn discredited 'naïve empiricism' with its claim to 'true history' as a type of 'new romance' (114). McKeon cites as examples of this genre various discursive modes of the new 'natural history'— scientific observation, documentary publication, legal validation and news reportage (72)—which were intended by the Royal Society historians to be 'naively empiricist' in their recording of true history instead of the 'pretty [t]ales' and 'romances' recorded by the Ancients (68). But from the perspective of empirical science itself, the exemplars of 'extreme skepticism' like Samuel Butler rejected these as no more true than the old romance. When it comes to the textual treatment of these questions of historicity and truth, *The Monk* is not easily understood as an exemplar either of 'naïve empiricism' or of 'extreme skepticism'. This is because, firstly, not only does it render a naïve empiricist account of mortal lives with their tangible facts, but also includes within this empiricist account the narration of the brazenly romance-like supernatural episodes almost as though they belong in this natural world. And secondly, the text is not sceptical about the possibility of empiricist natural reportage altogether. Instead, Lewis functions in a mode that one could term 'extreme empiricism', one in which—as I have already begun to demonstrate above—even the supernatural is presented as not romance but history governed thoroughly by the laws of empiricism. This generative tension between the modes of empiricist 'history' and supernatural 'romance' is revealed best in Agnes's account of the Bleeding Nun story. Agnes wavers uncertainly between classifying the story as romance or history, and the narrative strategically inclines towards the latter. Raymond notes Agnes's painting of the legend of the Bleeding Nun, replete with every horrific detail of the Nun's appearance and the shock it elicits among her audience. He enquires of Agnes whether the etching was a mere 'invention of [her] . . . own', gesturing towards its obvious romance-like elements. In response, Agnes lends the narrative a 'marvelous' fanciful aspect as she tells the story of the Bleeding Nun in a 'tone of burlesqued gravity' (Lewis 139). However, she also draws on collective and shared social knowledge, and the notion of historical time, thereby embedding this mysterious and supernatural story in recorded empirical history. Agnes grounds the figure and the story of the Bleeding Nun in the Lindenberg community's historical trajectory and its shared repository of knowledge when she asks Raymond incredulously: 'But can you possibly have lived at Lindenberg for three whole months without hearing of the Bleeding Nun?' (138–39). She reasserts the historicity of the supernatural narrative by legitimising it as history and knowledge—realms perceived as respectful of facticity and opposed to otherworldliness—by declaring to Raymond: 'All my knowledge of her History comes from her old tradition in this family, which has been handed down from Father to Son, and is firmly credited throughout the Baron's domains' (138–39). These claims of the tangible historicity and rational verifiability of the supernatural are cemented when the Bleeding Nun actually appears and when Raymond not just receives her outside the castle but also mistakes her for Agnes. Reinstating her in a historic narrative instead of in an inventive romance, Raymond recites a short verse that uses language of legal ownership to establish his proprietary right over the Bleeding Nun:

> Agnes! Agnes! Thou art mine!
> Agnes! Agnes! I am thine!
> In my veins while blood shall roll,
> Thou art mine!
> I am thine!
> Thine my body! Thine my soul! (Lewis 155)

This rhetoric is even adopted by the mysterious and otherworldly Bleeding Nun, who then repeats the verse, planting herself in this contractual agreement:

> Raymond! Raymond! Thou art mine!
> Raymond! Raymond! I am thine!
> In thy veins while blood shall roll,
> I am thine!
> Thou art mine!
> Mine thy body! Mine thy soul! (Lewis 160)

The Bleeding Nun then proceeds to evoke the idea of the modern economic contract, referring to notions of mercenary 'engage'-ment: 'His [Raymond's] own lips have made over to me his body and his soul: never will I give back his promise, never shall He know a night devoid of terror, unless He engages to collect my mouldering bones . . .' (165).

However, the most complex evocation of this ambiguity and overlap between the 'marvelous'/supernatural on the one hand and the 'historical' on the other—a binary associated with the debate on 'secularisation'—can be found in Agnes's seeming attempt to defend the historicity of the Bleeding Nun story. She declares that even her 'Aunt who has a natural turn for the marvellous, . . . *would sooner doubt the veracity of the Bible*, than of the Bleeding Nun', and follows this up by offering to narrate the history of the supernatural legend (Lewis 138–39; emphasis added). In this debate about whether the narrative of the Bleeding Nun is fictitious or historical, Agnes's reference to the Bible's truthfulness evokes the larger Enlightenment 'secularisation' debate with its attacks on the authenticity of the Biblical narrative. As Jonathan Sheehan notes, around 1700, Protestants in Germany and England had discovered that their 'canonical texts', like the Bible, 'had become or were threatening to become . . . *"strange, awkward, and new"*' (27). The Bible had taken on 'darker tones: it was obsolete, it was imperiled, it was deficient, it was insufficient as it stood to confirm the authenticity of the Protestant religions', being under attack by 'iconoclastic Catholics like the Oratorian scholar Richard Simon' or 'radical philosophers' like 'Baruch Spinoza, Thomas Hobbes, or Pierre Bayle' (27). Thus, with attacks by sceptics like Hume, who challenged the idea of religious miracles, and polemic cultural currents such as those Sheehan delineates, debates about the Bible were at the very heart of controversies about the truthfulness, historicity and veracity of religion. Agnes once again stirs the 'secularisation' debate when, having outlined the many sceptical attacks on religion, she references the idea of superstition from contemporary Enlightenment discourses that had begun to discard premodern Christian ritual as 'superstition'. When Raymond asks her if she believes in the supernatural tale of the Bleeding Nun she had just narrated, she responds indignantly: 'How can you ask such a question? No, no . . . I have too much reason to lament superstition's influence to be its Victim myself' (Lewis 141). Agnes therefore allows the Bleeding Nun narrative, as well as religious claims as a whole, to waver between the marvelous, fictional and false on the one hand and the truthful, historical and authentic on the other. And the novel as a whole moors these descriptions of the religious and the supernatural within the valorised eighteenth-century discourses of empiricism, rationality, commerce and legality. Into this polemical space, the author releases his novel, now a mere textual commodity designed to 'delight' in the modern eighteenth-century marketplace, free-flowing through its channels of uncertain commerce, untethered to any likelihood of literary permanence, and treading the 'dangerous' and anxious currents of purported 'secularisation':

> Go then, and pass that dangerous bourn
> Whence never Book can back return:
> And when you find, condemned, despised,
> Neglected, blamed, and criticized,
> Abuse from All who read you fall,
> (If haply you be read at all)
> Sorely will you your folly sigh at,
> And wish for me, and home, and quiet.
> . . .
> Now then your venturous course pursue:
> Go, my delight! Dear Book, adieu! (Lewis 3–4)

NOTES

1. The American and French revolutions in the eighteenth century ended the association between royal absolutism and the established Church. In Britain, this severance manifested later when, in the early nineteenth century, Catholics and Dissenters were gradually enfranchised.

2. In Locke's works, such as *Letter Concerning Toleration* and *The Reasonableness of Christianity*, influenced as they were by Edward, Lord Herbert of Cherbury, we see the emerging idea of the individual's right to choose religion based on reason.

3. Locke, writing in 1685, argued that, '[a]ll the life and power of true religion consists in the inward and full persuasion of the mind' (Ward 59). He clarified that the churches only have jurisdiction therefore over the '"externals" of worship', while the civil government 'provides for the temporal good' and therefore has sway over the 'outward prosperity of society'. And so, the boundaries between the two realms are 'fixed and immoveable' (59).

4. Watt draws on F. W. J. Hemmings' *The Russian Novel in France, 1884–1914* to quote the views of Eugéne-Melchior de Vogüé, the Catholic opponent of the French Realists who 'found an atheistic presumption in the novel's exclusion of the non-natural' (Watt 83–84).

5. Paul Lewis gestures towards this when he argues that Matthew Lewis writes 'rational, didactic fiction' so that, in his works, 'criminal actions are always labelled as crimes' and 'the final natural or supernatural explanations serve to remind us of the relations of characters and events to an order that has been operative throughout' (471).

REFERENCES

Adams, Nicholas. 'Kant.' *The Blackwell Companion to Nineteenth-Century Theology*, edited by David A. Fergusson, Wiley-Blackwell, 2010, pp. 3–30.

Blakemore, Steven. 'Matthew Lewis's Black Mass: Sexual, Religious Inversion in *The Monk*.' *Studies in the Novel*, vol. 30, no. 4, 1998, pp. 521–39. *JSTOR,* www.jstor.org/stable/pdf/29533296.pdf.

Branch, Lori. *Rituals of Spontaneity: Sentiment and Secularism from Free Prayer to Wordsworth.* Baylor UP, 2006.

Brooks, Peter. 'Virtue and Terror: The Monk.' *ELH*, vol. 40, no. 2, 1973, pp. 249–63. *JSTOR,* www.jstor.org/stable/pdf/2872659.pdf.

Caputo, John. *On Religion.* Routledge, 2001.

Grudin, Peter. '*The Monk*: Matilda and the Rhetoric of Deceit.' *The Journal of Narrative Technique*, vol. 5, no. 2, 1975, pp. 136–46. *JSTOR,* www.jstor.org/stable/30225558.

Hemmings, F. W. J. *The Russian Novel in France, 1884–1914.* Oxford UP, 1950.

Irlam, Shaun. *Elations: The Poetics of Enthusiasm in Eighteenth-Century Britain.* Stanford UP, 1999.

Lewis, Matthew. *The Monk.* Edited by Howard Anderson, Introduction by Nick Groom, Oxford UP, 2016.

Lewis, Paul. 'Fearful Lessons: The Didacticism of the Early Gothic Novel.' *CLA Journal, vol.* 23, no. 4, 1980, pp. 470–84. *JSTOR.* www.jstor.org/stable/44328598.

McKeon, Michael. *The Origins of the English Novel, 1600–1740*. Johns Hopkins UP, 2002.

Murphy, Richard. *Theorizing the Avant-Garde: Modernism, Expressionism, and the Problem of Postmodernity*. Cambridge UP, 1999.

Radcliffe, Ann. 'On the Supernatural in Poetry.' *New Monthly Magazine*, vol. 16, no. 1, 1826, pp. 145–52.

Sheehan, Jonathan. *The Enlightenment Bible: Translation, Scholarship, Culture*. Princeton UP, 2005.

Taylor, Charles. *A Secular Age*. Harvard UP, 2007.

Tzvetan Todorov. *Introduction a la litterature fantastique*. Editions du Seuil, 1970, pp. 133–43.

Veer, Peter van der. *Imperial Encounters: Religion and Modernity in India and Britain*. Princeton UP, 2001.

Viswanathan, Gauri. *Outside the Fold: Conversion, Modernity, and Belief*. Princeton UP, 1998.

Ward, Graham. *True Religion*. Blackwell Publishing, 2003.

Watt, Ian. *The Rise of the Novel: Studies in Defoe, Richardson and Fielding*. 1957. U of California P, 2001.

Zaret, David. *The Heavenly Contract: Ideology and Organization in Pre-Revolutionary Puritanism*. U of Chicago P, 1985.

Chapter Five

Nineteenth-Century Anxieties and Modern Perspectives

The nineteenth century is embossed on the popular and scholarly imagination as the watershed period of religious crisis and spiritual decline. Caputo notes that '[b]y the end of the nineteenth century God was indeed all but dead among the intellectuals' and religious faith had become 'scientifically dubious (Darwin), psychoanalytically twisted (Freud), and economically and politically reactionary (Marx)' (55–56). This impression of the nineteenth century is true not only of the historiographical accounts that followed the age but also of the contemporary narratives produced by those who lived and agonised at the time. Robert Lee Wolff's sizeable work, *Gains and Losses: Novels of Faith and Doubt in Victorian England* (1977), among other works of secondary scholarship, lists the hundreds of 'crisis of faith' novels that were produced in the nineteenth century, each of which provided a poignant and embattled account of the author's loss of faith and their disillusionment either with a faith denomination or with religion as a whole, often under the influence of modernising scientific currents or inter-denominational religious conflicts. Modern historiographical scholarship about the nineteenth century recounts a hackneyed story of *perceived* 'secularisation'. As noted in chapter two, A. N. Wilson and Bernard Reardon figure among countless others that recount this familiar narrative. Wilson notes how '[p]eriodically in the course of the century' many 'proclaimed that God was dead' and that 'that is how it appeared to many... who lived through those times' (xi). This scholarship succinctly retells this story, emphasizing: the tremendous influence of eighteenth-century sceptics like Gibbon and Hume; the historical narrativisation of Christ's life by those like David Friedrich Strauss and Ernest Renan that destabilised assumptions of Christ's divinity; the work of Biblical Criticism that dramatically altered the way people saw or interpreted the Scripture; the geological/scientific interventions (culminating in Darwin's *Origin of Species* in 1859) that demolished faith in a benevolent God; the publication of *Essays and Reviews* in 1861 that unleashed the central crises of the controversy; and the rise of Comparative Religion that threatened Western assumptions about Christianity's global supremacy. Historiographical accounts such as these abound. Nevertheless, several authors continue to problematise, in greater or lesser measure, the assumption of a gradual and irrevocable decline of faith.

My aim, in the lead-up to the three chapters which follow, is to cursorily review some of the most significant scholarship that has intervened, challenged and sometimes completely debunked the conventional nineteenth-century 'secularisation' narrative. It is useful to begin with Charles Taylor, who questions some of the most traditionally held assumptions of this 'crisis' story. He explains that, contrary to popular understanding, the shift away from orthodox Christianity took place in two phases—one that came before Darwin and one that came after. Taylor challenges the 'standard story of the Victorians' loss of faith' that oversimplifies the truth by placing emphasis only on 'Darwinian evolution, which is held so directly to have refuted the Bible' (378). Taylor refutes this version, reminding us that 'evolutionary theory didn't emerge in a world where almost everyone still took the Bible story simply and literally' and that, 'among other things, this world was already strongly marked by the ideas of impersonal order' (388). Even before Darwin, traditional Christianity had been challenged by the emergence of ideas of an 'impersonal order'. What is crucial to note, however, is that *both* alternatives available to people at this earlier stage were *'tinged with moral import'* (388; emphasis added). Departing from common scholarly assumption, Taylor emphasises that neither of these 'two understandings of [the] ... epistemological predicament' represented a scientific alternative designed to uproot spiritual faith. Both were perceived as essentially moral choices, and people faced the prospect of choosing what they felt to be the *more moral* of the two (388). The system of impersonal order was considered superior for its stance on the problem of theodicy, which could still maintain a belief in the 'benevolent over-all drift of things' while also accommodating for disturbing disasters (388). These conceptions of an impersonal order were, according to Taylor, 'bridges' which people were already beginning to cross to leave orthodox Christianity (76). In the later part of the nineteenth century, the second stage of the shift brought about by Darwin's ideas occurred—a shift that is generally considered to be the signal turning point and that is based on the idea of 'nature "red in tooth and claw"' which 'operates through extinctions, through the winnowing of the unfit' (54). The conventional narrative asserts that this was the moment science overturned belief. According to Taylor, at this point in time Darwin's theories shattered not orthodox Christianity—the shift away from which had already been effected in the first part of the century—but the prevalent theory of an impersonal order or a 'general design' which believed in the 'benevolent overall drift of things' (388). Taylor cites the example of Thomas Carlyle, Matthew Arnold, T. H. Green, and Mary Humphrey Ward, whose writings express the tensions of the choice they faced in the second half of the nineteenth century— between, on the one hand, an impersonal order on the cosmic level and, on the other hand, the more 'reductive, scientistic or utilitarian modes of order' that their 'sense of the weaknesses, ugliness or evils of their age forbade them to accept' (378). As such, Taylor revises our understanding of the 'secularisation thesis' by plotting the 'secularising' development on a staggered timeline and in a morally imbued landscape.

In *The English Churches in a Secular Society, Lambeth 1870–1930* (1982), Jeffrey Cox problematises the 'secularisation thesis' by objecting to the way churchgoing statistics is used as a ready mark of 'secularisation', and challenges those who subscribe to the notion without realising their complicity with a particular social ideology—an ideology that is hegemonic in its interpretation of the value, meaning or relevance of faith in our lives and that therefore ignores all other perspectives. Cox fractures the 'sociological theory of secularization' (or 'the religious counterpart of the theory of modernization') which, he notes, is cited by 'the great majority of social theorists, sociologists, and social historians' along with many others who are in fact even unconscious of their 'allegiance to any formal theory of social change' (9). According to Cox, the problem with this theory is that its champions cite 'evidence of the existence of a decline of religion in Britain as if it were conclusive evidence in support of their particular theory of the causes of this decline' (9). Cox's analysis leads in a different direction. He admits that religious institutions did start to wither away, and church attendance did begin to decline almost certainly by the 1880s and by the end of the 1920s virtually 'all Protestant statistics (except of church closures) were plunging inexorably' (7). However, Cox contests the common interpretation of this reality, objecting to the way historians gauge the success of nineteenth-century Christianity based on whether 'the churches [could] persuade the emerging urban working class to attend Sunday services' and consider Christianity to be failing because by the mid-nineteenth century it became evident that the churches were not succeeding at this task (4). Cox argues in favour of an alternative approach, reminding us of the religious vitality of the nineteenth century. He observes that the eighteenth-century religious revival animated all but 'the coldest, most rationalistic denominations' and 'generated new ones throughout the industrial areas', 'the mid-Victorian period ... swarm[ed] with religious activity' when compared to the last third of the twentieth century, and the Dissenters and Methodists 'appealed effectively to England's growing numbers of shopkeepers and artisans, and the challenges of Nonconformity and urban infidelity summoned an energetic response by the established church' (4). Cox remarks that the Church of England 'found new and significant social functions at both parochial and national levels' despite challenges (4), and was uncomparable in its geographical reach and its range of philanthropic activities with its network of thousands of clergymen placed in every remote neighbourhood which 'secular' social reformers could not rival. Based on this, Cox concludes that though not succeeding in 'attracting the entire nation to public worship', the churches did triumph in making 'public deference to religious values—and public acknowledgment of the importance of religion—almost universal among the upper and middle classes' (76). Ultimately, Cox's work emphasises this lived reality of religion, indirectly critiquing the approach that considers religion to be a tool of intellectual influence and measurable through statistical indicators—assumptions that undergird the 'secularisation thesis' itself.

This approach is powerfully overturned in *The Secularization of the European Mind in the Nineteenth Century* (1975) by Owen Chadwick who dismisses 'this simplistic model of social change, now largely confined to textbooks', in which '[i]ntellectuals are thought to act as the vanguard of popular beliefs and values' and the 'advanced' or 'progressive' values are understood to effect change by filtering down through the social scale over a few decades or centuries (23). Chadwick points out that '[n]ot all "advanced" ideas become popular attitudes as a matter of course', and 'ideas take on meaning from their social context' (8). He dismisses this basic template of intellectual history, most crucially because it is a methodological approach that, as he observes, bolsters the 'secularisation thesis'. Discussing the issue of the correct methodological approach for the subject of 'secularisation', Chadwick cites the rift between traditional intellectual history and the later kind of social history introduced by modern social science. He explains how the former assumes that intellectual history 'moves like the advance of a scientific theory'—that 'the cause of all is change in intellectual ideas and better logic; that clever men thought cleverly and unclever slowly followed' (11). He says that half a century ago, the subject of 'secularisation' would have been looked upon in this way and would have entailed a chronological study starting with Descartes, Bayle, the new science leading into the Enlightenment, passing via the Encyclopaedists into Kant or the Utilitarians and the new philosophers of the nineteenth century. Chadwick, however, disagrees with the underlying assumptions of this approach. Charles Taylor similarly departs from this logic by attacking the hackneyed story of Darwin displacing religion. Taylor remarks: 'I'm not satisfied with this explanation . . . [that] science refutes and hence crowds out religious belief.' He explains that his first objection is to the logic of the argument that 'the findings of Darwin [led] to the alleged refutations of religion' (4). Secondly, he questions how one can possibly deduce that this ideational shift was the reason that 'people abandoned their faith', even if 'they themselves articulate what happened in such terms as "Darwin refuted the Bible"' (4). Instead of this approach typical to intellectual history, Chadwick prefers the modern social-scientific approach which he says asks a different question, that is, 'what changes in economic or social order lay under the willingness of a society to jettison notions which hitherto were conceived as necessary to its very existence?' (11). Social history believes that '*social process caused* the intellectual process, that ordinary men and women experienced new forms of social life, and then clever men were clever in suiting their mental gymnastics to the new forms' (11–12; emphasis added). Chadwick explains that this idea of historical process was introduced by the social sciences; for instance, Marx argued that it is actually one's material life that determined the society in which one lived and produced the ideas that propelled that society. Another example of this social-scientific intervention, cited by Chadwick, is the one performed by Durkheim, who proposed the collective social consciousness—a consciousness distinct from the sum total of the individual consciousness of all members of society, and one that possesses a life of its own—and suggested that it was this collective social consciousness that threw up the idea of God at one time and that has now discarded it in the modern historical moment because it has outlived its utility (qtd. in Chadwick 11). Thus, Chadwick's analysis challenges the assumption of 'secularisation' and therefore the 'secularisation thesis' as a whole by demonstrating how a social-scientific approach produced by turn-of-the-century modernity overturns the usual intellectual rationale for modern 'secularisation'.

Interestingly, other scholarly interventions dismantle the 'secularisation thesis' by questioning the social-scientific model. One example is Callum Brown who, as I briefly explained in chapter two, debunks the social-scientific methodology by demonstrating the way it participates in the rationalist fallacy of privileging statistical evaluation. He explains that social-scientific parameters such as quantifiable statistical indicators are therefore unsuitable for evaluating the religious pulse of modern societies because the discipline of social science was the historical product of the time and the forces that birthed the 'secularisation thesis' itself.

Among studies that focus more specifically on nineteenth-century Britain from a literary point of view and implicitly challenge the 'secularisation thesis' are John D. Barbour's *Versions of Deconversion: Autobiography and the Loss of Faith* and Timothy Larsen's *Crisis of Doubt: Honest Faith in Nineteenth-Century England*. These works develop concepts like 'deconversion' and 'reconversion', respectively, to dismantle the 'crisis' story. Barbour discusses what he calls the genre of nineteenth-century deconversion narratives, such as John Ruskin's *Praeterita* (1885–89) and Edmund Gosse's *Father and Son* (1907), significantly observing that '[d]ocuments of deconversion look remarkably like stories of conversion' in the 'rhetoric of a crisis of faith and the dramatization of a climactic scene of agonized choice' and in the 'positive convictions attained after losing faith in Christianity' (57–58). Barbour also notes that 'the reasons for deconversion and the rhetoric used to indict conforming Christians' in the deconversion novels are 'especially indebted to the character of evangelical Protestantism' (58), and the novels therefore follow the structure of the evangelical conversion narratives ever so familiar from Protestant spiritual autobiographies since the end of the seventeenth century.[1] Like Gosse and Ruskin, '[d]oubters presented their lives as more ethically rigorous and committed to fundamental truth' than the 'lives of Christian believers, as represented by their own earlier hypocrisies and evasions' (58).[2] Thus, according to Barbour, nineteenth-century narratives conventionally understood as harbingers or manifestations of 'secularisation' are better classified as 'deconversion' narratives that are manifestly moral/religious in their appropriation of distinctly 'Christian rhetoric and values' (57). In contrast to 'secularisation' which narrates 'a gradual fading away of beliefs, as religion simply ceases to inform a person's life, to make any real difference', deconversion narratives involve 'the narration of the significant events that call a faith into question, an analysis of choices, and usually a rather dramatic reversal' where '[o]ne's former faith is presented as not just irrelevant but as wrong or misguided'—all the while indirectly foregrounding the significance of religiosity itself (2–3). Larsen similarly contests the conventional story of Victorian 'secularisation' by introducing the idea of 'honest doubt' and by citing sincere nineteenth-century 'reconversions' to orthodox Christianity (239). Larsen contests the Victorian 'crisis of faith' narrative by reminding us that the doubt experienced by key cultural figures in fact originated in the sincerity of their faith (239). Larsen studies the Secularist movement and shows that 'reconversions were a major reality' in the movement (89), providing accounts of individual 'plebeian' Secularist leaders who, after having abandoned Christian faith for Secularism, later experienced a 'reconversion' or return to orthodox Christianity. In arguing thus, Larsen controverts the usual account of 'secularisation' as a unilinear movement from belief to unbelief. Additionally, Larsen raises a crucial disciplinary question pertinent to scholars of literature. He cites the many works of 'intellectual history', 'literary studies', and general Victorian historiography that bolster the 'secularisation' story and alleges that literary studies plays a crucial role in perpetuating this stereotype. Observing the preponderance of this rubric in literature courses and conferences, Larsen warns us against allowing this 'sizeable literary theme' to '[blur] into a misperception of the Victorians themselves' (66).

It is with a view to redressing this imbalance and rectifying this misrepresentation that I take up the study of several nineteenth-century literary texts in the three chapters which follow, focusing on a historical period that was most central to the articulation, formulation, mainstreaming and reification of the idea of 'secularisation' in literary and scholarly narratives. In chapters six, seven and eight, I will closely examine three different groups of texts to understand how a postsecular reading of nineteenth-century literature may reveal the complexities underlying the Victorian experience of faith and doubt, and the ambiguities that demolish a straightforward narrative of religious decline.

NOTES

1. These nineteenth-century 'crisis of faith' narratives are infused with accounts of 'deconversion' that interestingly echo the trope of 'conversion' found in Protestant spiritual autobiographies produced during the Evangelical Revival where a narrator recounted an inward and definitive turning to God (Hindmarsh 1–3). David Bebbington, in *Evangelism in Modern Britain: A History from the 1730s to the 1980s* (1989), explains that the Evangelical tradition of the late eighteenth and early nineteenth century, that was reflected in the evangelical Protestant spiritual autobiographies, 'gave exclusive pride of place to a small number of leading principles' like activism, Biblicism, crucicentrism and, most importantly, conversionism. The 'call to conversion', which is 'the content of the gospel', was considered to be of the greatest importance in the Evangelical tradition (Bebbington 5). Undergoing the conversion experience was crucial and central to the life of any believing Evangelical. Conversions were 'the goal of personal effort, the collective aim of churches, the theme of Evangelical literature'— and were represented as the emotionally intense 'great crisis of life'. Narratives of conversion were common and were characterised by their 'patent sincerity' and their 'inclusion of agony, guilt and immense relief' (Bebbington 5).

2. There were, however, others like Harriet Martineau (who adopted the positivist philosophy of Auguste Comte and substituted a 'scientific model of self-interpretation for the traditional patterns of biblical hermeneutics'), and later autobiographers like Charles Darwin, Herbert Spencer, Samuel Butler and Henry Adams (who 'approach their lives as if examining a scientific specimen that demonstrates universal laws') who alter the form as well as the content of conversion (Barbour 59).

REFERENCES

Augustine. *The Confessions*. Translated by Henry Chadwick, Oxford UP, 2009.

Barbour, John D. *Versions of Deconversion: Autobiography and the Loss of Faith*. U of Virginia P, 1994.

Bebbington, David W. *Evangelism in Modern Britain: A History from the 1730s to the 1980s*. 1989. Routledge, 2002.

Brown, Callum. *The Death of Christian Britain: Understanding Secularization, 1800–2000*. Routledge, 2009.

Bunyan, John. *Grace Abounding: With Other Spiritual Autobiographies*. 1666. Edited by John Stachniewski and Anita Pacheco, Oxford UP, 2008.

Caputo, John. *On Religion*. Routledge, 2001.

Chadwick, Owen. *The Secularization of the European Mind in the Nineteenth Century*. Cambridge UP, 1990.

Cox, Jeffrey. *The English Churches in a Secular Society, Lambeth 1870–1930*. Oxford UP, 1982.

Darwin, Charles. *On the Origin of Species*. 1859. Introduction by William Bynum, Penguin, 2009.

Gosse, Edmund. *Father and Son*. 1907. Edited by Michael Newton, Oxford UP, 2009.

Hindmarsh, D. Bruce. *The Evangelical Conversion Narrative: Spiritual Autobiography in Early Modern England*. Oxford UP, 2005.

Larsen, Timothy. *Crisis of Doubt: Honest Faith in Nineteenth-Century England*. Oxford UP, 2006.

Newman, John Henry. *Apologia Pro Vita Sua: Being a History of His Religious Opinions*. 1864. Edited by Martin J. Svaglic, Oxford UP, 1967.

Reardon, Bernard M. G. *Religious Thought in the Victorian Age: A Survey from Coleridge to Gore*. Longman, 1980.

Ruskin, John. *Praeterita: Outlines of Scenes and Thoughts Perhaps Worthy of Memory in My Past Life*. 1885–89. Oxford UP, 2012.

Shea, Victor, and William Whitla, editors. *Essays and Reviews: The 1860 Text and Its Reading*. U of Virginia P, 2000.

Taylor, Charles. *A Secular Age*. Harvard UP, 2007.

Wilson, A. N. *God's Funeral: The Decline of Faith in Western Civilization*. W. W. Norton & Company, 1999.

Wolff, Robert Lee. *Gains and Losses: Novels of Faith and Doubt in Victorian England*. Garland Publishing, 1977.

Chapter Six

The New Woman of Faith and Fears in Cholmondeley's Red Pottage

Cholmondeley's *Red Pottage* (1899) narrates the heartbreaking journey of the Victorian New Woman, embodied partly by Rachel West, who wallows in poverty and subjects herself to endless suffering while striving to rescue the unfortunate around her. The author offers an account of Rachel's conscientious reflection and loving sympathy describing how she 'looked out dumbly over the wilderness of roofs' that stretched out for miles beneath her garret window, while the 'suffering of the world was eating into her soul; the suffering of th[e] vast trailing East London, where people trod each other down to live' (34). As she looks she realises the culpability of the modern world in the wrongs being enacted daily against the wretched, for before her eyes the sight of the roofs suddenly turns into 'a sullen furrowed sea of shame and crime which, awaiting no future day of judgment, daily gave up its awful dead' (35). Challenging a long-held staple of nineteenth-century scholarship, I examine the New Woman of Cholmondeley's creation to ask if this indeed is the prototype of a creature of unbelief as critics argue, represented by the likes of Sue Bridehead in Thomas Hardy's *Jude the Obsure* (1895) who audaciously tears up the Bible. With the 'suffering of the world . . . eating into her', one has to wonder if this template of the New Woman's body does not debunk the caricatured version circulated in *Punch* and portrayed as overly or aberrantly sexual. In this chapter, I adopt a postsecular perspective to study the literary New Woman of the nineteenth century, focusing on Mary Cholmondeley's *Red Pottage* (1899)—an earnest tale about Hester Gresley's arduous struggle to become an author and Rachel West's tormenting journey through poverty—to understand the New Woman as a figure that does not critique religion but the 'secular' imaginary which imposes a woefully narrow definition of religiosity. Though I only discuss *Red Pottage* intensively, my observations resonate with a significant section of other New Woman novels, some of which I refer to intermittently like George Gissing's *New Grub Street* (1891) and *The Odd Women* (1893), Ella Hepworth Dixon's *The Story of a Modern Woman* (1894), and Grant Allen's *The Woman Who Did* (1895) and *The Type-Writer Girl* (1897). I will suggest how the experience of pain and bodily suffering in these texts evokes templates of religious experience that dismantle 'secularist' concepts of faith, bodily agency and liberty.[1]

Red Pottage follows the unconventional lives of two friends and prototypes of the Victorian New Woman, Hester Gresley and Rachel West. After the success of her first novel about London's dismal East End, Hester is shown engrossed in the composition of her second novel—a text critical of dogmatic religion—while living under the shelter of her sentless clergyman brother and vicar of their village of Warpington, James Gresley. Hester produces her novel with reverent dedication and painstaking effort despite her consuming fatigue and failing health. Her masterpiece is accepted by a publisher for a generous sum of money. The text then takes a turn for the tragic when James, who severely disapproves of her writing and views, chances upon her recently completed manuscript and becomes livid with what he considers to be its profane critique of institutionalised religion. In the quiet of the night, he heartlessly burns the manuscript, sending Hester into a prolonged nervous illness. The other key character, Rachel, is a wealthy heiress who falls in love with Hugh Scarlett, shortly after he terminates his affair with Lady Newhaven. Lord Newhaven discovers his wife's affair and compels Hugh to draw straws in private to settle who between them must die as retribution. Lady Newhaven, unaware of Rachel's love for Hugh, confides in her, and the two of them wait in suspense to find out who has drawn the shorter straw and would die. Hugh draws the ill-fated straw in the deadly game but lacks the courage to kill himself, and Lord Newhaven ends his life instead in a show of righteous bravado. When Rachel is informed of Hugh's cowardice through a letter Lord Newhaven wrote to her before his suicide, it results in a temporary estrangement between the lovers and Hugh tragically ends his life during this separation by walking into a frozen lake. As the novel closes, Hester and Rachel support each other in their darkest hour and emerge as beacons of hope and strength despite—or perhaps because of—the disasters they suffer with the burning of the book and the death of Hugh.

My aim is to study how Cholmondeley's fin-de-siècle Künstlerroman represents the first generation of feminists—first-wave feminists protesting political, economic and social inequalities who were rendered into the literary New Women[2]—and the template this sets up for feminism's relation to faith. This question is particularly pertinent today when critical debates have surfaced about the extent to which women's agency is circumscribed by or can exist within domains of religious allegiance. This is a topic I address at length and from a different perspective in chapter nine. Regardless of what our individual stance may be on the question of women's freedom within traditional religious discourses such as those surrounding abortion or the hijab, it is productive to examine the early fictional counterpart of liberatory first-wave feminism to glean a better understanding of what freedom means— an understanding that is then able to incorporate other forms of feeling which ordinarily baffle the 'secular' imagination. On the question of religion, Hester—who labours indefatigably to write her extended novelistic critique of dogmatic Christianity—does espouse Christianity herself, however unorthodox, while condemning narrow denominational conflicts and blind conservatism. And Rachel fights a gruelling battle with spiritual bankruptcy in the West End and material poverty in the East End, toiling in a brutally competitive evolutionary universe and struggling as a woman to earn her livelihood while lamenting the absence of a benign Christian god. My focus is not on denominational theological contentions that surface through the voice of the author or the characters. Instead, my postsecular analysis will be directed towards the commentary that the literary figure of the New Woman offers about the reign of 'secular' modernity—a narrative which has gifted us a legacy of narrow definitions, both of religion and of feminist freedom. As Saba Mahmood insightfully summarises, the 'secular-liberal and progressive sensibilities' that underlie our understanding of rightful and free modernity are based on a 'secularized conception of religiosity' that has a specific 'Protestant genealogy'. It implies a 'privatized and individualized concept of religion . . . [that] has come to command a normative force in modernity and is often upheld as the measure against which the adequacy of other religious traditions is measured and judged' (xiii). This 'secularized conception of religiosity' considers religion to be 'a set of beliefs expressed in a set of propositions to which an individual gives assent' (xiii) and regards it as a 'dangerous affront' if there is the 'slightest eruption of religion into the public domain' (xxiii). As discussed in chapter two, both Talal Asad and Geoffrey Oddie trace the modern transition that took place when religion shifted from being a set of practical rules and rituals and became abstracted and universalised as an objective creed or doctrine. Furthermore, the flow of colonial power ensured the centrality of this Protestant Christian trajectory, making it the necessary template that non-Western religions felt impelled to emulate in order to qualify as modern. Departing from this prescriptive route, and taking a cue from postsecular critics who operate with non-Western traditions that offer alternative paradigms for religious experience, this chapter examines the formats of painful sacrifice and bodily suffering that the New Woman adopts—formats which help widen the notion of feminist freedom in order to incorporate feelings and experiences considered disempowering by the 'secular' imaginary. This conceptualisation of the role of the body differs fundamentally from the one underlying the 'Protestant conception of religiosity' where a distinction is made 'between a privatized interiority that is the proper locus of belief and a public exteriority that is an *expression* of this belief' (Mahmood xv; emphasis added). Mahmood further explains that '[i]n this view, while rituals and bodily practices might represent belief, they are not essential to its acquisition' (xv). As opposed to this, claims Mahmood, the

Egyptian piety (*da'wa*) movement (3) offers a template in which the practice of donning the hijab is felt to be a bodily act that is not just 'symbolic' of the subject but 'is both an expression of, and a means to, *the realization of the subject*' (xi; emphasis added). This alternative (non-Western) paradigm for understanding the role of the body in the making of one's religious subjectivity is foundational to my account of how bodily experiences constitute the New Woman subject. Questioning the notion of propositional faith and the assumption of an unassailable unified body, the New Woman in *Red Pottage* offers us a postsecular understanding of what it could *also* mean to be agentive and free. Following the Enlightenment, when Darwinian theorisations had prepared the ground for modern 'secularism' and a (Victorian) 'crisis of faith', the New Woman offers an interesting format for religious experience that problematises the 'secularisation thesis', and becomes relevant for our complex modern-day debates about women's agency in faith.

The nineteenth-century perception and modern reception of the literary New Woman as irreligious finds occasional mention in secondary scholarship. In her essay on Sarah Grand's *The Heavenly Twins* (1893), Naomi Lloyd acknowledges that the 'New Woman as a "modern maiden" is ... assumed to emerge from a predominantly secular cultural context' (177). An iconic moment, as mentioned earlier in this chapter, takes place when Sue Bridehead, a New Woman figure from Hardy's *Jude the Obscure*, suggests an irreverent and scholarly ('secular') approach to the Bible by declaring to Jude that she could 'make ... [him] a *new* New Testament', just as she had done for herself at Christminster when she 'altered' her 'old' New Testament by 'cutting up all the Epistles and Gospels into separate *brochures*, and rearranging them in chronological order as written' to make it 'twice as interesting as before, and twice as understandable' (178). This overt expression of seeming unbelief carries a 'sense of sacrilege' that shocks Jude, so that he responds to this test of loyalty by rejecting Sue's suggestions and saying, 'I take Christianity' (178).[3] The New Women characters in several other nineteenth-century novels also appear to feed into this contemporary Darwinian 'crisis of faith' narrative in the way they lament the godless evolutionary universe that subjects them to the merciless law of competition in their pursuit of a livelihood and sense of purpose. In *Red Pottage*, poverty-stricken Rachel inadvertently takes the job of another woman struggling to earn a living. When the woman blames her for this injustice, Rachel ruminates: '[W]e grind each other for our daily bread with our eyes open. I have got that woman's work. I have struggled hard enough to get it, but . . . I had only got on to the raft by pushing some one else off it' (35). Mary Erle, the New Woman in Ella Hepworth Dixon's *The Story of a Modern Woman*, concludes in the midst of her endless miseries that '[s]he was the plaything, the sport of Destiny, and Destiny always won the game' (184). In Grant Allen's *The Type-Writer Girl*, the New Woman heroine, Juliet Appleton, fights to keep herself afloat through insulting jobs in what she sarcastically calls the heartless evolutionary 'Struggle for Life' (32). In Grant Allen's *The Woman Who Did*, Herminia Barton, the New Woman protagonist, talks of how the cruel evolutionary world, full of 'the crying inequalities and injustices of man or nature', often pushes one to ignore 'the maimed lives, the stricken heads and seared hearts, the reddened fangs and ravening claws of nature' and to 'curl . . . up selfishly' instead of 'recognizing the seething mass of misery' or 'redressing' it (124). And though, faced with this dismal reality, she 'long[ed] to pray—if only there had been anybody or anything to pray pray to'—she is left in this godless world 'clasp[ing] her bloodless hands in an agony of solitude' (133–34).

The contention that the New Woman is undebatably representative of religious scepticism is problematic, and has been contested in recent studies which connect this figure with alternative spiritualities that were at the height of their popularity in the late nineteenth century and that allowed the New Woman alternative paradigms for her religiosity and concurrently her feminist agenda. Noting this, Lloyd writes that '[r]ecent historical studies of alternative spirituality and fin-de-siècle feminism prompt a revisiting of the singularly secular origins of the literary New Woman' (177). She explains that the 'Evangelical alignment of middle-class women with spirituality in the early nineteenth century rendered religion a primary source of cultural authority for these women' so that on 'encountering religious doubt, many chose to rework, rather than to relinquish, religious belief' (177–78). Studies by Joy Dixon, Alex Owen and Ann Heilmann provide instances of these reworkings,[4] showing how the late nineteenth century was characterised by '[f]eminist spiritualities' which 'emerged as late Victorians, seeking alternative, spiritually-based discourses of gender and sexuality, unearthed minority traditions within orthodox religion, and/or moved beyond orthodoxy altogether' (Lloyd 178).

The aim in this chapter is not to identify the particular religious strand with which the New Woman aligns herself, whether orthodox or unorthodox Christianity, or colonial religiosities. My admittedly more theoretical interest, in light of contemporary debates on feminism and its contentious relation to faith, is in studying how this first generation of literary feminists offer several templates of self-sought pain and suffering, agonised experiences, bodily submission and volitional sacrifice that are derived through their presence in the public sphere and that carry religious meaning. I ask how this approach to the New Woman's body portrays alternative ways of negotiating the public realm and of empowering oneself through religious subjectivities that go beyond 'secular' conceptions of liberty, power and freedom. Given that the New Woman reverently welcomes pain upon her own body, the emphasis is on the reimagined role of the body, and this resonates significantly with the centrality attributed to women's bodies in alternative spiritual traditions such as Theosophy and Spiritualism that acquired tremendous popularity and influence in the late nineteenth century. Scholars like Marlene Tromp and Alex Owen explore this substantially reimagined and radical role of the woman's body in fin-de-siècle Spiritualism focusing on the part played by the bodies of female mediums in Victorian spiritualist séances and full-form materialisations, and Joy Dixon examines the same thematic in Theosophical traditions. Their concluding observation, significant for the current study of the devout New Woman, is that late-Victorian alternative religiosities reimagined the spiritual space as one that combined feminist consciousness and a reconfiguration of the role of the female body. Though this is not the direction my analysis will take, it is therefore useful to remember that the New Woman, herself located on the cusp of feminist agency and bodily reconfiguration (through the self-infliction of pain), indirectly echoes the discourse surrounding these alternative religiosities.

The importance of telling this story lies in how long it has been untold; the predominant narrative has been structured around the 'Victorian binary of the "secular man" and the "spiritual woman"', a gender binary underlying the 'secularisation' narrative which speaks only of a *masculine* 'crisis of faith' because in this largely unquestioned narrative 'faith [is] . . . gendered feminine . . . [and] "doubt" . . . masculine' (Dixon, 'Modernity, Heterodoxy, and the Transformation of Religious Cultures' 212–13).[5] Joy Dixon, Ruth Jenkins, and Joanna Dean observe the gendered nature of this narrative of 'doubt'. Dixon cautions against accepting the well-established idea of the nineteenth-century 'separate spheres', and the 'categories which underpin the gendered piety' associated with this idea, that scholarly research adopts.[6] Dixon reminds us that these categories, that is, the pious domesticated angel of the house and the irreligious husband whose masculine temptations threaten the spirituality of the household, are *all* 'nineteenth-century creations' based on 'nineteenth-century understandings of "religion"' (211). This is crucial because the construct of the spiritual domesticated angel is a Victorian narrative that was used to bolster the 'secularisation' discourse by showing the exclusiveness of religion to the private (female) sphere and its erosion from the public (masculine) realm—and it is precisely this stereotypical binary that the figure of the New Woman overturns.[7] The New Women in these novels offer a different paradigm for women's religiosity— no longer limited to the private sphere and no longer free of the modern challenges to a belief in God, but functioning in the midst of the visibly godless public realm and sculpting their own spiritual meaning within this very template through the surrender of their bodies to pain and suffering. And it is through this intervention that the New Woman undercuts the 'secularisation thesis', suggesting a fuller understanding of faith.

Examining Mona Caird's New Woman novel, *The Daughters of Danaus* (1894), Casey A. Cothran notes how Caird provides poignant 'descriptions of physical and mental pain' and 'the vision of "endurance"'—showing ultimately how *'suffering can convey meaning'*

(63–64; emphasis added). According to Cothran, the New Woman heroine, Hadria Fullerton, 'recognizes that the weakening of her physical body is a direct result of acting as daughter, housewife, and mother', and it is by 'making her own painful confinement within the domestic sphere into a sad spectacle' that Hadria 'encourages others to re-envision the roles of all women in late Victorian culture' (64). Most importantly, speaking of the inscription of suffering on the New Women's bodies and the agentive role this provides them, Cothran notes that this novel 'can be seen as part of a larger cultural examination of the violence enacted on women's bodies in the decades both preceding and following the turn of the century' (64). Cothran explains that Caird's novel 'acts as a marker between the 1888–1891 murders of Jack the Ripper (where a man was believed to have gruesomely destroyed women's bodies)' and the 'militant feminist suffragettes of the early twentieth century (who did violence on their bodies for political gain)'—so that the novel ultimately 'evidences new ways of interpreting the damaged bodies of women, *positing suffering not as a sign of victimization but as a means of protest*' (64; emphasis added). Showing how 'Caird's fictional work reacted to and interacted with a national audience, participating in a critical discourse about women's bodies within that society', Cothran captures from a socio-historical standpoint the 'shifting pattern of cultural perspectives on women and suffering' (64). Evidently, the significance of the agonised and suffering body is crucial to other New Woman novels such as Cholmondeley's.

A good place to start is by noting how frequently and meaningfully the New Woman in *Red Pottage* is characterised by testing experiences and unrelenting suffering that are ultimately engraved on her body. When Rachel struggles to earn a livelihood amidst poverty, one can already see in her face—'as in the faces of seamen [where] we [can] trace the onslaught of storm and sun and brine'—a beauty that comes from rigorous struggle and 'conflict and endurance' (6–7). It is an expression, we learn, that betokens 'strong resistance from within of the brunt of a whirlwind from without' (7). This experience is presented as a feature and asset of the divine, earned through arduous tumult, and borne with indefatigable determination. This is an experience of both good and evil alike, such as the kind that shapes the nature of the (spiritually) wise, and is directly paralleled with the travails of Christ. The novel sets up a comparison between the inscription of painful experiences on the body of Rachel and Christ. The latter is described thus: 'The Mother of Jesus must have noticed a great difference in her Son when she first saw Him again after the temptation in the wilderness' (7). The encounter with the ruthless evolutionary world becomes the temptation in the wilderness for the New Woman, much like the Satanic temptation faced by Jesus in the gospel, and Rachel emerges from it bearing a bodily mark—'a great difference' (7). Elsewhere, we read about the other New Woman prototype, Hester, and the mark her experience leaves on her body when the narrative mentions her 'seven-and-twenty . . . years' of unmitigated suffering and the way the wisdom and insight she derived from the experience inscribed itself on her body so that she 'showed her age in her eyes' (54). In many instances, the New Woman has these pains and attendant fatigues embossed on her body in the process of trying to survive poverty and brutal competition through authorial labours. Mary Erle, in *The Story of a Modern Woman*, feels 'wretchedly weak' from the 'strain of writing [that] was intense', 'bending over a desk since nine o'clock' and awake all night 'with every nerve in her body quivering' (132–33). In Gissing's *New Grub Street*, Marian Yule works tirelessly in the British Museum following the instructions of her father, churning out for him anonymous journal articles. We find her exhausted and despondent, lamenting 'the aching sadness of her heart, the dreariness of life as it lay before her', unable to 'fix her attention upon' the 'books open before her' till finally 'she let her hands fall and her head droop.' (193–94). Such chafing physical weariness also appears in the case of Herminia Barton in *The Woman Who Did* when she writes 'with fiery energy, for her baby's sake, on waste scraps of paper, at stray moments snatched from endless other engagements' and despairingly sends it to a publisher, 'in fear and trembling' (142).

This draining experience that the New Woman selflessly welcomes upon her body results in endless enervation and evident agony. In fact, the conscientious surrender to painful suffering emerges as the hallmark of the New Woman's ethical dedication.

Thus, Hester congratulates Rachel on the way she has learnt of the realities of life during her stay in the East End, in the process undergoing 'an agonized awakening' (136). We note that while 'all the great realities of life—love, hatred, temptation, enthusiasm' remain for Sybell Loftus (a woman caught up in the frivolities of society) 'merely pretty words to string on light conversation', Rachel emerges from this painful interlude truly enriched (136). Thus, Hester compares Rachel directly to the Virgin Mary (of whom Simeon prophesies that 'a sword will pierce your own heart also') and congratulates her on her hardship: '[T]he sword that pierced your heart forced an entrance for angels, who had been knocking where there was no door—until then' (136). Hester therefore interestingly uses the Biblical metaphor of the sword—the empowering instrument of God that enriches by cutting to the core—to suggest the way in which Rachel acquires meaning from her privation.[8] The New Woman novels are, in fact, replete with descriptions of the New Woman's suffering, pain and sacrifice. Iconic New Woman heroines—Mary Erle, Juliet Appleton, Marian Yule and Herminia Barton—struggle in a visibly Darwinian universe governed by the ruthless laws of evolution. This is a fate pointed out by Sally Ledger, who discusses Caird's *The Daughters of Danaus* and notes its 'Darwinian-inflected, pessimistic discourse on the possible roles for women in the late nineteenth century' (Ledger 27–28). In *The Woman Who Did*, Alan Merrick, for example, speaks of all that Herminia had 'sacrificed, how deeply . . . [she had] suffered, for the sake of . . . [her] principles' (166). Even Herminia's novel is described as an embodiment of 'the experiences and beliefs and sentiments of a *martyred woman*' (141–42; emphasis added). In *The Story of a Modern Woman*, Mary Erle's novel is discarded by the publishers for being too authentic—'a bit of real life' with 'twenty-seven years of actual experience in it' and therefore 'too sad, "too *painful*"' (130; emphasis added)—something that we learn 'wouldn't have pleased the British public' (122). Pain as a concept and an experience occupied a critical position in the cultural landscape of the nineteenth century. Steven Bruhm observes that for writers in the late eighteenth and early nineteenth centuries, spectacality, or, the spectacle of pain, was critically important, noting how Romantic literature in particular was replete with painful bodies. Lucy Bending explains how the decline of faith in Christianity towards the second half of the nineteenth century was partly because the painful physical suffering on earth could no longer be easily reconciled with the idea of a loving God. In *Victorian Pain*, Rachel Ablow explains that pain in the Victorian Age led to 'the inevitability of scepticism' (140) because the nineteenth-century 'improvements in analgesics, new understandings of nerve function, and the introduction of vaccination' made 'pain . . . seem potentially eradicable'. This cast a shadow on the issue of human pain, which till then had seemed to be the result of God's unavoidable and benign will and which now began to seem 'potentially incompatible with a loving God', thereby raising 'serious theological questions' (2).[9] In *Red Pottage*, for example, one of the chapters begins evocatively by quoting from Owen Meredith's 'Lyric XXVIII', which highlights the inability of all religions to explain unmerited human pain and suffering: 'And we are punished for our purest deeds, / And chasten'd for our holiest thoughts; alas! / There is no reason found in all the creeds, / Why these things are, nor whence they come to pass' (qtd. in Cholmondeley 270).

Lucy Bending notes that besides the intellectual and theological problem with Christianity (that came out of a 'revolution in scientific and theological thinking' in fields like geology, Biblical criticism, etc.), what were also important were 'moral objections to Christianity' (24). By the 1870s there arose what was called the 'problem of pain' (6). In Christian theology, the belief in doctrinally sanctioned pains—such as those surrounding everlasting damnation and Christ's atonement—was connected to the pains faced by human beings on earth, the latter being considered by this logic to be divinely sanctioned. However, later in the century, there was a waning of belief in a painful physical hell (following especially the heresy trials in the 1860s of clergymen deviating from doctrinal explanations of pain and suffering).[10] At the heart of the increasing unpopularity of the idea of a physically tormenting hell was the notion that hell pains were supposed to be moral and not physical, a distinction that Juliet foregrounds in *The Type-Writer Girl*. While struggling in the brutal evolutionary universe of Venice with love and moral surrender in her heart, Juliet wakes up one day, after having sacrificed the love of her life for the sake of friendship, and experiences a 'dull pain in . . . [her] left side', about which she says, 'It was moral, not physical' (136). Given the way human faith in eternal damnation and a physical hell had been challenged, the belief in the justifiability of earthly pains also came into question. Pains in this world 'which had been seen as an expression of God's justice, became by the end of the century the expression of God's injustice' (Bending 28). The 'pains of earth' now became a stumbling block, 'partly as a result of chloroform's undercutting [of] the status of pain as a natural phenomenon, partly in response to the new Darwinian paradigm, and partly to fill the gap left by the decline of religion as a viable justification for physical suffering' (27–28). Thus, the developing turbulence surrounding the question of pain was fundamentally linked to the putative 'crisis of faith'. Crucially, *Red Pottage* locates itself within this larger context, resuscitating to some extent the moral and regenerative value of earthly pain. As an agent welcoming pain upon herself, The New Woman is—as I observed earlier—even compared to the Christ-figure, whose atonement was a theological staple of doctrinally sanctioned and theologically valorised pain used to justify earthly suffering in the debates surrounding pain. Thus, Rachel, upon whose 'grave face the word "Helper" was plainly written' (6), is shown to desire the spiritual power of Christ—the religious archetype of the one who suffers pain to relieve (redeem) others. As Rachel tries to dissuade Lady Newhaven from selfishly and covertly desiring Lord Newhaven's death and a subsequent marriage with Hugh Scarlett, we learn that she herself, despite being deeply in love with Hugh, 'would have given everything she possessed at that moment for one second of Christ's power to touch those [Lady Newhaven's] blind eyes to sight' (143).

The experience of pain becomes an important mode of meaningful growth in *Red Pottage*. Hester says, referring to the need for loving others and willingly welcoming pain upon oneself for the sake of true happiness:

> Every year I live I am more convinced that the waste of life lies in the love we have not given, the powers we have not

used, the selfish prudence which will risk nothing, and which, *shirking pain, misses happiness as well*. No one ever yet was the poorer in the long-run for having once in a lifetime 'let out all the length of all the reins'. (134; emphasis added)

This approach to pain, where one goes beyond the limits of self-centredness to 'risk' something in a gesture of collective duty and in a realisation of social connectedness, reflects one of Ablow's two approaches to the nineteenth-century 'problem of pain'. Ablow discusses how the nineteenth century was divided between two understandings of pain that also dominate our modern perception of this experience. The first 'casts the pain of the other primarily as an epistemological problem—the thing we cannot, but most need to, know' (famously advanced by Elaine Scarry in recent times)—an approach that Ablow argues 'is bound up with a particular account of liberal subjectivity as self-conscious, prior to the social, and private' (4). The other approach that Ablow identifies as more significant for the nineteenth century 'emphasizes how pain is always already part of a social world', a view espoused by modern figures like Ludwig Wittgenstein, Stanley Cavell and Veena Das (4). Ablow studies a range of nineteenth-century texts indicating how they show that '[p]ain is not self-evident, private, and isolating' (140), as distinct from the epistemological accounts of pain. This approach in which pain is understood as a shared social experience of suffering that connects individuals resonates with the New Woman's battles and toils in an interconnected social landscape from the novels we have been studying. Ablow's analysis therefore suggests how several nineteenth-century texts also offer, by presenting the experience of pain as a shared social experience, 'a revised notion of liberal subjectivity, not as prior to the social, but instead as inevitably enmeshed within it' (21).[11]

It is useful to note briefly that this immanentist approach that views the social body as an integrated and connected whole also likely drew from the larger nineteenth-century cultural context in which alternative spiritualities like Theosophy and Spiritualism—with their reimagining of the role of the body—were beginning to command unprecedented popularity and influence in Britain in the later decades of the nineteenth century (as explored, among others, by J. Jeffrey Franklin, Peter van der Veer, Joy Dixon and Alex Owen). Dixon writes that '[t]he Theosophical Society was an important source for immanentist thinking' which became influential in the late nineteenth century (*Divine Feminine* 123). Immanentist ways of thought offered a strong critique of modern Western liberalism which posit 'an atomistic vision of society as an aggregation of autonomous individuals' by proposing that '[o]n the physical plane individual bodies might appear to be separate and unconnected, but on the higher planes—the astral, mental, or spiritual planes—bodies were connected in very real ways' (123–24). Thus, as Dixon explains, 'Theosophy's occult body politics involved a critique of liberal individualism' with its assumptions of the autonomous and unassailable individual body, positing instead that 'the universe was not a collection of discrete parts but one organism' (123–24)—a form of thinking that finds reflection in the shared experience of (bodily) pain demonstrated by the New Woman.

Interestingly, in *Red Pottage*, we see how characters attempt to challenge this liberal notion of an integrated unassailable body—a view that understands pain as a private and isolated experience—and instead see pain as something that is socially shared and that shatters personal bodily boundaries to connect disparate individuals through the bond of sympathy.[12] The text therefore presents the body as permeable and vulnerable, amenable to suffering for the sake of others and capable of acquiring meaningful agency in the process. Hester, for instance, speaks of her inability to dwell in a unitary body: '[M]y mind gets loose from my body and wanders away to an immense distance, to long, dreary, desert places. And then if you come in I make a great effort to bring it back . . . And—my mind gets farther and further away every day . . . [and] sometime—I really can't bring it back any longer' (337). As noted earlier, Dixon explains how, under the influence of Theosophical occult body politics, the 'liberal vision of the state as an association of autonomous individuals was challenged by an organic vision that eroded the boundaries between the individual and the community' (*Divine Feminine* 123). This new immanentist vision challenged the liberal view of the body and emphasised instead a 'fluidity and permeability . . . of the body', that is, saw the body as 'literally as well as metaphysically connected to all other bodies' (*Divine Feminine* 123). Such is the vision infusing the New Woman who drifts from the confines of her own discrete body—an experience that ultimately allows her to welcome the pain of others upon herself and in the process feel virtuous sympathy for them. In Grant Allen's *The Type-Writer Girl*, Juliet compassionately embraces Elsie, who did not secure a job at Romeo's firm because she was 'hopelessly incompetent' when compared to Juliet. Juliet says that Elsie's 'gratitude [to Juliet for her kindness] was a satire on Christian charity in this town of London', and then remarks that because the 'struggle for life' had 'not quite choked out . . . [her own] soul', she invited Elsie 'for a cup of tea and an ounce of *sympathy*' (93; emphasis added). Similarly, in *Red Pottage*, Rachel has a tormenting moment of contemplation when she encounters 'the poor creature'—the woman who lost to Rachel in the struggle for procuring employment. The meeting initiates her ethical journey towards remedying women's social inequalities. We are told that '[s]omething in the poor creature's words', 'something vague but repulsive in her remembrance of the man who paid her for the work by which she could barely live', dropped 'like lead into Rachel's heart' (34). Hester too debunks the traditional and narrower sense of bodily experience and the limited sympathy for others that stems from it. She cites the example of conventional society women like Sybell Loftus, according to whom 'one can only sympathize with what one has experienced' and who are therefore 'always saying, "as a mother", or "as a wife"' (135). Exposing the superficiality of this straitened understanding of bodily experience, Hester notes that '[i]f that were true the world would have to get on without sympathy' because 'no two people have the same experience' (135–36). The New Woman's (in this case, Hester's) guiding ethic instead seems to reinforce the humane and implicitly spiritual quality of 'sympathy' that she attains by *widening* the usual constrictive definitions of experience—that is, experience understood as exclusively of one's own and limited to the physical outline of one's *own body*. Instead of this stultifying sense of selfhood and the liberal notion of isolated body-based experience, what is suggested is the possibility of spiritually transcending the body. Thus, Hester speaks of making 'sympathy' possible by remedying a 'want of imagination' that characterises superficial society women like Sybell who 'cannot readily enter into the feelings of others' or put themselves 'in their place' (135). This ability to allow one's body to serve as a site for its own transcendence is something that the Bishop notes in Hester. Hester is able to transcend her body and its own little agonies, allowing it to feel the pain of others so as to cultivate sympathy for her fellow sufferers, in the process subjecting herself to pain for the sake of others, much like Rachel who sits 'looking out into the distance beyond the narrow confines of her [own] agony' (233). The Bishop points to Hester's volitional experience of this pain, using linguistic descriptors of motion that suggest the disruption of stable bodily boundaries, saying she is 'passionate' and 'too much *swayed* by every little incident' and that '[e]verything makes a vivid impression on her and *shakes her to pieces*' (88; emphasis added). This spiritual experience disrupts and transcends the unified physical body—the corporeal limits of which are often disabling—even at the cost of pain in order to help others. In *The Woman Who Did*, Allen clarifies that this surrender to pain and suffering was in fact the most deeply spiritual response that one could offer when barraged with the seemingly 'secularising' despair of a Darwinian universe. Thus, the narrator, and implicitly Herminia Barton, ponders the dark and relentless struggle and concludes:

> A crowned Caprice is god of the world:
> On his stony breast are his white wings furled.
> No ear to hearken, no eye to see,
> No heart to feel for a man hath he.
> But his pitiless hands are swift to smite,
> And his mute lips utter one word of might
> In the clash of gentler souls and rougher—
> 'Wrong must thou do, or wrong must suffer.'
> Then grant, O dumb, blind god, at least that we
> Rather the sufferers than the doers be. (134)

In *Red Pottage*, pain and suffering are often shown to help in *the rise to a higher self*, such as when Rachel gains morally from her agonised existence in the East End. This echoes the hierarchies of suffering that found expression in several nineteenth-century debates on pain, and the corresponding gendered or evolutionary attainments these varying levels of suffering were supposed to signify. One of the many voices contributing to these debates was that of Charles Voysey, a member of the Broad Church, who detailed 'scales of sensitivity, ranging from the insensateness of the worm to the painful vulnerability of the human', clearly linking 'perceived heightened physical sensitivity and Christian manliness' (Bending 34). The ideal man, by Voysey's logic, had to 'embrace not just the *means* of dealing with suffering, but the suffering itself'—a quality that the New Woman manifests in what I have been suggesting is a spiritually empowering move (34; emphasis added). Furthermore, observing the intensification of these discussions in the late nineteenth century, Bending explains that while the 'ability to suffer [pain] was seen to unify' all men (and women) of 'whatever race, creed, or social class', this 'inclusivity . . . was put under enormous pressure in the last two decades of the nineteenth century' (178). Evolutionary scales of suffering were often established by discrediting the suffering of certain groups of humans or certain species of animals, that is, by reading 'the pain of individual human sufferers . . . in accordance with particular preconceptions, rather than in the light of suffering endured in the body' (177). This 'idea of evolutionary scales of pain' was used, for example, to demarcate 'the savage from the civilized, and the poor from the rich', providing the basis for 'a progressive scale from non-pain to pain perception, with the worm firmly at the lower end', such as in *Jude the Obscure* (197). This notion of painful suffering leading one to a higher state is expressed most clearly in *Red Pottage*, and its evolutionary premise is implied especially when the novel narrates Hugh's conflicted, lovelorn and painful state in terms of a rise to a *higher* self. Though speaking of a male character and the story of his unrequited love, the passage expresses mankind's eternal inner turmoil while suggesting the larger issue of the New Woman's painful sacrifice that lies at the heart of the novel:

> The strain of conflict was upon Hugh—the old, old conflict of the seed with the earth, of the soul with love. How many little fibres and roots the seed puts out, pushed by an unrecognized need within itself, *not without pain, not without a gradual rending of its being, not without a death unto self into a higher life*. Love was

dealing with Hugh's soul as the earth deals with the seed, and—he *suffered*. (308; emphasis added)

In *Victorian Sacrifice*, Ilana Blumberg writes that '[a]t mid-century, British Christians were largely agreed in understanding personal suffering and sacrifice in imitation of Christ as critical elements of genuine religious experience' (6). '[S]piritual sacrifice' was understood to be 'the hallmark of a pious life on earth', especially according to the 'evangelical demand conveyed to the reading and listening public', and many sermons 'sought to address the practicalities of such a lofty demand, seeking to translate it to the realm of everyday action' (6). And while 'the force of the sacrificial ideal was felt keenly by religious Victorians' and Christian writers adopted the 'ethical imperative' of 'self-sacrifice in imitation of Christ,' this imperative also extended to those Victorians who were 'not conventionally devout' and 'the more secularized Victorian notion of "duty" . . . retained at its core a sense of painful, self-lacerating sacrifice' (Blumberg 7).[13] Blumberg explains that while an extreme binary developed initially between a desired maximalist altruism (self-sacrifice) and a feared individualistic egoism, mid-Victorian novelists moved away from this ethic of self-sacrifice to a worldview in which mutual benefit was the desired ideal for the individual. In this vision, the individual sought to equally gain what they gave from their interaction with society. Undoubtedly, therefore, the discourses, beliefs and assumptions surrounding the ethic of self-sacrifice were complex and polemical, and the novel functions in this space by valorising the New Woman's self-sacrifice while still ensuring her emancipation and empowerment. Hence, it is important to look at alternative reading approaches that show us how the idea of welcoming pain upon one's body or surrendering oneself—where the 'sacrifice' that seems like a 'death unto self' ultimately leads to a 'higher life' (Cholmondeley 308)—is a uniquely *feminist* mode of action that bypasses masculinist violence and offers a deeper spiritual payoff. This notion of sacrifice as empowering causes us discomfort because, as Mahmood points out, 'liberal presuppositions [that discredit sacrifice as an empowering modality of action] have become naturalized in the scholarship on gender' (13). However, the figure of the New Woman from our novels show

how pain and sacrifice may offer a spiritually empowering format for the exercise of feminist agency—the mechanics of which are explained by Sarah Coakley in her chapter, 'In Defense of Sacrifice', in *Feminism, Sexuality, and the Return of Religion*. The editors of the book, Linda Martín Alcoff and John Caputo, cite Coakley when urging us to 'rethink the relationship of freedom to sacrifice and purgation, and to see the latter as a means to overcoming the false desires—the falseness of desire itself—which is the real obstacle to achieving autonomy' (Alcoff and Caputo 5–6). Coakley's chapter focuses on the condition of the modern working (feminist) woman no longer limited to the domestic realm, and analyses how faith works itself out through, and finds expression in, the *worldly* sphere. As such, Coakley's reading speaks directly to the situation of the New Woman—located in the public realm—and allows us to see the relevance of Victorian studies to the contemporary world, that of the New Woman to the modern professional woman, and that of the first wave of feminist representation in literature to modern debates about women's agency in faith. Borrowing the Biblical story of Isaac's sacrifice as the central metaphor in her chapter, Coakley explains that her 'interest in casting Isaac as an "honorary woman" lies in his perilous negotiation of the line'—which is 'well known to feminist women in the contemporary workplace'—'between submission to the logic of a *false* patriarchal sacrifice (in which male violence and scapegoating dominate), and the choice of an authentic and discerning "sacrificial" posture of another sort . . . (in which genuine consent is given to the *divine* call to purge and purify one's desires in order to align them with God's)' (25).[14] Coakley examines the 'biblical narrative of the sacrifice, or "binding", of Isaac' by his father to posit that Isaac 'is the type of the one who triumphs over human powerlessness, not by a false, compensatory will-to-power and further patriarchal violence, but through the subtler power of a transformative, divine *interruption*' (18). Isaac, according to Coakley, 'can be read as gender-labile, the "type" of feminist selfhood transformed' because even though he is 'ostensibly [the] powerless one' he 'emerges from his ordeal . . . unscathed, re-enlivened, and utterly transformed' (18–19). Coakley's thesis here is that 'only sacrifice, *rightly understood*, can account for a feminist transformation of the self that is radically "theonomous", rooted and sustained in God' (19). She says 'that it is only in the crisis of a divine "sacrifice" . . . and an accompanying divine interruption of the normal human workings of power and violence, that a theonomous self is formed that can overcome the secular feminist impasses' (19). This means that the impasse on the question of what constitutes the *real* empowerment of women is overcome by endowing them with *true* 'freedom' or 'agency' that goes beyond the narrow understanding of these terms in modern 'secular' feminism (19). Coakley concludes prophetically by stating that the '"sacrificial" ordeal of our feminist hero Isaac . . . remains on offer; its transformations are undeniably costly, but they are the price of freedom in the richest sense' (20).[15]

While contemporary periodical, journalistic and literary discourse (including *Punch* cartoons) frequently portrayed the New Woman as a creature of (implicitly transgressive) sexual pleasure, often taking their cue from the new feminist protests against sexual double standards (such as Josephine Butler's campaign against the Contagious Diseases Act), the New Woman in these novels designs her body to be a carrier of a higher (religious) cause—a 'sacrifice' to which she constantly swears allegiance. Braving social criticism, Herminia Barton in Allen's *The Woman Who Did* sacrifices social respectability and economic stability by entering into a free union with Alan Merrick and later undertaking to raise her daughter alone after Alan's death, despite great socio-economic and personal suffering as a single unwed mother. Shunned by all, including her clergyman father and her disdainful would-be father-in-law, and thwarted in her attempts to become a successful author, she sacrifices everything and ultimately dies offering the world the gift of her daughter—a symbol of a pure lineage ('free love') untainted by the exploitative institution of marriage. In *The Type-Writer Girl*, Juliet Appleton bravely struggles with destitution and scorn for the barest means of subsistence, and sacrifices her love for Romeo by persuading him to marry her rich friend, Michaela, whom she knows to be in love with him. In the last scene, as Juliet departs from Michaela forever after a tearful adieu, there is a poignant suggestion that Michaela awakens to the truth of Juliet's sacrifice and her lifelong ethical travails. In Gissing's *The Odd Women*, Rhoda

Nunn briefly entertains the possibility of love and marriage with the rakish Everard Barfoot, before sacrificing this socially valued offer and choosing to remain true to her sisterhood with the struggling 'odd women'. And in *The Story of a Modern Woman*, both Alison Ives and Mary Erle sacrifice their romantic dreams for their principles, the former turning away from Doctor Dunlop Strange and the latter from Perry Jackson and Vincent Hemming, implicitly dedicating themselves to the painful and arduous task of uplifting women, often from their degrading lives of indigence and despair in the East End. In *Red Pottage*, the central preoccupation is with Hester's tireless labours and her sacrifice of all pleasures as she produces her religious novel—a journey that is taken to signify immense spiritual growth in the text. The essential difference between the masculinist realm of ruthless competition and the female realm of potential feminist and spiritual sacrifice is initially emphasised in *Red Pottage* when the Bishop, Hester and Rachel sit together and speak of the failings of women. They speak of how women are fundamentally different from men in that they lack the masculinist spirit—'[w]omen have not . . . the *esprit de corps* which the most ordinary men possess' and this is evident in how, only through great 'difficulty can one squeeze out of a man any fact that is detrimental to his friend' (84). In an apparent critique of women, the Bishop says, and Hester and Rachel agree, that women 'give away their best woman friend at the smallest provocation, or without any provocation at all'. However, the essential thing to note about this alternative ethical realm that is being posited for women is that, lacking the masculinist '*espirit de corps*', they actually 'lead unselfish lives' and, 'if that same friend whom she has run down is ill, the runner down will nurse her day and night with absolutely selfless devotion' (84). One of the most poignant moments in the text arises later when Hester faces the violence of the world in its most brutal form as her brother burns her novel, the product of her devoted labours, and she is tempted to retaliate in the harshest spirit of (worldly and masculinist) violence by hurting Regie, her brother's son, for whom she holds great affection. We are told: 'Hester turned upon the child [Regie] like some blinded, infuriated animal at bay, and thrust him violently from her' (277). As '[h]e fell shrieking', '[s]he rushed past him out of the room, and out of the house, his screams following her', and exclaimed, 'I've killed him' (277). Subsequently, following an attempt to recover her book from the ashen remains of the fire, she burns her hands and despairingly voices not just the death of her book but also the futility of the chain of violence that had consumed, by the very logic of retaliation, both the book (that James had burnt) and Regie (whom she had hurt). As she stands up in '[h]er gown [that] was burned through where she had knelt down,' she says despondently: 'Quite dead . . . Regie and the book.' At this moment when the text foregrounds the futility of violent retaliation, and thus the value of quiet suffering, nature responds with 'a few flakes of snow . . . [that fall] in a great compassion' (277). Hester then 'set[s] off running blindly across the darkening fields' and arrives at the Bishop's home, where she confesses to him her culpability in this cycle of violence: 'They have killed my book . . . They have killed my book. They burned it alive when I was away. And my head went. I don't know what I did, but I think I killed Regie. I know I meant to' (277–78). Following this, she enters a phase of deep suffering and illness that is marked not only by her dejection about her burnt book, but also predominantly by her anguish at having resorted to heartless violence. Her surrender to the patriarchal law of retaliation distresses her and threatens to empty her of her spiritual essence. The Bishop explains that Hester has 'fears' and 'brain fever' because she still thinks that she has killed Regie (282). To Doctor Brown, who tends to her, Hester says lifelessly in 'a monotonous voice', 'Regie is dead, you old gray wolf . . . I killed him in the back-yard. The place is quite black, and it smokes.' Explaining her terrible suffering, the Bishop says 'the only thing we can do for her is to show Regie to her. If she sees him she may believe her own eyes' (283). Quite rightly, Hester emerges from this emotional stillness only when she sees Regie again. And in this exuberant moment, that is marked not only by happiness but also by the very affirmation of *the principle of love*, a 'change [comes] . . . over Hester's face'. She pulls Regie close, and her 'tears . . . [fall] at last, quenching the wild fire in her eyes' (288). Emerging from the vicious logic of violence, Hester pardons the Gresleys. She says, 'Do you think I still blame poor James for his bonfire, or his jealous little wife who wanted to get rid of me? Why should I? They acted up to their lights' (335). Furthermore, at this point after the New Woman heroine has emerged from the patriarchal law of violent retaliation, the text achieves its final intervention through the figure of the Bishop who reproves Hester for her transactional understanding of the human–God relationship. Hester begins by expressing her ill-formed expectation of transactionality: 'In all those days when I did not say anything, it was because I felt I had been deceived. I had done my part. God had not done His. He should have seen to it that the book was not destroyed' (336). Most evocatively, it is at this stage that a distinctly feminist reimagining of this relationship with the divine is achieved, expressed not by the New Woman but by the Bishop, and worked out through the figure of the New Woman. The Bishop criticises her contractual expectation from God, and interestingly compares her rhetoric and understanding of the divine to that of a (misdirected) man, saying that she is behaving 'like a man who has had a blow, who staggers about giddy and dazed, and sees the pavement rising up to strike him', whereas the 'pavement is firm under his feet all the time' (336). Discrediting this typically masculinist imagining of the divine, the Bishop reassures Hester of the constant presence of the overseeing divine force, and explicitly articulates the need for God's intervention. At this transformative moment, the body of the New Woman is offered up, through suffering, to the workings of God, beyond the assurances of self-possession or rationalistic self-control. Echoing the 'passionate *self-surrender*' that James Gresley had earlier found 'reflected in her [Hester's] eyes', the Bishop now emphasises the empowering notion of self-sacrifice to Rachel (156; emphasis added):

> We have got to trust the one person whom we always show we tacitly distrust by trying to take matters out of His hands. *We must trust God*. So far we have strained ourselves to keep Hester alive, but she is past our help now. She is in none the worse case for that . . . *We must leave her to the best Friend of all. God has her in His hand*. For the moment the greater love holds her away from the less, like the mother who takes her sick child into her arms, apart from the other children who are playing round her. *Hester is in God's keeping, and that is enough for us*. (338; emphasis added)

As Brenda Ayres explains, 'when Hester meets her darkest hour, when her brother has burned her book for its critical assessment of the clergy, . . . she flees, on foot, the ten-mile distance to the bishop' and 'he does exactly what a man of the cloth should do: *he puts her in God's hands*' (154–55; emphasis added). Following Hester's willing self-surrender and the implicit divine intervention, the novel ends with meaningful accomplishments for both the New Women and the world surrounding them—with Hester and Rachel pursuing larger goals in India, Australia and New Zealand, and with a postscript that assures us that 'the old light [was] rekindled in Hester's eyes' and that 'Hope and Love and Enthusiasm never die' (376).

Red Pottage leaves us then on this note of trusting submission and bright hope, having offered us the promising figure of the New Woman—who ethically surrenders to sacrifice and pain and breaks free of her own bodily autonomy and the masculinist logic of violence to connect socially through sympathy—and having embossed her on the 'secularist' cultural landscape of the late nineteenth century as an alternative model of both feminist agency and deep religiosity.

NOTES

1. Barbara Caine notes that the 'celebration of women's self-sacrifice, which is seen as having the capacity to bring social and moral transformation' was 'a quite common feature of much Victorian feminism' (80–81). And, more specifically, as Tara MacDonald observes, 'various scholars have emphasized the *New Woman*'s predilection for self-sacrifice' (129; emphasis added). I look, however, at how pain, suffering and self-sacrifice were being reinstated not as a (possibly conservative) moral imperative towards social change but as a larger virtue indicative of an empowering and rewarding redefinition of the body and spirituality.
2. I refer repeatedly in this chapter to how the Victorian New Woman, emerging in the late-nineteenth and early-twentieth century as a caricatured icon in journalistic literature and a venerable (if problematic) character in novels (by or about New Women), formed the interesting fictional counterpart of the 'first wave' of

feminist activism in the public realm. In this context, I examine the figure as one of the earliest and most interesting portrayals of feminist subjectivity in English novels. I speak of feminism here in terms of its first organised manifestation as a sociopolitical process and not feminist consciousness itself, the literary representation of which can obviously be traced back to time immemorial (from works by Mary Wollstonecraft or Aphra Behn, to the ancient oral literature of the classical ages).

3. Interestingly, Sue continues to proclaim the purity (religiosity) of her impulse and her underlying loyalty to the Bible by declaring that 'people have no right to falsify the Bible' (178).

4. Lloyd refers to the explorations of alternative religiosities in Alex Owen's *The Place of Enchantment: British Occultism and the Culture of the Modern* (2004), Joy Dixon's *Divine Feminine: Theosophy and Feminism in England* (2001), Ann Heilmann's *New Woman Strategies: Sarah Grand, Olive Schreiner, Mona Caird* (2004) and her article, 'Visionary Desires: Theosophy, Auto-Eroticism and the Seventh Wave Artist in Sarah Grand's *The Beth Book*'.

5. Joy Dixon notes that 'doubt was often symbolically represented as estrangement from one's wife'—as shown by Elisabeth Jay in *Faith and Doubt in Victorian Britain* (1986), and the narrative was 'dramatised [as] an explicitly masculine crisis of faith'—as in Samuel Butler's *The Way of All Flesh* (1903) and Edmund Gosse's *Father and Son* (1907) ('Modernity, Heterodoxy, and the Transformation of Religious Cultures' 213). Ruth Y. Jenkins, in *Reclaiming Myths of Power* (1995), notes how '[r]eading ... [the] male writers and analysing their crises [of faith] remain central to understanding the complexity of Victorian religious and ethical attitudes' (19). Joanna Dean observes how the 'religious crisis in literature, from its origins in Thomas Carlyle's *Sartor Resartus* (1833–1834), J. A. Froude's *Nemesis of Faith* (1849), and J. H. Newman's *Loss and Gain* (1848), has been a masculine one, closely tied to the religious maturation and vocational difficulties of young college men' (47).

6. There is a long list of works that explain the way the nineteenth century operated on the basis of the 'separate spheres' gender ideology which established the construct of the pious, virtuous and domesticated 'angel of the house' on the one hand, and the worldly man of the public sphere on the other. Some of the most important among these are Leonore Davidoff and Catherine

Hall's *Family Fortunes* (1987), Callum G. Brown's *The Death of Christian Britain* (2001), Ruth Jenkins's *Reclaiming Myths of Power*, Sue Morgan's *Women, Religion and Feminism in Britain 1750–1900* (2002), Sue Morgan and Jacqueline de Vries' *Women, Gender and Religious Cultures in Britain 1800–1940* (2010) and Barbara Taylor's *Eve and the New Jerusalem* (1983).

7. One must acknowledge here the volume of scholarly work that details how Victorian women were empowered through participation in religious activities and even institutions. There is no doubt, therefore, that despite the contemporary (and also perhaps the perpetual scholarly) stereotype of the domesticated religious housewife and her implicit powerlessness, the rapidly expanding religious roles for women provided her with various forms of (social and spiritual) agency and self-expression. In *Women, Gender and Religious Cultures in Britain, 1800–1940*, Joy Dixon refers to Joan Scott to remind us that we must not 'assume the abiding homogenous collectivity called "women" upon which measurable experiences are visited' (212). And Sue Morgan and Jacqueline de Vries, editors of the same volume, note that their operative assumption is that women 'were both the inheritors and makers of their own religious cultures'. 'Religious discourses', they assert, 'were never passively received within religious institutions or in the wider culture, instead they were constantly reinterpreted by women and invested with new meanings' (2–3). Though, as summed up by Joy Dixon, the 'separare spheres' ideology rendered women without any real authority in institutionalised religion (whether in the established or the Nonconformist churches), it did provide them with the tremendous symbolic importance of being the more 'spiritual' sex. Seminal works study the agency gained by women through religion. This includes Julie Melnyk's *Women's Theology in Nineteenth-Century Britain* (1998), Mary Wilson Carpenter's *Imperial Bibles Domestic Bodies* (2003), Sarah A. Willburn's *Possessed Victorians* (2006), Rebecca Styler's *Literary Theology by Women Writers of the Nineteenth Century* (2010), and Gail Turley Houston's *Victorian Women Writers, Radical Grandmothers, and the Gendering of God* (2013). In addition to works on nineteenth-century women and alternative religiosities to which I referred in a previous endnote, some significant others relevant here are Charlotte Despard's *Theosophy and the Woman's Movement* (1913), Tatiana Kontou's *Women and the Victorian Occult* (2011),

Alex Owen's *The Darkened Room* (1989), Marlene Tromp's *Altered States* (2006) and Kumari Jayawardena's *The White Women's Other Burden* (1995).

8. Two of many such examples of Biblical passages include Hebrews 4:12 and Isaiah 49:2. (Speaking of the Word of God) Hebrews 4:12: For the word of God is alive and active. Sharper than any double-edged sword, it penetrates even to dividing soul and spirit, joints and marrow; it judges the thoughts and attitudes of the heart. (Speaking of the Word of God) Isaiah 49:2: He made my mouth like a sharpened sword, in the shadow of his hand he hid me; he made me into a polished arrow and concealed me in his quiver.

9. As Ablow notes in *Victorian Pain*, both 'medical and religious professionals struggled with the problem of how to maintain faith in a benevolent God when one generation is made to suffer what another is able to remediate' because of developments in pain-ameliorative advances in the sciences. (2)

10. This was a development mostly led by the Broad Church, while the Catholics, Anglo-Catholics and Evangelicals were more resistant to any such doctrinal shift.

11. Ablow also talks about the prevalence of the epistemological model of pain and how it drew from eighteenth-century notions of sympathy and the belief that the knowledge of pain inevitably leads to the desire to relieve it. This unmistakably contributes to the nexus of meanings and notions I am discussing. But my reading draws its force from Ablow's overarching discussion about the social and shared nature of pain, an aspect that ties up with other analyses by Joy Dixon and Lucy Bending that I discuss throughout this chapter.

12. Also crucial in this area is Talal Asad's theorisation of pain, to which I will refer in the following chapter in trying to understand colonial models of faith and suffering. Asad explains how secular regimes, founded on a liberal understanding of the self-sufficient autonomous body, considers this body unassailable, and any attempt to invade it through pain as disabling.

13. Blumberg notes that, according to Owen Chadwick, even when the Agnostics 'drop[ped] the creed linked with inherited morality, they nevertheless assumed that the morality itself was "absolute and must be preserved"' (qtd. in Blumberg 7).

14. This kind of sacrifice is distinguished from the type of sacrifice generally associated with women as mothers, to which Nancy Jay refers in *Throughout Your Generations Forever: Sacrifice, Religion, and Paternity* (1993).
15. Coakley explains that the angelic 'interruption' recorded in the episode of Isaac's sacrifice is important 'for the rethinking of sacrifice and the rendering of it [is] compatible' with what she calls the 'reflexive, purgative, divine "gift"' (27).

REFERENCES

'A Few Lyrics of Owen Meredith: Set to Hindu Music by Sourindro Mohun Tagore.' *Internet Archive*. 25 June 2015. https://archive.org/details/in.ernet.dli.2015.38272/page/n5.

Ablow, Rachel. *Victorian Pain*. Princeton UP, 2017.

Alcoff, Linda Martín, and John D. Caputo. 'Introduction: Feminism, Sexuality and the Return of Religion.' *Feminism, Sexuality, and the Return of Religion*. Indiana UP, 2011, pp. 1–16.

Allen, Grant. *The Type-Writer Girl*. Edited by Clarissa J. Suranyi, Broadview P, 2003.

---. *The Woman Who Did*. John Lane/Robert Bros, 1895.

Asad, Talal. *Formations of the Secular: Christianity, Islam, Modernity*. Stanford UP, 2003.

---. *Genealogies of Religion: Discipline and Reasons of Power in Christianity and Islam*. Johns Hopkins UP, 1993.

Ayres, Brenda. '"Moth and Rust": Cholmondeley's Assessment of the Church of England.' *Mary Cholmondeley Reconsidered*, edited by Carolyn W. de la L. Oulton and SueAnn Schatz, Pickering & Chatto, 2010, pp. 147–60.

Bending, Lucy. *The Representation of Bodily Pain in Late Nineteenth-Century English Culture*. Oxford UP, 2000.

Blumberg, Ilana M. *Victorian Sacrifice: Ethics and Economics in Mid-Century Novels*. Ohio State UP, 2013. *Project MUSE*, muse.jhu.edu/book/27534.

Brown, Callum. *The Death of Christian Britain: Understanding Secularization, 1800–2000*. Routledge, 2009.

Bruhm, Steven. *Gothic Bodies: The Politics of Pain in Romantic Fiction*. U of Pennsylvania P, 1994.

Butler, Samuel. *The Way of All Flesh*. 1903. Modern Library (Random House Inc.), 1998.

Caine, Barbara. *Victorian Feminists*. Oxford UP, 1992.

Carlyle, Thomas. *Sartor Resartus*. 1836. Edited by Kerry McSweeney and Peter Sabor, Oxford UP, 2008.

Carpenter, Mary Wilson. *Imperial Bibles, Domestic Bodies: Women, Sexuality, and Religion in the Victorian Market*. Ohio UP, 2003.

Chadwick, Owen. *The Secularization of the European Mind in the Nineteenth Century*. Cambridge UP, 1975.

Cholmondeley, Mary. *Red Pottage*. 1899. Harper & Brothers Publishers, 1900.

Coakley, Sarah. 'In Defense of Sacrifice: Gender, Selfhood, and the Binding of Isaac,' *Feminism, Sexuality, and the Return of Religion*, edited by Linda Martín Alcoff and John D. Caputo, Indiana UP, 2011, pp. 17–38.

Cothran, Casey A. 'Mona Caird and the Spectacle of Suffering.' *New Woman Writers, Authority and the Body*, edited by Melissa Purdue and Stacey Floyd, Cambridge Scholars Publishing, 2009, pp. 63–88.

Davidoff, Leonore, and Catherine Hall. *Family Fortunes: Men and Women of the English Middle Class, 1780–1850*. U of Chicago P, 1987.

Dean, Joanna. *Religious Experience and the New Woman: The Life of Lily Dougall*. Indiana UP, 2007. *Project MUSE*, muse.jhu.edu/book/4026.

Despard, Charlotte. *Theosophy and the Woman's Movement*. Theosophical Publishing Society, 1913.

Dixon, Ella Hepworth. *The Story of a Modern Woman*. 1894. Edited by Steve Farmer, Broadview P, 2004.

Dixon, Joy. *Divine Feminine: Theosophy and Feminism in England*. Johns Hopkins UP, 2001.

---. 'Modernity, Heterodoxy and the Transformation of Religious Cultures.' *Women, Gender and Religious Cultures in Britain, 1800–1940*, edited by Sue Morgan and Jacqueline de Vries, Routledge, 2010, pp. 211–30.

Franklin, J. Jeffrey. 'The Life of the Buddha in Victorian England.' *ELH*, vol. 72, no. 4, 2005, pp. 941–74. *Project MUSE*, doi:10.1353/elh.2005.0033.

---. *The Lotus and the Lion: Buddhism and the British Empire*. Cornell UP, 2008.

Froude, James Anthony. *Nemesis of Faith*. 1849. New York Garland, 1975.

Gissing, George. *New Grub Street*. 2nd ed. Edited by Katherine Mullin, Oxford UP, 2016.

---. *The Odd Women*. 1893. Edited by Patricia Ingham, Oxford UP, 2008.

Gosse, Edmund. *Father and Son*. 1907. Edited by Michael Newton, Oxford UP, 2009.

Hardy, Thomas. *Jude the Obscure*. Harper & Brothers, 1896.

Heilmann, Ann. *New Woman Strategies: Sarah Grand, Olive Schreiner, Mona Caird*. Manchester UP, 2004.

---. 'Visionary Desires: Theosophy, Auto-Eroticism and the Seventh-Wave Artist in Sarah Grand's *The Beth Book*.' *Nineteenth-Century Contexts*, vol. 26, no.1, March 2004, pp. 29–46. doi: 10.1080/08905490410001683282.

Houston, Gail Turley. *Victorian Women Writers, Radical Grandmothers, and the Gendering of God*. Ohio State UP, 2013.

Jay, Elisabeth. *Faith and Doubt in Victorian Britain*. Humanities P, 1986.

Jay, Nancy. *Throughout Your Generations Forever: Sacrifice, Religion, and Paternity*. U of Chicago P, 1992.

Jayawardena, Kumari. *The White Women's Other Burden: Western Women and South Asia During British Rule*. Routledge, 1995.

Jenkins, Ruth. *Reclaiming Myths of Power: Women Writers and the Victorian Spiritual Crisis*. Bucknell UP, 1995.

Kontou, Tatiana. *Women and the Victorian Occult*. Routledge, 2011.

Ledger, Sally. *The New Woman: Fiction and Feminism at the Fin de Siècle*. Manchester UP, 1997.

Lloyd, Naomi. 'The Universal Divine Principle, the Spiritual Androgyne, and the New Age in Sarah Grand's *The Heavenly Twins*.' *Victorian Literature and Culture*, vol. 37, no.1, 2009, pp. 177–96. *JSTOR*, www.jstor.org/stable/40347220.

MacDonald, Tara. *The New Man, Masculinity and Marriage in the Victorian Novel*. Routledge, 2015.

Mahmood, Saba. *Politics of Piety: The Islamic Revival and the Feminist Subject*. Princeton UP, 2011.

Melnyk, Julie. *Women's Theology in Nineteenth-Century Britain: Transfiguring the Faith of Their Fathers*. Routledge, 1997.

Morgan, Sue, editor. *Women, Religion and Feminism in Britain, 1750–1900*. Palgrave Macmillan, 2002.

Morgan, Sue, and Jacqueline de Vries. 'Introduction.' *Women, Gender and Religious Cultures in Britain, 1800–1940*, Routledge, 2010.

Newman, John Henry. *Loss and Gain*. 1848. Edited by Trevor Lipscombe, series editor Joseph Pearce, Ignatius P, 2012.

Owen, Alex. *The Darkened Room: Women, Power, and Spiritualism in Late Victorian England*. U of Pennsylvania P, 1990.

---. *The Place of Enchantment: British Occultism and the Culture of the Modern*. U of Chicago P, 2004.

Scarry, Elaine. *The Body in Pain: The Making and Unmaking of the World*. Oxford UP, 1985.

Scott, Joan Wallach. *Gender and the Politics of History*. 1988. Columbia UP, 2018.

Styler, Rebecca. *Literary Theology by Women Writers of the Nineteenth Century*. Ashgate Publishing, 2010.

Taylor, Barbara. *Eve and the New Jerusalem: Socialism and Feminism in the Nineteenth Century*. Harvard UP, 1993.

Tromp, Marlene. *Altered States: Sex, Nation, Drugs, and Self-transformation in Victorian Spiritualism*. SUNY P, 2006.

Veer, Peter van der. *Imperial Encounters: Religion and Modernity in India and Britain*. Princeton UP, 2001.

Vicinus, Martha. *Independent Women: Work and Community for Single Women, 1850–1920*. U of Chicago P, 1985.

Willburn, Sarah A. *Possessed Victorians: Extra Spheres in Nineteenth-Century Mystical Writings*. Ashgate Publishing, 2006.

Yamaguchi, Midori. *Daughters of the Anglican Clergy: Religion, Gender and Identity in Victorian England*, Palgrave Macmillan, 2014.

Chapter Seven

The British 'Crisis of Faith' in Fin-de-Siècle Novels of Colonial India

The fin-de-siècle was a time of anxiety-ridden ruminations surrounding the British 'crisis of faith', not just in the metropolitan heartland but also in the colonies. In this chapter, I examine the way these tensions register in late nineteenth-century and early twentieth-century British novels set in colonial India. I argue that these texts, seemingly invested in representing the idolatrous colonial religion, quietly project British domestic religious anxieties about the perceived contemporary 'secularisation', and extract from colonial religious alterity a critique of 'modern' rationalistic (Protestant) Christianity and its 'secularist' assumptions of a 'crisis'. As part of this study, I look at Philip Meadows Taylor's *Seeta* (1872), Headon Hill's *The Rajah's Second Wife* (1894), Alice Perrin's *The Stronger Claim* (1903) and *Idolatry* (1909), with brief references to Maud Diver's *Lilamani* (1911). Though located in the colony[1] and manifestly preoccupied not only with the alleged inadequacies of colonial faiths but also with the need for conversion to Christianity, these novels are undergirded by a consuming engagement with the British narrative of religious 'decline' at home. I show how British authors, functioning under the overbearing perception of domestic unbelief, reacted to this crisis by deploying the colonial space as a fecund setting for crafting concepts like authentic divinity, true religiosity and civilised worship—thereby attempting to install an authoritative Western voice behind all colonial discussions about the nature and validity of native religion. Furthermore, the novels become more an externalised site for (a distanced and relatively covert) British national religious introspection. The texts repeatedly discuss the staples of the polemical British 'secularisation' debate— the issue of miracles, religious historiography, the divinity of Christ and the authenticity of the Bible—seemingly commenting on colonial religion but actually questioning and redefining the domestic British experience of a religious 'crisis'. Ultimately, these works attempt to restore a sense of religious wonder and spiritual love that go beyond the crippling binary alternatives of desiccated Christian faith and sceptical religious doubt offered by the post-Enlightenment Western 'secular' paradigm.[2]

One of the most representative novels is Alice Perrin's *The Stronger Claim*—a tale about the religious tussles of Paul Vereker, the mixed-race son born to a British father and an Indian mother. The mother's Indian family is described as slothful, covetous, avaricious and repugnant in their habits and even the Indian weather is portrayed as inclement and unwelcoming, verging on famines and cholera epidemics. Paul, however, is fascinated by idolatrous Hinduism, riveted by a pagan charm that hardly earns the approval of the author. When Paul's parents die, he is sent to England for an upbringing befitting an Englishman. He later returns to India with an English wife, only to revisit the haunting charm of his childhood fascinations that alienate him from his English relatives. The novel climaxes with a chaotic scene involving Paul's suggestively mystic surrender to Hindu religiosity.

Philip Meadows Taylor's *Seeta*—a novel set in the social and religious atmosphere of the Sepoy Mutiny—revolves around the marriage of Seeta, a Hindu widow, and Cyril Brandon, an Englishman, and offers an interesting narrative about faith, doubt and conversion. Seeta is the beautiful and virtuous young widow of Hurree Das, who was killed in a dacoits' burglary plot. Widowed and determined to testify against the miscreants, Seeta earns the attention of the Commissioner Sahib in charge of the legal proceedings, Cyril Brandon. Brandon is critical of the fate of the Hindu widow and wishes to rescue her from her misfortune and from a conspiratorial attack on her and her household by

Nawab Dil Khan. Over a period of time, a gradual development of affection and admiration between the English civil servant and the Hindu widow culminates in a marriage that we learn can be solemnised only by Hindu rites because it is impermissible in Christianity. Following the ceremony, Seeta experiences uncertainty and apprehension about religious pollution because of her cross-cultural union, but she is allowed to maintain the sanctity of her daily existence in her living quarters provided by Cyril. The cultural contrast between Seeta and Judge Mostyn's wife and sister (Rose and Grace) becomes evident, as does Cyril's developing extramarital attraction for Grace. A contemplative Seeta nearly undergoes a spiritual conversion to Christianity, and dies trying to save her husband. Following her death, Cyril marries Grace, and normative English domestic life is restored.

Perrin's *Idolatry* revolves around Oliver Wray, a dedicated British missionary located in India who immerses himself passionately in the task of abolishing idolatry from the country. At the heart of the story is the Englishwoman Anne, who fancies Dion Devasse, a colonial administrator, and pursues him from London to India. Disoriented by and often dismissive of colonial realities, she grudgingly recognises a magnetic attraction towards Oliver even as she maintains her primary interest in Dion. Oliver introduces her to a colonial civilisational and spiritual reality very different from her own which continues to overawe her even after her return to the cosy comfort of London life and English churches. The novel ends with her quietly lamenting the absence of Oliver in her life and with a narrative reconfirmation of Oliver's missionary commitment through news of his latest missionary ventures.

The Rajah's Second Wife by Headon Hill (pseudonym of Francis Edward Grainger) portrays the life of Amy, an Englishwoman who marries the Hindu Rajah Harichand of India (Jhalwa). The king formally aligns himself with Hinduism, the religion of his subjects, while also proudly declaring his newfound allegiance to Christianity. The Rajah's dalliance with Christianity is disliked by his minister (or Dewan), Govindjee, as well as by a large section of his subjects. John Deacon, the missionary, pities Amy's plight for what he considers to be her delusion about the sincerity of her husband's Christianity, and hopes to convert the Rajah in reality through long and promising personal theological debates with him. Underneath his honest efforts, he continues to harbour a quiet love for Amy which puts him in an ethical dilemma about whether or not to save the life of the Rajah when he learns about a native uprising.

Lilamani (published in America as *The Awakening*), by Maud Diver (born Katherine Helen Maud Marshall), is built on the premise that the Indian woman's inherent virtue and innocence distinguishes her from and elevates her over the forward Western women of the time—a binary represented in the text by Lilamani and Audrey. While Audrey is portrayed as the quintessential British New Woman pursuing advanced medical studies, Lilamani is contrasted as an embodiment of native virtue, holiness and spiritual dedication. Uninterested in professional pursuit, committed to a traditional ideal of marriage and implicitly immersed in the religious ethic, Lilamani epitomises a cultural critique of the English New Woman. It is therefore notable that it is Lilamani who is able to inspire love, longing and admiration in the heart of Nevil Sinclair, the man of Audrey's unrequited affections.

This set of works has been selected from among the vast number of fin-de-siècle novels set in colonial India, and especially the Mutiny novels, that deal with colonial Indian religious tensions surrounding Christian conversions because of their heavy focus on the contemporary British 'secularisation' debates. The authors of these works, composed between 1870 and 1914, occupy a central position within turn-of-the-century fiction. Francis Edward Grainger, who wrote under the pseudonym Headon Hill, was a British journalist and author of popular fiction including nonfantastic thrillers, police procedurals, and spy fiction. All the other authors were prolific practitioners in the domain of Anglo-Indian fiction. Both Alice Perrin and Maud Diver—'wives and daughters of Anglo-Indians' (Woodcock 100)—were well suited to offer an insider's account of the empire from the colonial margins as Perrin came from an old Anglo-Indian family and Diver married a soldier serving in India (Mannsaker 34). Meadows Taylor was similarly an insider, an 'administrator-novelist' with several decades of experience working for the Nizam of Hyderabad, and was furthermore 'a leading colonial writer', distinct from 'his contemporary administrator-novelists by his benevolent, paternalistic admiration of Indian culture' (Sen, Jhansi 1756). With the exception of Headon Hill, these authors and their works have received ample scholarly attention for their complex colonial dynamics. Melissa Edmundson Makala and Frances M. Mannsaker examine the inqualities of interrracial relationships in Perrin, and Indrani Sen investigates how Perrin's work complicates the mental health of the Western woman in colonial India. Philip Meadows Taylor's *Seeta* has been received as a crucial exemplar of the genre of Mutiny novels. Indrani Sen suggests that this work reshapes the genre by portraying the figure of Rani of Jhansi not as cruel and licentious as in other Mutiny novels but as a 'warrior woman' and freedom fighter. Nancy L. Paxton remarks that *Seeta* discards the rape narrative typical of Mutiny novels to achieve a coloniser–colonised reconciliation through interracial marriage. And Aishwarya Lakshmi observes that the novel constructs the colony as a feminised domestic space morally bound to its colonial masters in a hierarchical relationship represented through the metaphor of an unequal marriage. Maud Diver has been studied for her depiction of interracial dynamics by Loretta M. Mijares, and for her anti-feminist stance on the fin-de-siècle women's movement by Hager Ben Driss and Hagen Ben Driss. However, despite several such scholarly studies, there has been no sustained examination of the religious anxieties underpinning these novels separately or together. I undertake to study these novels as a group arguing that though not necessarily homogenous in their approach to the question of religion, they collectively present a composite picture of contemporary British tensions about declining religiosity, challenging the dominant nineteenth-century perception of 'secularism' and implicitly problematising the ubiquitous twentieth-century 'secularisation thesis' founded on this perception.

A FAITH FOREIGN, A FEAR FAMILIAR

One of the most remarkable aspects of this set of novels about colonial India is the way they stage the presence of Christian faith on the colonial landscape. The Church in nineteenth-century

India is at times portrayed as a comforting source of wholesome spiritual and social community for the British characters, especially those who freshly arrive and look to strengthen their ties with their homeland. For instance, in *The Rajah's Second Wife,* on the Sunday immediately after her arrival, Amy 'bearing up bravely amid the stupendous changes in her life, found herself longing for the support of public worship, to which she had always been accustomed' (Hill 64). We discover that she desires the protection of this religious institution because she felt that even if she were to be 'outside the pale of English society,' yet 'the ministrations of her Church formed common ground whence no one had the right to thrust her' (64). Defying contemporary Western claims of a religious 'crisis', the texts reiterate the solace and meaning that Christianity signifies in the lives of its followers. The value of domestic British faith is affirmed in *The Rajah's Second Wife,* at least for the 'real Christians', in marked contrast to what is shown to be the vapid poverty of the prospective Indian convert's native spiritual reservoir (35). Rajah Harichand says longingly to the British missionary, John Deacon: 'You Christians—real Christians, I mean—seem so happily confident in all your difficulties that it makes an outsider like myself a little envious sometimes.' To this, John says, assured of his own faith: 'That happiness and confidence are open to you, sir, this very day, if you would but put forth your hand and take them' (35). Taylor's *Seeta* also performs a sleight of hand by portraying the 'struggles' of the Indian convert to Christianity as so painfully rigorous that it inadvertently undermines the British 'crisis of faith'. The narrator observes that Seeta's 'struggles' as 'a heathen, with intellect and education powerful enough to understand' the 'truth', are particularly acute because the situation asks that 'every consideration, before held most sacred and precious, not only . . . be risked, but abandoned entirely for a new faith, and altogether new affections and associations' (Taylor 389). By portraying Seeta's tumultuous journey of religious conversion, the experience of the British domestic 'crisis of faith' is indirectly rendered less serious, demanding and perilous than that of colonial conversion to Christianity. This becomes most manifest in the narrator's succinct remark about the 'struggles' of Seeta as she attempts to convert: 'Such struggles, even in Christian hearts yearning to feel the truth, are often long and terrible; how much more, then, those of a heathen' (389). Such a narrative strategy glosses over Western scuffles with unbelief and cements the perception of a formidable and unassailable British domestic religiosity. While staging the dilemmas and demerits of colonial religion, the novels demolish the 'secularisation' narrative by rehearsing and disavowing the standard historical and scientific scholarly arguments that undergirded nineteenth-century domestic 'crisis of faith' narratives. This is best showcased in *The Rajah's Second Wife* in the descriptions of Harichand's growing friendship with John Deacon and his shift towards Christianity. In rhetoric familiar from the British religious debates of the time, the novel narrates how the Rajah passes '[f]rom scoffing unbelief' to the 'more hopeful regions of *honest doubt*' and finally to a surrender to Christianity (Hill 139; emphasis added).[3] John Deacon remarks that Harichand's feeling of doubt 'was no unassailable fortress' because it was 'based on nothing more solid than the stale old arguments of cheap infidelity,' and 'surrender would be only a question of time' (139). However, before this final surrender, Harichand passes through a phase when his 'scepticism', that had been 'at first merely careless', becomes 'more obstinate than profound' (219–20). In response to this scepticism, John Deacon undertakes to debunk the eighteenth- and nineteenth-century arguments against religion on which it was premised. To demolish Harichand's religious doubt—presented as unwieldy and illogical—John dismantles the claims of eighteenth-century scepticism (of Hume against miracles, and Voltaire against superstition, religious violence or intolerance) which foreshadowed the nineteenth-century 'crisis of faith' debates (fueled by Darwinian science and Biblical Higher Criticism). John falls 'with sledge-hammer force upon all the second-hand claptrap [that the Rajah] . . . had cribbed from Hume and Voltaire' (220). John also fractures the familiar nineteenth-century 'secularisation' arguments. On the issue of the 'historical accuracy of the Bible', John 'proved it [the Bible] to him [the Rajah] by comparing it with other histories written and accepted by infidels'. To settle the debate over the divine origin of Scripture, John proves 'the Bible . . . [to be] the revealed

Word of God' by 'citing the fulfilment of a score of prophecies'. Furthermore, John overturns the science-vs-religion conflict—a staple in the contemporary debates on religion. When the Rajah 'allege[d] the stale old argument that the Bible and the discoveries of modern science are irreconcilable', John 'called in the testimony of the stars, of the earth's strata, and of chemistry to show that the two were as one upon every vital issue' (220–22). John also addresses the supernatural claims of Christianity—in particular, the veracity of miracles and the divinity of Christ—that were being strongly contested in contemporary discourse with the counterargument that miracles were not rationally possible and Christ was not a divine incarnation but a historical personage. When 'at last, beaten from point to point, Harichand fell back on the last resource of doubting the miracles and denying the divinity of Christ', John responds:

> You say that the miracles may be accounted for by juggling or mesmerism—that in India at this day there are conjurers who perform equally marvellous feats. I ask you, has any one of these jugglers, or any other *man* since the creation of the world, ever succeeded in raising the dead to life? There is no such record, you say. Very well; I ask you further, has any *man*, other than Him whose resurrection is written in the book of which you have just admitted the historical accuracy—has any man, I say, ever before or ever since been able to burst the bonds of the grave, and *himself* return in the flesh to this lower world? Had this power been human, would it not have been exercised by these wonderful jugglers of yours and by others? Would no one else through all the centuries have found out the secret? Remember, the love of life is strong. (220–22)

Interestingly, John implies a parallel between the dilemma of the unconverted sceptical native and that of the British doubter by reiterating the hackneyed arguments of the Western 'secularisation' debate, supplying each with a forceful refutation. Thus, the text shows the British missionary defending religious faith and its supernatural claims against the barrage of Western post-Enlightenment rationalism. Furthermore, the missionary suggests that the sceptical native, and implicitly also the British doubter whose concerns he shares, wishes in actuality to surrender to religious faith despite professions of unbelief or doubt. As he observes, in all of the Rajah's arguments 'it was defeat, not victory, that he [the Rajah] was courting' (219). As such, the novels project the colonial battleground, on which domestic religious tensions are projected and negotiated.

In particular, the novels resonate with the nineteenth-century polemics surrounding the viability of religious miracles—a theme critical to the 'secularisation' discourse as we have seen— and repeatedly challenge the possibility of the miraculous when associated with Hinduism. At a time when this aspect of Christianity was under the harshest attacks by historical and scientific scholarship, the contentiousness of the issue is revived in connection with Hinduism. The narrative of *Seeta* indirectly devalues Hinduism's claim to miracles and in the process reinstates the legitimacy of Christian miracles, offsetting Western rationalism. The novel describes the buildup to the Sepoy Mutiny noting that this was a direct result of the wild rumours that incited the colonial natives— rumours that could proliferate only because of the gullibility of the Indian mind, made susceptible by claims of Hindu miracles. The narrator remarks that the 'childish credulity of the ordinary Hindoo native of India' is unparalleled and 'his mind is prepared, as it were, to receive any human exaggeration and invention without question, and for any cause' because he has been '[t]rained in his youth to believe the astonishing, and to him beneficent, miracles of his gods'[4] (Taylor 233). Referring to the rumour of the Sumbut that spread rapidly before the Sepoy Mutiny, the narrator notes that perhaps it was 'not strange that when the purport of the weird Sumbut 1914 was disseminated, any rumour whatever that might arise, *any* portent that was visible or imagined, *was accepted as a divine revelation*, and believed in faith' (Taylor 233; emphasis added). This condemnation of misplaced Hindu credulousness derives from the textual disapproval of false Hindu claims of religious miracles—a critique that serves as a foil to what are suggestively the true miracles of Christianity. The insinuation that Hinduism is an unsubstantial faith becomes the pretext for the novel's disparagement of the 'modern' desiccated Christian experience in Britain. Instead, what is recreated in the colony, against which colonial religions (like Hinduism) are offset and critiqued, is a reimagined Christianity that exceeds the British domestic rationalistic template.

CHRISTIAN FAITH AND ITS 'OTHER'

A substantial part of each of these novels demonstrates the superiority of Christian faith over colonial religion, specifically over Hinduism, while participating in crucial contemporary debates about the meanings and forms of religiosity. Before I layer this reading with more ambiguous indicators of a colonial challenge to 'modern' rationalistic Christian faith, it is important to note the primary textual emphasis on the preeminence of Christian faith.

Set against the reimagined Christianity of the colonies, Hinduism is critiqued, especially through the character of Taylor's prospective convert and eponymous heroine, Seeta. Seeta is portrayed as an instructive prototype of a woman converting devoutly from Hinduism to Christianity. Besides the tractable simplicity of the native colonial woman susceptible to religious faith, Seeta also displays an intuitive understanding of the supposed superiority of Christianity over idolatrous Hinduism. When she watches the church services intently, accompanied by her supportive friends (Mrs Mostyn, Grace Mostyn, Lucy Home, Mrs Hill and Mrs Pratt), she is overcome by a combination of reverence and discomfort. The narrator remarks condescendingly: 'I think if she had followed her own instincts she would have gone forward at once, and fallen prostrate before the table, and there prayed in her own simple fashion; but nobody she saw did that' (Taylor 358). These impulses or habits informed by a Hindu upbringing is contrasted with the profound impact and emotional power of the Christian service where, when she hears the 'litany to Him "that despiseth not the sighing of a contrite heart"', her heart swells with 'silent ecstasy'. As she surrenders to, and immerses herself in, Christian faith, we learn that so 'full her heart was of devotion that as yet she could only think, but not express'. And in this moment when Seeta discovers the essence and value of Christianity, the narrative symbolically crowns her with a halo as if to endorse the Hindu woman's spiritual transformation: '[B]y chance one of the rays from the clerestory fell on her, and surrounded her as with a glory all the time she sat' (358). Reveling in her spiritual experience of Christian worship and suffused with the hallowed peace it brings her, she nevertheless remains conscious of the gulf that hinders her, a Hindu, from participating in the Eucharist.[5] Diver's *Lilamani* presents a similar instance of a native Indian woman transforming under the influence of Christianity. The narrative builds the spiritual crescendo towards the moment when Lilamani surrenders to the worship of Christ: 'To-day the presence of others troubled her not at all. For to-day, by her husband's wish, she was privileged to worship, with him, that Great One, that "Brilliance at the core of Brilliance," whose diverse names and forms are but the manifold garments of His revealing' (276–77). Lilamani devotes herself unquestioningly to Christ— to this 'thing of beauty and awe'—and sees in the (Protestant) architectural design of the church a distillation of Christian religiosity: 'The church itself, plain and unpretentious, like most of its kind abroad—had yet its pervasive atmosphere of sanctuary, above all in the region of the altar—shrine, she named it—where the white-robed figure, tall candlesticks and sober embroideries were glorified by sun-rays streaming through stained glass' (276–77). Lilamani and Nevil begin to inhabit a state of spiritual conjugal bliss which sanctifies their union in ways that elude expression. As the narrator remarks about the couple's state of mind after their church worship—they were 'too deeply and diversely stirred for common speech' (277).

In Taylor's novel, Seeta is also shown eventually realising the ineffectiveness of the Hindu idol. On returning home from a spiritually uplifting church prayer, she feels alienated from her cherished idol of Krishna. She goes into her 'little oratory' and touches her forehead with 'the ashes from the sacred fire' and then 'prostrate[s] herself before her little altar', only to discover that her idol—a 'silver image of Krishna . . . that her grandfather and Aunt Ella had confided to her with earnest injunctions for its worship'— now 'seemed to blink at her sleepily with its sapphire eyes' (Taylor 359). In a climactic moment, she realises that even though she 'cried to it [the idol] in the words of her own liturgy which she had by heart', those 'prayers seemed to her cold and comfortless' (359).

She postulates the Hindu idol's ineffectiveness, contrasting it with the consolation offered by the Christian God, and reveals the impact that Christian liturgy has on her:

> [T]here came up involuntarily in her heart, the Christian wail, 'O God, merciful Father, that despisest not the sighing of a contrite heart, nor the desires of such as be sorrowful,' and she felt that, through God's mercy, 'the craft and subtilty of the devil or man had indeed, for her, been brought to nought,' and that she was safe—safe from the horrible violence that had been intended. (359–60)

In *Educating Seeta* (2010), Shuchi Kapila discusses the way the native Indian woman was presented in Anglo-Indian romances as 'educable, docile, devoted, and loyal, in other words, the ideal colonial subject' (2). Within the context of Britain's colonial 'system of "indirect rule"' over India, where governance was implemented through benevolence (education and reform) and not coercive force, these romances grew out of the Western project of producing 'literary-political fantasies'. Kapila explains that these romances 'encode a political fantasy of creating through a process of benevolent rule, native subjects acculturated to European values who welcome colonial rule and ally themselves with British interests' (3). This 'political fantasy' is played out through the 'interracial relationship' between the dominating Englishman-educator and the pliable Indian woman. Kapila notes that novels like *Seeta* and *Lilamani* are 'interracial romance[s] . . . in the high orientalist mode' in which the women function as 'melancholy, "idealized," exotic beauties,' who represent 'not only the glories of Hindu culture but also its repressive aspects' and who are eventually rescued by the Englishmen (16). Echoing Kapila's insights, *Seeta* and *Lilamani* show their titular characters similarly paired and contrasted with benevolent Englishmen, and depict how the protagonists' educable docility easily translates into their spontaneous preference for Christianity as the 'superior faith'.[6] The native women's unprompted surrender to Christianity offers a chiselled, meaningful and deliberate counterpoint to the phenomenon of late-nineteenth-century Western women rejecting traditional Christianity in favour of heterodox religious alternatives. Kumari Jayawardena describes the role played by Western women in 'the revolt against Christianity in the West, the rise of numerous alternative beliefs, and the link-up between such tendencies in the West with religious revival and emerging nationalism in the colonies' (15). She observes that 'anxiety and loss of faith led to a revival of interest in earlier forms of belief . . . in arcane knowledge, in the occult, magic, spiritualism, astrology', Theosophy, Vedanta and Kali worship and 'curiosity about religions of the non-Christian world' (112–13). This led to the general shift towards Eastern faiths that was represented by spiritualism and Theosophy. Jayawardena notes that this eastward move came out of the 'anti-systemic and heterodox movements that emerged in the west in the 19th century, which questioned the social and ideological orthodoxies of the day and rejected the notion of Christianity as the only true religion' (107–08).[7] While explorations of Western women's involvement in the empire, especially in South Asia, abound—such as in the works of Pat Barr, Kirsty Reid, Mary Ann Lind, Rosemary Raza, Indira Ghose, Barbara Ramusack, Antoinette Burton, Susmita Roye, Rajeshwar Mittapalli, Sangeeta Ray, Clare Midgley and Indrani Sen—Jayawardena's is particularly rewarding for the subversive (and de-Christianised) Western woman it discusses, which the colonial Hindu woman's adoption of Christianity emerges as significant.

The novels' portrayal of Christianity's relative superiority over colonial faiths is anchored in their representation of its inherent simplicity. This is contrasted with the abstruse, unappealing and even corrupt nature of colonial faiths like Hinduism. In *Lilamani*, for example, when Nevil asks Lilamani if the Christian 'fashion of worship' pleases her, she replies succinctly: 'Yes. It is more simple—more solemn than ours. It speaks to the soul' (Diver 277). In Perrin's *Idolatry*, Ramanund, a prospective convert, simultaneously recognises the original purity and current corruption of Hinduism, and powerfully voices his yearning for the simplicity of Christian faith. While Ramanund reveres the 'wisdom and piety' of his native faith, he also struggles with it because 'so complicated and entangled was the teaching with the wildest allegory' and 'so hampered [was it] with priestly tradition' and 'so bewildering' that the 'original purity and purpose was hard to seize and hold' and he 'craved for simpler guidance—for more direct and tender help' (Perrin, *Idolatry* 183). This portrayal echoes the stereotypical representation of Hinduism in British (Protestant) colonial discourse—as a faith resembling Catholicism and thus rife with priesthood, idolatry and ritual. In contrast to colonial faiths, Protestant Christianity and its Scripture is valorised in the novels for its uniquely appealing trait of simplicity that also serves as the marker of a superior English culture. In *England's Secular Scripture* (2011), Jo Carruthers studies Reformation England of the sixteenth and seventeenth centuries, noting that 'an aesthetic revolution' took place at this time in which simplicity took on 'a whole new set of associations' and assumed 'the mantle of both Protestant theology and the new . . . Protestant English identity' (7). Though 'visual simplicity had been an important symbol within religious life in England' long before the sixteenth century, the understanding of this aesthetic had been very different. For the Church Fathers, the Scripture's simplicity was the 'chosen form of communication that spoke of God's efforts to speak to humankind on their own level' (9). In this pre-Reformation view, the 'simplicity of form expressed, not belied, the complexity and distance of the divine to the human,' signifying 'uniqueness and even the complexity and ineffableness of the divine' (9). However, the Reformation brought a shift and simplicity now came to characterise *the unfettered access to the divine* that Protestantism, as opposed to Catholicism, provided through scripture. Thus, while 'seemingly innocent and benign', simplicity in the Reformation emerged as 'a peculiarly Protestant aesthetic and concept' that shaped an 'oppositional sense of English identity'— that is, Englishness as anti-Catholic (3). This early modern aesthetic continued to function in the eighteenth and nineteenth centuries as 'primarily [an] oppositional aesthetic that denigrate[d] both external and internal enemies' (49)—marking the distinction 'in national terms' between the English and the '(usually Catholic) foreigners' as well as the 'internal opposition' between 'the "true" English . . . [and the] inferior classes' (50). As instanced in *Lilamani* and *Idolatry*, this charged notion is deployed strategically in these nineteenth-century colonial Indian novels to demarcate the colonial 'others', defined by their foreign faith (Hinduism) but lacking in the typically (Protestant) English quality of simplicity. Similarly in *Seeta*, during discussions about whether Seeta would convert to her husband's faith, Hinduism is described through its ancientness as 'the old belief in which she had been reared' and its foundations in 'deep and often grand metaphysical arguments', while Christianity is marked by its nearly 'childish' simplicity (388). Seeta's religious trajectory from Hinduism to Christianity is delineated thus: '[T]he *simplicity* of Christian truth had, at first, indeed, appeared childish, if not contemptible; and yet how they had perceptibly grown upon her!' (Taylor 388; emphasis added). The novel wonders whether Hinduism's vast theological underpinning was crumbling when confronted by the appeal of Christian simplicity: 'Were the foundations of the old Hindooism—the grand citadels of the Vedas and the "Bhugwut Geeta," the metaphysics of Patanjula, giving way?' (372). The text represents the English as unversed in theological expertise and incapable of dogmatic nuances, initially pondering if this is a failing: 'If Mrs Pratt or Cyril had been as deeply versed in Hindoo theology as Seeta was, they might have had many a fervid battle' (373).[8] But this finally becomes a way for the narrative to demonstrate the superiority of Christian simplicity as a religious template that rises above dogmatic complexity. The novel poignantly summarises what Christianity offers in opposition to 'all . . . [of Seeta's] learning': '[Cyril Brandon and Mrs Pratt] could only oppose *the simple truths* and faithful realities of their own belief. Nothing of dogma was ever mentioned; only a Saviour's atonement for sin, His present help in all trouble, and faith to realize His gracious promises' (373; emphasis added). Eventually, this presumptively superior English aesthetic has its desired religious effect because, like 'stormy waves beating against a rock' and gradually altering their form, Seeta too 'grew fond of these arguments: fonder and fonder as it appeared' (373).

The privileging of simplicity in the novels also translates into discussions about the Bible and what was perceived to be its distinguishing feature in relation to Hindu scripture—transparent and rationalist accessibility. This attribution of simplicity drew from the larger colonial context in which the Bible acquired a charged cross-cultural relevance and popularity as a *cultural* instead of a theological text—having developed into what Jonathan Sheehan calls the 'cultural Bible'. Sheehan explains how the nineteenth-century 'cultural Bible', that grew out of its precursor (the 'Enlightenment Bible'), was a work 'whose meaning, significance, and function ensured its vitality in a *postconfessional and post-theological age*' (27–28; emphasis added).[9] It was therefore received in the colonies less as a theological text, more as a work emblematic of 'English' culture and was uniquely accessible to the native population because of its perceived simplicity. This turn towards cultural translatability and open access, facilitated through the ethic of simplicity, is interpreted ambiguously both as a secularising development and a bulwark against secularisation. According to Sheehan, this shift to simplicity did not constitute 'secularisation' but was instead responsible for an internal change within religion (Protestant Christianity) that *staved off* 'secularisation'. The novels portray the charged simplicity of the Scripture and its complex allure for the colonial natives, locating the colonial conversations and conversions in this ambiguous space between religiosity and secularism. An engagement with the simplicity of the Bible is evident in Taylor's novel when Seeta explains to Cyril the emotional and spiritual comfort the Bible brought to her when she felt discarded by her community at Shah Gunje:

> I met with this passage in one of the books you gave me to read, 'Come unto me, all ye that are weary and heavy laden, and I will give you rest.' They are God's words, . . . So I used to take the book to the garden and read it, and I used to say, 'I am weary, Lord, very weary, give me rest.' . . . rest came with you, and He had heard me. O! I was sorely grieved then, Cyril; . . . Was it wrong to pray to your God? Would He care for me? (273)

To this appeal Cyril replies delightedly, guessing that 'a dawning of true light [had] come into her mind': 'God is your God as well as mine; He never turns from those who cry to Him in their need, and in humble faith' (273). Seeta's response summarises the primary and most winning quality of simplicity that she associates with the Bible: '[T]here is the same in the Geeta; but your book is so tender, so simple, that a child could understand it, and who but

Brahmins can understand the mysteries of the Geeta?'[10] (273–74). Seeta further explains the effect the words of the Christian God had on her, noting with quiet confidence how these passages from the Bible 'comforted . . . [her] more than the "Bhugwut Geeta"' (273). Again in Perrin's *Idolatry*, Hindu scripture is faulted for its lack of transparent simplicity and therefore for its inaccessibility to rationalist interpretation. Ramanund tells Oliver, for example, about how he had read 'only the ancient wisdom of . . . [the Hindu] Holy Books' and about how he had struggled because 'they are so many, and so bewildering, no man may hope to read them in a lifetime' (105–06).

In the discussion that follows I show how, at a deeper level in these novels, the apparent superiority of the Christian faith is problematised and colonial religion is shown to demonstrate alternate templates for religious experience that privilege faith over reason, divine mystery over transparent knowledge and surrender over control. As a whole, this corpus establishes possibilities for deeper forms of religious experience that exceed contemporary Western 'secularist' frameworks.

CHALLENGING REASON THROUGH TEMPLATES OF FAITH

The Protestant notion of simplicity that 'promoted a whole set of beliefs about English character', and dismissed emotion and divine mystery in favour of 'superiority, transparency, rationality and self-possession' (Carruthers 2, 50), also prescribed 'discerning reading' through 'prioritization of rationality and the suppression of emotion' (13). While the novels partially valorise the simplicity of the Christian faith and Scripture over colonial faiths, this section shows that they ultimately critique this ethic of simplicity along with its prescribed modes of rationalist reading. The texts—most significantly *Seeta*—accomplish this by offering an alternative model for the reading and interpreting of Scripture. This template for religious reading can be understood best by resorting to Alan Jacobs's *A Theology of Reading* (2001) where he explains the need for 'charitable interpretation' in all our reading processes and prescribes what he calls the 'hermeneutics of love' (8).[11] Despite the historical gap between Taylor's *Seeta* and Jacobs's contemporary scholarship, the latter discusses what could be considered a theological understanding of 'knowledge'—an approach that Seeta exemplifies through her reading of the Bible. With the help of Jacobs's philosophical intervention, we are able to identify in Taylor's novel a narrative attempt at bridging the fissure that emerged *within* Christianity during the Reformation and Enlightenment—between knowledge on the one hand, and experiential faith, love and prayer on the other. While Jacobs, writing in our times, is primarily invested in devising alternate literary/critical reading practices for our everyday application, his work also supplies a useful framework for understanding the colonial Indian novels. Reading these texts retrospectively, we find a parallel to Jacobs's insight in the reading technique adopted by the colonial woman who supplements 'knowledge' with faith and love—the need for which was being felt by Victorian Christianity as it reeled under the impact of polemical and personal 'crisis of faith' narratives. Dismantling our usual practice of equating knowledge with information, Jacobs writes of the possibility of a different kind of knowledge. He notes: 'We love people because of what we know about them, to be sure, but we also come to know them more fully because we love them. Certain kinds of knowledge of people . . . are available only to those who love them' (43). Referring to Martha Nussbaum's *Love's Knowledge* (1990), Jacobs explains that the love for someone allows us to possess an 'intimate knowledge' of this person—a template of knowledge that exceeds the logic of the factual (6).[12] In his work, *On Religion*, Caputo asseverates that the definition of a religious person is one who is in love, and the loveless is one who is faithless, implying that it is only possible to know God by loving God (1–4). These scholarly approaches therefore challenge and fuse the binary of 'knowledge' and 'faith' that the 'secularisation' crisis was most vigorously constructing, confronting and battling. As Talal Asad explains in *Genealogies of Religion* (1993), this opposition of 'knowledge' to 'love'/'feeling'/'faith' is a problem that arises only in the 'modern' Western understanding of religiosity that dominated the nineteenth and twentieth centuries. Asad observes that for 'pious learned Christians of the twelfth century, . . . knowledge and belief were not so clearly at odds' (47). Instead, Christian belief was then built on a different kind of knowledge altogether—a 'knowledge of theological doctrine, of canon law and Church courts, . . . [and] of the lives of the saints'—that is, a knowledge of the domain of faith (47). The late nineteenth and early twentieth century was forced into the heart of this polemical confrontation of knowledge and faith, with scholarship (textual knowledge of the Scripture, historical knowledge, scientific knowledge) challenging the fundamentals of the Christian doctrine and posing (what was perceived to be) a 'crisis of faith'. Interestingly, departing from the 'secularist' binary of knowledge-versus-faith, the colonial native reading the Bible empoweringly exemplifies an *alternate* model of knowledge that is based on what Jacobs calls the 'hermeneutics of love'. Seeta most eloquently opens up this possibility of religious knowledge by proposing a knowledge based on love, thereby restoring the sense of divine mystery to religion that is otherwise devalued in the novels through their privileging of the aesthetic of simplicity and the 'cultural' Bible amenable to rationalist interpretation. Seeta describes to Cyril the effect of a 'passage in one of the books' he had given to her to read. Having read 'God's words'—'Come unto me, all ye that are weary and heavy laden, and I will give you rest'—she says '*I know, and they comforted me*' (273; emphasis added). Almost immediately, she adds—'*I do not know to whom I prayed*, but rest came' (273; emphasis added). Her confidence about how she *knows* them to be God's words ('I know') seems to contradict her candid confession of her lack of knowledge ('I do not know to whom I prayed'), but in fact it alerts us to the distinction between factual information on the one hand and a deeper knowledge deriving from loving comprehension on the other. Despite Seeta's initial championing of Christian religious simplicity, she finally downplays this rationalistic ideal that assumes the possibility of a transparent human comprehension of the divine. She exposes the impossibility of such factual knowledge, and models an empowering surrender to the unfathomable divinity. Recounting her efforts at, and satisfaction from, reading the Bible—first in English and then more comfortably in the 'Hindee' translation—Seeta admits: 'I am never tired of reading now, though much of it makes me weep, and be angry too: but I cannot understand many portions yet' (274). Discarding conventional factual information (or, 'understand[ing]') of the Scripture, Seeta prefers emotional engagement with the text as a way to most meaningfully comprehending it. In this recuperation of love and surrender as a mode for Bible-reading, the mainstream rationalistic narrative of faith and doubt is problematised.[13] Even as Cyril attempts to help Seeta, she forestalls him: 'No, you must not teach me, . . . I have understood much, and God will teach me more, if He will' (274). Demonstrating humble contentment with partial information and choosing to defer to God's judgment about the necessity of human knowledge, the devotee models what Jacobs prescribes as religious humility. Quoting from W. H. Auden's *The Dyer's Hand* (1948), Jacobs suggests the need for moderating what we consider to be our fundamental 'right to know' and remarks that true knowledge is that which we can truly live up to—the kind of eligibility that we are not best placed to decide upon by ourselves. Jacobs draws a passage from Auden that is worth quoting:

> [I]n our culture, we have all accepted the notion that the right to know is absolute and unlimited. . . . We are quite prepared to admit that, while food and sex are good in themselves, an uncontrolled pursuit of either is not, but it is difficult for us to believe that intellectual curiosity is a desire like any other, and to realize that correct knowledge and truth are not identical. To apply a categorical imperative to knowing, so that, instead of asking, 'What can I know?' we ask, 'What, at this moment, am I meant to know?'— . . . that seems to all of us crazy and almost immoral. (qtd. in Jacobs 21–22)

This critique of the modern rationalistic understanding of religion can be observed again in the text when Seeta attends a Christian communion for the first time. Taylor describes Seeta's experience, constantly emphasising not only her spiritual fulfilment but also her inability to comprehend the divine. As an indication of this, the narrator informs us that for Seeta the 'excellent divine's delivery *was none of the plainest*' (359; emphasis added). This is not the case for the Western audience, suggestively of the rational bent, who 'understood it, practical and seasonable as it was' (359)—clearly comprehending only the surface. By contrast, Seeta is shown to experience intellectual bafflement, not tremulously or regretfully but as an enriching mode of religious engagement. The narrator observes that though 'Seeta *did not understand* much' of the sermon, and though 'she *could not follow* all the service', because 'its length, and the changes in it, *bewildered her*', she actually derived spiritual fulfilment through this very incomprehension (358–59; emphasis added). Thus, as she watches the service, Seeta's heart becomes a 'humble reverent spirit' full of 'devotion', 'swell[ing] with gratitude in a kind of silent ecstasy, which she had never before experienced' (359). As distinct from the Western churchgoers, Seeta's poignant emotional experience during the service suggests her far more meaningful understanding of the loving spirit of Christianity. Her friends watch 'the silent soft tears dropping gently from her eyes, while her reverent glances were now and then upraised, and her lips moved to her thoughts'. Of all things that appealed to her, 'most of all [was]. . . that supplication in the litany to Him' (358). Crucially, in this surrender she finds agency, and from her wondrous incomprehension she derives fulfilment. Through these interesting colonial encounters with religious alterities, deeper formats for religious experience seem to emerge which fracture 'modern' Protestant injunctions of simplicity and rationality.

The novels do not fail to impress upon the readers the centrality of the colonial landscape in this restructuring and deepening of the experience of faith. On the one hand, as explained above, the colonial native, as opposed to the Westerners, embodies the prototype of the worshipper who is fully aware of the miraculous nature of faith and the surrender this demands. Thus, in Maud Diver's novel, Lilamani's experience of Christianity is contrasted with that of the unbelieving English masses. Speaking of the church service Lilamani attended, the narrator says: 'The handful of "Christian peoples," hypnotized by ceaseless repetition, found the service, with its scanty music and unimpressive sermon, a rather lifeless affair. But to one privileged "heathen" it seemed a thing of beauty and awe' (Diver 276–77). Nevil defends Lilamani to his relatives, contrasting a 'declining' Western ability to experience the religious with the Indian woman's ability and desire to inhabit this spiritual realm of 'miraculous' uncertainty: 'She [Lilamani] knows the Bible better than some of us do; and *religion means a great deal more to her than to the average Christian*' (162; emphasis added). Not only this, the British characters themselves are shown to more fully experience religious awe when they encounter Christian faith in the colony. In Perrin's *Idolatry*, for example, Dion watches the native Indians perform their holy rituals at the Ganges, and afterwards confesses its religious power while disparagingly reporting this scene to Judge Stapely: 'Oh! well, at any rate we ain't idolaters; *though I must say I noticed enough reverence and devotion this afternoon to put many of us to shame!*' (39; emphasis added). On his way back from the Ganges, Dion chances upon Oliver Wray preaching Christianity to a native audience and this stirs in Dion emotions that are different and stronger than those he had ever felt before in Britain: 'He [Dion] felt puzzled by his own sensations and not a little impatient with them. Why should he be so affected by this example of his national faith as opposed to idolatry, when any amount of customary "church" at home had failed to arouse in him the smallest emotion?' (37–38). Dion further emphasises how this sight awakens him to the experience of the miraculous and the mysterious—or the 'impossible' in Caputo's formulation (Caputo 67)—that lies at the heart of religious experience: 'The preacher's face and voice had stirred within him an indefinable sense of mystery' (Perrin, *Idolatry* 37). Dion even assigns Oliver a position of regious authority, describing him as '[a]n Englishman . . . with a face like an apostle on a stained-glass window' (41), for the awe he is able to evoke in him. The situation is similar for Anne, who begins with a routinised approach to religion—such as when she visits the Indian church and sits down 'mechanically, with the rest of the congregation'—but ultimately undergoes a spiritual transformation as Oliver's sermon puts her 'under a spell' and Oliver's voice rings out exhorting the masses to religious surrender: 'The Voice of one crying in the Wilderness, Prepare ye the way of the Lord, make His paths straight' (154).

The novels also suggest that the civilisational ancientness and spiritual depth of India facilitates a more meaningful experience of faith as a whole. In Perrin's *Idolatry*, for example, Oliver says to Anne that the literature and philosophers of India '*often contain the highest spiritual thought*' (120; emphasis added). In *The Stronger Claim*, Paul Vereker remarks about India's ethical systems and therefore suggestively also about Indian spirituality: 'Think of these people who three thousand years ago evolved the Laws of Manu—one of the grandest systems of ethics that has ever been known—remember the culture, thought, and philosophy that has lasted through all those centuries!' (Perrin, *The Stronger Claim* 218). Emphasising once again the importance of the unknowable and the miraculous in faith, Paul announces his proud allegiance to his wife: 'This is a country that is old in original wisdom, she is steeped in knowledge, and beauty, and *mystery*! I tell you, Selma, I am glad I belong to her—I am proud of it!' (200; emphasis added). Speaking of the forthcoming 'great religious [Hindu] fair', Paul flaunts the ancient glory of the Hindu religious celebration to Selma, and chastises those who judge Eastern religion from a Western standpoint. Speaking enthusiastically of the great 'opportunity for studying the religious thought and feeling of the country' that will be offered by the upcoming fair, he excitedly anticipates this spiritually electrifying experience: 'Fancy two or three millions of people all impelled to the same spot by a sense of religion—what a wonderful atmosphere!' (218). The power of this image derives greatly from the implicit juxtaposition of this colonial (frenzied) religious devotion with the nineteenth-century desiccated (Protestant) Christian landscape. In the climactic scene of the novel, there is a similar acknowledgement of this colonial religious excess when Selma watches the confluence of thousands of Hindu pilgrims at the religious fair entranced: 'It seemed to be almost unreal to be viewing from these high red walls a scene that had been enacted year after year for many centuries, and that was now as much *alive with religious belief and enthusiasm* as it had been two, or perhaps three, thousand years ago' (288–89; emphasis added). Furthermore, as Selma watched this 'seething concourse of human beings' and the religious frenzy of the natives with their 'ceaseless clamour of prayer and praise', she begins to have only a 'dim understanding of the spell of this wonderful country'. A strong 'sense of the *mystery* of far-off ages touche[s] her spirit' (288–89; emphasis added). Overtaken not just by the frenzy but also by the 'mystery' inherent to the miraculousness of faith, Selma admits to the workings of the religious power that she knows has overtaken her husband.

A similar confrontation between the dry religious practice of the modern West and the inarticulable depth and mystery modelled by colonial faiths can also be seen in Perrin's *Idolatry*. In this novel, we are shown the stark contrast between the superficial British upper-class life on the one hand, and the deeply spiritual Thanesur Buddhist shrine on the other. The narrator puts on display the facile routine of London life with its preoccupations and camaraderie—a social circle of 'little jokes and happenings, broken-off engagements, unexpected marriages, [and] one or two scandals' about which the Westerners 'gossiped shamelessly'—a world deeply antithetical to the ancient and mysterious religious landscape that surrounds Dion and Anne at Thanesur (Perrin, *Idolatry* 170–71). They travel to the Buddhist shrine: the 'great tower', a 'massive erection with its crooked, battered crown standing full in the sunlight' (171)—a site where 'Wray reminded his hearers that . . . Buddha had preached his first sermon' (156–57). Upon arrival, Anne's mixed feelings of deep reverence and wonder on the one hand and consuming terror on the other begin to surface. Speechless and 'awed', she awakens to the religious significance of the site: 'So it was here that the voice of Buddha had cried his great creed so long, long ago!' (171). Experiencing the inexplicable and magical hold of colonial religiosity as the sacred site 'over[comes] her', Anne confesses that she 'could not go any nearer, she could not lie . . . in such an environment' (172). Spontaneously, she develops an aversion towards the 'trivial talk' with Dion that she typically enjoyed, and is appalled at the gaping rift that separates it from the engrossing profundity of colonial faith which she encounters at this site (171). Quietly contemplating the religious significance of the place whose 'silence, . . . [and] wild loneliness . . . [had] aroused her wonder', she ponders about the Buddha's sermon at Thanesur: 'Had it really happened?' The sheer force exercised by colonial religion in general, and the Thanesur shrine in particular, becomes evident in the way it evokes not only deep awe but also 'sudden repulsion, almost a terror of the place' (171–72).

The inexplicable force of colonial religion is similarly emphasised in Perrin's *The Stronger Claim*. In this novel, the protagonist Paul Vereker of mixed religious lineage displays how Hinduism begins to possess his Christian self once he returns to India. At the Hindu fair in the climax of the novel, a huge commotion starts from within the atmosphere of colonial religious frenzy, escalating further with the Hindu priests on one side and the Christian missionary on the other. Paul stands unable to decide between the two religions and the crowd's fervour rises to a tumultuous pitch in no time. Paul is trampled underfoot and 'fatally injured', which leaves Mr Goring (his friend, the Englishman Collector) unsympathetic, and Selma aghast (Perrin, *The Stronger Claim* 296). He is rescued and carried outside while he 'whisper[s] beseechingly' to be taken 'into the light' (296). The Hindu mob's rapture and hysteria rises to a climactic pitch as 'the sunset . . . crimson[s] the waters' and the 'noise of the multitude'—the 'clang of bells and conches, the cries of prayer and praise'—soar (296). In the midst of this religious vortex, Paul, with Hindu blood in his veins and a name bearing heavy Christian iconicity, voices the 'stronger claim' in his final words to the Hindu priests: 'Oh! Baba-jee! . . . Behold! I am come!' (296–97). Rerouted from England to India, his land of origin, Paul surrenders himself to the Hindu deity in this grand gesture that concludes the novel. Reaching the apotheosis of devotion, and fervour, the narrative closes by announcing and inscribing the magnetic call and spiritual power of Hinduism: '[I]n the atmosphere of the faith that by heritage was in his veins, Paul Vereker's spirit answered to the call of the gods' (297).

A similar openness to, or immersion in, the alternate templates offered by colonial religion is to be found in the Western encounter with idolatry in the texts, most directly in the case of Paul Vereker. While Seeta in Taylor's novel suggests the inertness of the Hindu idol, watching her Krishna idol 'blink at her sleepily', Paul experiences the full extent of its power. Departing radically from the conventional nineteenth-century British aversion towards idolatry,[14] the text portrays a unique religious dynamic where what to his English wife 'meant idolatry' was for Paul the mark of something greater (Perrin, *The Stronger Claim* 219). For Selma, the Hindu idols were 'grotesque idols in the niches of the walls, ... watching her with malign amusement' (220). Paul, however, is perfectly at ease with the 'recumbent red figure of the idol' at the 'shrine of the monkey-god' (Hanuman) and with 'the great polished stone—the symbol of Siva—damp, and shining' (217–20). Pointing to 'the grinning red figure', and dismantling the fear behind idolatry, Paul says that he does not wish to 'idealise' India 'but behind all the falseness and impurity, behind the gross ugliness of that idol', he sees the 'worship of the great invisible forces that regulate the world' (218–19). Paul's conversion to Hinduism is therefore portrayed in *The Stronger Claim* as a religious reorientation that the 'secularised' West and lacklustre Protestant Christianity needed to undergo—a reorientation that all of these novels implicitly facilitate. This force of colonial religion and its idolatry is recognised not only in the tractable figure of Paul Vereker in *The Stronger Claim*, but also in the recalcitrant Oliver Wray in *Idolatry*—the British missionary who had committed his life to eradicating idolatry from colonial India. The narrator observes that Oliver was 'conscious himself of the terrible fascination of this Power of Darkness—when ... the idols in their sanctuaries looked on with eternal passivity and cold, stony stare' (Perrin, *Idolatry* 114). Despite his deep-seated aversion to idolatry, Oliver could understand not only 'the degradation of idolatry' but could also 'well imagine the frenzied emotion of it all, the splendour, the madness ... of idolatry' (114).

Throbbing with mystery, flushed with reverence, pulsating with miracles, the colonial framework of religion forces upon the Westerner a scathing reflection of his own discourse of doubt while also offering him a measure of reassuring faith. Channeling the tensions that pervade the British landscape, the novels compel an outpouring of domestic 'secularising' polemics—debates about the legitimacy of religious faith or fears regarding declining religiosity—and enable an interface with alternative formats of belief, simultaneously releasing buried sources of domestic faith. Dissociating from the nineteenth-century legacy of post-Enlightenment scepticism, the English agents of faltering faith like Dion or Anne are able to relive their religiosity in the homeland because of their interim hiatus in the colony. In greater or lesser measure, the English characters (such as Nevil,

Paul, Selma, Anne and Dion) are shaken out of their stereotypical notions of, or indifference towards, colonial faith and compelled—by characters such as Seeta, Lilamani or Oliver—to recognise the possibility of a deeper religiosity that colonial faiths teach them to uncomfortably acknowledge, if not joyfully experience. Epitomising this transformation is Anne, for whom the British church and Christian experience stands transmogrified after her return from India. She watches mesmerised as the grandiose English church service recalls to her mind her transforming religious experience in the unembellished Indian church where she had felt spiritually transported by Oliver's sermon.

> [T]he lofty English church, with its pillars and aisles and vaulted roof, its colour and fragrance, melted from Anne's sight, and she was back in a bare building that had undecorated walls and simple accessories, and the hard, bright glare of an Eastern sun streaming through its unstained windows. She was gazing at a figure in the pulpit, at a rapt, earnest face, at grey eyes that gleamed with the faith and courage of the soul behind them; she was listening, breathless, to a voice that vibrated with fervour and enthusiasm . . . Anne stood for a moment, dazed and uncertain. Then the soft air of the warm, dusty, London evening, the rattle of a passing hansom and the thunder of a motor omnibus restored her self-possession.
> (Perrin, *Idolatry* 390)

Despite this mundane concluding note of English routine and rationalistic self-possession, the colonial religious encounter across the novels jolts the anxious English nation into a fierce questioning of the 'crisis' narrative and a renewed hope of religious self-surrender.

NOTES

1. The only novel that is not actually set in colonial India is Maud Diver's *Lilamani*. However, I include it because it engages with the same set of anxieties and forms of religious experience that I study in this chapter.
2. It is important to note that some of the most extensive segments in the novels that I will not examine seem to critique colonial religion, reflecting conventional Western prejudice against

colonial idolatry, spiritual frenzy or pageantry and superstition. This pervasive revulsion at Hinduism is especially true of *The Stronger Claim* which is populated with overtly racist characters displaying horrified disgust around the natives and especially at their performance of colonial religious rituals.
3. In chapter five, I refer to John Barbour's analysis of the idea of 'honest doubt' as it appeared in nineteenth-century religious discourse.
4. The childishness of the colonial native—a staple of colonial discourses—is connected here to a contemplation on the possibility of miracles and the comparative merits of miracles across different religions. This latter discussion features abundantly in nineteenth-century texts and a fuller exposition is outside the scope of this book. However, as an interesting indicator, one can look at Ram Mohun Roy's works. R. S. Sugirtharajah discusses how Roy purges Christianity of the miraculous when he distills what he considers to be central to the Christian faith in *Precepts* (*The Precepts of Jesus: the guide to Peace and Happiness; extracted from the books of the New Testament, ascribed to the four Evangelists*, 1820). Suggesting that Christianity disseminates only the moral teachings of Christ and not the miraculous elements, Roy notes in *Precepts* that the weak and polemical claims of miracles can lay Christianity open to challenge because the Christian miracles fade in glory when compared to those in colonial religious narratives (Sugirtharajah 33–35).
5. While this passage indicates the eminence of Christian faith over Hinduism at one level, I will later discuss how this section has another interpretive overlay—a colonial religious challenge to rationalistic Christian faith.
6. Kapila's work examines the figure of the native Indian woman *not* as a site of silence but as one of protest and destabilisation, signaling a mid-century shift away from the 'rescue' narrative to romances that foreground resistance. My study also identifies Seeta and Lilamani as figures of rebellion, and proposes that it is precisely their simple and unquestioning acceptance of Christianity that undercuts the complex contemporary Western polemic of 'secularisation'.
7. Jayawardena notes that Spiritualism was '[o]ne of the manifestations of . . . [the] reaction' to the 'crisis of faith' and the developing 'curiosity about religions of the non-Christian

world' (112–13). The Theosophical Society rejected 'universalist claims of Christianity' (Jayawardena 119) and developed connections with 'those Hindus, Buddhists and free-thinkers in India and Sri Lanka who were opposing Christianity and the proselytizing and educational activities of missionaries' (Jayawardena 116–17).

8. We learn that Seeta is well versed in Hindu theology: 'She had been an apt scholar of Wamun Bhut, one of the best disputants of the Vedantic Brahmins of the Noorpoor province', and 'she had all his arguments by heart, and often became fierce over them' (Taylor 372).

9. Describing the varying stages of Bible reception through history, Sheehan notes that from the early modern confessional age, in which 'the theological function of the Bible guaranteed its place at the very center of European religion and letters', there was a shift to the Enlightenment Bible and finally to the 'cultural Bible'. Sheehan delineates that by the 1780s and 90s the Enlightenment age of Bible translations in Germany was over and the ground had been prepared for the transformation of the Bible 'from a work of theology to a *work of culture*' (220–21; emphasis added) with the 'collaps[e] [of] the diverse Bibles of Enlightenment into a singular cultural Bible' (223)—one that would be invested with a 'new [cultural,] post-theological authority' (224).

10. The novel contains a subtextual critique of the Hindu caste hierarchy and posits this as part of the reason why Seeta is drawn to Christianity—a faith that welcomes all. Seeta says to Cyril: 'They [Hindu Brahmins] will not even teach them [Hindu Scripture] to Soodras like me; and He who spoke the words which are in your book [the Bible], told all to come to Him, like little children, without fear. But the Geeta does not say so' (Taylor 274).

11. Referring to the central twofold Christian tenet of loving God and loving one's neighbour, the central question Jacobs returns to time and again is: 'What would interpretation governed by the law of love look like?' (10). Jacobs, therefore, devotes his book to showing the need and the way to read—not just the Scripture but 'any and every kind of text'—'according to the principles of Christian charity' (11)

12. Jacobs provides an illuminating example from Shakespeare's *Much Ado About Nothing* (Act 4, Scene 1). He studies the scene where, after the 'plot of John the Bastard has come to fruition',

Claudio repudiates Hero based on the 'ocular proof' of infidelity he is offered but Beatrice continues to trust her. In place of the usual equation of information ('ocular proof', etc.) with knowledge, Jacobs suggests the possibility of a different kind of knowledge. Even more enlightening is the example of Beatrice, whose 'certainty' about Hero's innocence 'stems rather from her intimate personal knowledge of Hero' (5). Making the distinction between *connaitre* and *savoir*—roughly, 'knowledge of' rather than 'knowledge about'—Jacobs says that not knowing anything of the facts of the situation, it is this 'knowledge *of* Hero that Beatrice possesses, on the basis of which she forms her unwavering certainty about Hero's innocence. Referring to Martha Nussbaum, Jacobs explains that it is 'the kind of love that Beatrice and Hero feel for each other' that 'is productive of this intimate knowledge' (qtd. in Jacobs 6).

13. Not only was it faith that was coming under the attack of the rationalistic historical-scientific forays of the time, it was doubt too that was being defined exclusively in rationalist terms—something that, as I show in the fifth chapter, scholars like John D. Barbour and Timothy Larsen try to remedy. Barbour and Larsen challenge this rationalistic construction of doubt by coining concepts like 'deconversion and 'reconversion' (alongside 'honest doubt') respectively, that describe journeys away from (and around) faith through the vocabulary of faith itself instead of adopting a rationalistic rhetoric that does not recognise the critical role of spirituality and love in the very process of religious doubt.

14. The history of Western social and religious (Protestant) repulsion towards idolatry has been well documented in secondary scholarship, and finds one of the most detailed elaborations in Geoffrey Oddie who studies the 'basic missionary presuppositions' against idolatrous Hinduism (24–33).

REFERENCES

Asad, Talal. *Genealogies of Religion: Discipline and Reasons of Power in Christianity and Islam*. Johns Hopkins UP, 1993.

Auden, W. H. *The Dyer's Hand and Other Essays*. Faber and Faber, 1948.

Barbour, John D. *Versions of Deconversion: Autobiography and the Loss of Faith*. UP of Virginia, 1994.

Barr, Pat. *The Memsahibs: The Women of Victorian India*. Martin Secker and Warburg Ltd, 1976.

Burton, Antoinette. *At the Heart of the Empire: Indians and the Colonial Encounter in Late-Victorian Britain*. U of California P, 1998.

---, editor. *Burdens of History: British Feminists, Indian Women, and Imperial Culture, 1865–1915*. U of North Carolina P, 1994.

---. *Dwelling in the Archive: Women Writing House, Home, and History in Late Colonial India*. Oxford UP, 2003.

---. *Gender, Sexuality and Colonial Modernities*. Routledge, 2011.

Caputo, John. *On Religion*. Routledge, 2001.

Carruthers, Jo. *England's Secular Scripture: Islamophobia and the Protestant Aesthetic*. Continuum, 2011.

Diver, Maud. *Lilamani: A Study in Possibilities*. Hutchinson, 1911.

Driss, Hager Ben, and Hagen Ben Driss. 'Women Writing/Women Written: The Case of Oriental Women in English Colonial Fiction.' *Middle East Studies Association Bulletin*. vol. 35, no. 2, 2001, pp. 159–17. *JSTOR*.

Eliot, George. *Adam Bede*. 1859. Edited by Mary Waldron, Broadview, 2005.

Ghose, Indira. *Memsahibs Abroad: Writings by Women Travellers in Nineteenth-Century India*. Oxford UP, 1998.

---. *Women Travelers in Colonial India: The Power of the Female Gaze*. Oxford UP, 1998.

Ghosh, Durba. *Sex and the Family in Colonial India: The Making of Empire*. Cambridge UP, 2006.

Hill, Headon. *The Rajah's Second Wife*. Ward, Lock and Bowden Ltd, 1894.

Jacobs, Alan. *A Theology of Reading: The Hermeneutics of Love*. Westview P, 2001.

Jayawardena, Kumari. *The White Women's Other Burden: Western Women and South Asia During British Colonial Rule*. Routledge, 1995.

Kapila, Shuchi. *Educating Seeta: The Anglo-Indian Family Romance and the Poetics of Indirect Rule*. Ohio State UP, 2010.

Kirsty Reid. *Gender, Crime and Empire: Convicts, Settlers and the State in Early Colonial Australia*. Manchester UP, 2012.

Lakshmi, Aishwarya. 'The Mutiny Novel: Creating the Domestic Body of the Empire.' *Economic and Political Weekly*. vol. 42, no. 19, 2007, pp. 1746–53. *JSTOR*.

Larsen, Timothy. *Crisis of Doubt: Honest Faith in Nineteenth-Century England*. Oxford UP, 2008.

Lind, Mary Ann. *The Compassionate Memsahibs: Welfare Activities of British Women in India, 1900–1947*. Praeger, 1988.

Makala, Melissa Edmundson. 'Between Two Worlds: Racial Identity In Alice Perrin's *The Stronger Claim*.' *Victorian Literature and Culture*. vol. 42, no. 3, 2014, pp. 491–508. *JSTOR*.

Mannsaker, Frances M. 'East and West: Anglo-Indian Racial Attitudes as Reflected in Popular Fiction, 1890–1914.' *Victorian Studies*. vol. 24, no. 1, 1980, pp. 33–51. *JSTOR*.

Midgley, Clare. *Feminism and Empire: Women Activists in Imperial Britain, 1790–1865*. Routledge, 2007.

---, editor. *Gender and Imperialism*. Manchester UP, 1998.

Mijares, Loretta M. 'Distancing the Proximate Other: Hybridity and Maud Diver's *Candles in the Wind*.' *Twentieth Century Literature*. vol. 50, no. 2, 2004, pp. 107–40. *JSTOR*.

Nussbaum, Martha C. *Love's Knowledge: Essays on Philosophy and Literature*. Oxford UP, 1990.

Oddie, Geoffrey A. *Imagined Hinduism: British Protestant Missionary Constructions of Hinduism, 1793–1900*. Sage Publications, 2006.

Paxton, Nancy L. 'Mobilizing Chivalry: Rape in British Novels about the Indian Uprising of 1857.' *Victorian Studies*. vol. 36, no. 1, 1992, pp. 5–30. *JSTOR*.

Perrin, Alice. *Idolatry*. Chatto & Windus, 1909.

---. *The Stronger Claim*. 1903. Chatto & Windus, 1908.

Ray, Sangeeta. *En-Gendering India: Woman and Nation in Colonial and Postcolonial Narratives*. Duke UP, 2000.

Raza, Rosemary. *In Their Own Words: British Women Writers and India, 1740–1857*. Oxford UP, 2006.

Roye, Susmita, and Rajeshwar Mittapalli, editors. *The Male Empire under the Female Gaze: The British Raj and the Memsahib*. Cambria P, 2013.

Roy, Raja Ram Mohun. 'The Precepts of Jesus: The Guide to Peace and Happiness.' *Google Books*. 22 November 2007. <https://books.google.co.in/books?id=G3gOAAAAQAAJ&printsec=frontcover&source=gbs_ge_summary_r&cad=0#v=onepage&q&f=false>.

Sen, Indrani. *Woman and Empire: Representations in the Writings of British India, 1858–1900*. Orient BlackSwan, 2007.

---. 'The Memsahib's "Madness": The European Woman's Mental Health in Late Nineteenth Century India.' *Social Scientist*. vol. 33, no. 5/6, 2005, pp. 26–48. *JSTOR*.

---. 'Inscribing the Rani of Jhansi in Colonial 'Mutiny' Fiction.' *Economic and Political Weekly*. vol. 42, no. 19, 2007, pp. 1754–61. *JSTOR*.

Sheehan, Jonathan. *The Enlightenment Bible: Translation, Scholarship, Culture*. Princeton UP, 2005.

Sugirtharajah, R. S. *Asian Biblical Hermeneutics and Postcolonialism: Contesting the Interpretations*. Orbis Books, 1998.

Taylor, Philip Meadows. *Seeta*. 1872. 5th ed., Kegan Paul, Trench and Co., 1881.

Woodcock, George. 'A Distant and A Deadly Shore: Notes on the Literature of the Sahibs.' *Pacific Affairs*. vol. 46, no. 1, 1973, pp. 94–110. *JSTOR*.

Chapter Eight

Romancing Religious Hybridity
SCIENCE, RELIGION, AND THE TENSIONS OF THE 'SECULAR' IN CORELLI'S *A ROMANCE OF TWO WORLDS*

> Know that not one smallest world in all the myriad systems circling before thee, holds a single human creature who doubts his Maker. Not one! Except thine own doomed star! Behold it yonder—sparkling feebly, like a faint flame amid sunshine—how poor a speck it is. . . . Yet there dwell the dwarfs of clay—the men and women who pretend to love while they secretly hate and despise one another. (Corelli, *Romance of Two Worlds* 82)

In this chapter I study Marie Corelli's *A Romance of Two Worlds* (1886), not only her first but one of her most wildly successful novels, that offers us a complex portrayal of the politico-cultural tensions that constituted the understanding of religion in nineteenth-century Britain. I explore how Corelli's novel presents a 'hybrid Christianity'—a combination of traditional Protestant Christianity, colonial religions/Buddhism and scientific principles of electricity (Franklin, 'The Counter-Invasion of Britain by Buddhism' 30). I analyse how this construct of British Christianity debunks the 'secularisation thesis' by first implying the ways in which this thesis is imbricated within the post-Enlightenment 'secularist' paradigms, and then by challenging these templates—through both an awakening of imperial guilt about colonial injustices, and a reinterpretation of the meanings of pain made possible by alternative postcolonial postsecular frameworks.

Corelli, 'something of an enigma' to her readers (Ives and Hawkins 205), and the 'most financially successful author of the 1890s' (Stiles 23), began her career in February 1886 with *A Romance of Two Worlds* (referred from here on as *Romance*), a hugely popular novel, for the publishing of which Richard Bentley & Son went against the negative reviewer advice in a bold stroke of genius (Federico 1). As Jill Galvan points out, Corelli 'boasted a fan in Italy's queen, was granted a visit by William Gladstone, ... received heartening words from poet laureate Alfred Tennyson', and was widely known to be a raging favourite with Queen Victoria ('Christians, Infidels, and Women's Channeling in the Writings of Marie Corelli' 85). As Aaron Worth notes, the 'popular association of the Queen with Corelli and her work was widespread' in the fin-de-siècle, and the fascination began with Corelli's very first novel for which the Queen requested a special presentation copy from George Bentley (40).

Also significant for my reading of the novel is the fact that, as several scholars attest, Corelli's works were immensely popular in the colonies. Sharon Crozier-De Rosa notes that Corelli was one of only two women who in the 1900s appeared in both British and Colonial 'top ten' reading lists (4). Robert Fraser notes that Corelli 'acquired in the eyes of colonial readers the status of a near-deity' (176). Fraser observes that Corelli was 'universally appreciated in Africa and the Caribbean' and that her didactic romances 'were extensively imported, locally reprinted and stocked in most libraries as well as being multifariously translated, adapted and abridged' in India and Ceylon (176). Prodosh Bhattacharya, in his chapter on Corelli's literary influence on India, outlines in detail the extensive translation, publication, and reprinting of Corelli's works not only in nineteenth-century colonial India but also much later. He further notes the way Bengali translations of her novels became commentaries on several contemporary sociopolitical and cultural issues for Indian readers (219–44). So remarkable was her popularity in Africa that, as Fraser writes quoting Achebe, in a little book published in Nigeria in the nineteenth century, Corelli ranked among the world's 'superwomen' alongside Joan of Arc and Mary Magdalene (Fraser 176; quoting Achebe 36). Crucially,

Fraser notes that there was 'nothing passive about this cult' because colonial societies used 'diverse strategies of interpretation' to pick from her 'writings and from her moral and social attitudes, explicit or implied' (176). Scholarship on Corelli consistently emphasises the strategies through which and the consciousness with which she sculpted her image, not only for a domestic but a global readership, as the highest selling author of her times.

Corelli is often viewed as unconcerned with the issues of imperialism which she did not address directly in her works. However, the historical context of her writings make it imperative that we read her works, as I do in this chapter, for the suggestive commentary that she offers on this overarching fin-de-siècle political reality of the Empire. Of particular significance in this regard is the degree to which she allowed alternative forms of colonial religiosities (such as Buddhism, Theosophy and Hinduism, with their distinctively un-Christian ideas of karma and reincarnation) to figure in the syncretic form of Christianity that she espoused in her works, most prominently in *Romance*. Elaine M. Hartnell observes that though Corelli frequently aligns herself with Christianity, several of her texts displace and redefine the tenets of virtually all the mainstream Christian traditions and posit as Christianity a much more syncretic theology that embraces reincarnation. Ayers and Maier note, drawing on Master's biographical account of Corelli, that though born a Christian (as the allegedly illegitimate daughter of the Scottish journalist and songwriter Charles Mackay, and Mary Elizabeth Mills), Corelli was deeply interested in Theosophy, lectured at the Theosophical Lodge of Leeds, and was practically a Theosophist alongside Blavatsky (Ayers and Maier 167, 164; quoting Masters 301).

According to Crozier-De Rosa, Corelli tapped into the fin-de-siècle anxieties surrounding the Empire, and was strongly critical of the cultural phenomenon of the British New Woman because of the ways in which this figure undermined British imperial interests and claims of 'civilisational' superiority. She emphasises Corelli's self-appointed role as the 'guardian of the public conscience' and the way in which Corelli tried to elicit 'proper' feelings of shame and guilt from her readers (1). Though Crozier-De Rosa suggests that Corelli's aim was to safeguard the British public and imperial interests and to make her audience feel guity for the way the New Woman undermined the British 'civilisational' claims, I take a different route to show how Corelli's text in fact saturates the reader with a lingering sense of guilt at the perpetrations of colonial wrongs.

In *Romance*, the unnamed first-person narrator, a female concert pianist, is shown to suffer from physical and spiritual fatigue that leads to a kind of nervous infirmity, depression and insomnia—a condition that, according to Stiles, would be diagnosed in the nineteenth century as 'nerve exhaustion or neurasthenia' (161). On the advice of her doctor, she goes to the French Riviera to recuperate, where she meets Cellini, an Italian artist, who puts her in a tranquil slumber by administering a potion that also produces divine visions. Learning from Cellini about Dr Casimir Heliobas, the 'physical electrician' who had cured him, the narrator seeks him out in Paris to find a cure for her disordered nervous system (Corelli 33). She learns from him about 'The Electric Creed' of Christianity—the form of religion that he believes in and that forms the basis of his doctoral practice (103). This notion that is central to the novel is a remarkable textual amalgamation of medicine and religion that suggests the pre-existing congruence of science and faith—elements commonly perceived to be 'irreconcilable extremes' whose clash supposedly triggered the nineteenth-century 'decline of faith'. The narrator reads and learns from Heliobas's own manuscript about this form of 'hybrid Christianity' that combines elements of astral travel,[1] hypnotism, spiritualism, automatic writing, positivism, colonial religions (including Buddhism, Theosophy and Hinduism), and modern science (with its technological inventions like electricity, the telegraph, the telephone, or the phonograph)—all of which were supposed to debunk or challenge mainstream Christianity but are here drawn upon as being in many ways *intrinsic* to Christianity, or 'electric Christianity', probably as a narrative attempt to minimise these perceived threats to the religion.[2] Drawing on Franklin's essay on the representation of Buddhism in Corelli, I will refer to this form of Christianity as 'electric-aesthetic Christianity', a term that Franklin uses to communicate the combined force underlying this religious creed—the principle of electricity on the one hand and the implicit aesthetic imperative on the other ('The Counter-Invasion of Britain by Buddhism' 28).[3] The narrator concludes the novel by saying that this is a faith that fundamentally believes in 'THE EXISTENCE OF POWERFUL ELECTRIC ORGANS IN EVERY HUMAN BEING, WHICH WITH PROPER CULTIVATION ARE CAPABLE OF MARVELLOUS SPIRITUAL FORCE' (144)—a truth for which the world is not yet ready, '[t]he time is not yet ripe' (144). Heliobas is shown to be proficient in electrical remedies, which he has learnt from his close study of ancient Eastern thinkers. Heliobas uses his hypnotic powers and administers potions to the narrator, throwing her into a trance, and then utilises his electric powers to temporarily separate her soul from the body, after which her soul floats through the inter-galactic space to other spheres and gazes at the other planets of this 'electric Christian' universe, as well as at the Christian Heaven and Hell that also form a part of this setting. In this out-of-body journey to the Great Circle of the universe, accompanied by the guardian-angel Azul, the narrator sees other planets where people gratefully worship God instead of doubting him as they do on Earth—an episode that expresses a scathing critique of the increasing unbelief associated with the fin-de-siècle. She sees Heaven which is incredibly large and looks like '[a] Sphere . . . marvellous and dazzling; a great globe of opal-tinted light, revolving as it were upon its own axis, and ever surrounded by that scintillating, jewel-like wreath of electricity, whose only motion was to shine and burn within itself for ever' (87). She sees Christ, described as 'God's cable between us and His heaven' (105), and encounters a strange Hell where everyone leads future lives while still labouring under the memories of past mistakes. She returns from her astral travels as a staunch believer in 'electric Christianity'. The novel ends with the tragic death of Heliobas's sister Zara, who had befriended the narrator during the course of the narrator's treatment, and her death is presented as her life's culminating spiritual crescendo. Following the heart-breaking loss of his sister, Heliobas leaves Paris for Egypt and parts ways with the narrator, while painting for her a hopeful and happy image of their meeting several times in the future.

THE 'CRISIS OF FAITH' CONUNDRUM: ANXIETIES AND REMEDIES

Romance is a novel deeply preoccupied with the late-nineteenth-century fears of declining religiosity and, thus, forms an intriguing centrepiece in my re-examination of the 'secularisation thesis'. That the novel is supposed to exhibit a pervasive sense of Victorian Christian morality is evident in Aaron Worth's explanation of the Queen's fascination with it. He notes, 'The usual explanation for the Queen's passionate attachment to such works as *A Romance of Two Worlds* . . . lies in their elaboration, and celebration, of a shared moral code, that inflexible system of Christian morality which would come to be called "Victorian"' (40).[4] In fact, in a letter she wrote to her publisher Bentley on 15 November 1886, Corelli hoped that *Romance* would soothe 'the minds of those unhappy ones who have been unsteadied by modern atheistical books and doctrines, and feel themselves utterly wretched, not knowing where to turn' (Stiles 21).[5] The overarching Christian framework of the novel and its manifest attempts at, and pride in, bringing back to the Christian fold those who had wandered into unbelief or into other spiritual avenues, is evidenced by the grateful letters from readers that Corelli received and attached to subsequent editions of the novel that followed the first edition of February 1886. Federico also notes that Corelli received fan letters from readers who were 'interested in theosophy and psychical research, from an "earnest seeker after Truth," from a clergyman who was saved from suicide by reading it, and from an atheist who was converted to Christ' (Federico 6; referring to Corelli, *Romance* 146–57, 148). The Prologue of her novel manifestly acknowledges her predominant anxiety surrounding the contemporary 'crisis of faith' narratives:

> At a time when the great empire of the Christian Religion is being assailed, or politely ignored by governments and public speakers and teachers, I realize to the fullest extent how daring is my attempt to prove, even by a plain history of strange occurrences happening to oneself, the actual existence of the Supernatural around us; and the absolute certainty of a future state of being. (3)

In particular, Corelli addresses the post-Enlightenment mandating of evidentiality as the basis for any religious truth-claim—an approach that was used, as I have discussed earlier, in eighteenth- and nineteenth-century 'secularising' narratives to discredit the idea of Christian miracles. Critiquing this notion of numerical validity and evidential proof, Corelli clarifies in her Prologue that in *Romance*, she only intends to narrate what she herself has experienced and therefore 'do[es] not expect to be believed', because *'men and women of to-day must have proofs, or what they are willing to accept as proofs'* before they believe 'anything that purports to be of a spiritual tendency;—something startling—some miracle of a stupendous nature' (3; emphasis added). What is significant also is that the Prologue indicates Corelli's conscious choice of the genre of the 'romance' in writing this novel. Ives and Hawkins suggest that in using the romance as a genre, Corelli is not just opposing one kind of literary style in favour of another, but also 'one type of truth with another' (212). Federico connects Corelli's 'love of romance and her distaste for literary realism' (16). Hipsky notes how Corelli 'aggressively advocated for the romance as the literary mode to combat realism' (144). This choice of genre plays a pivotal role in Corelli's debunking of realism's prescriptive bias towards 'proof' as the basis of all truth—a project that also simultaneously dismantles post-Enlightenment 'secularising' narratives that considered faith to be unsustainable in the face of evidentiary requirements.

The burden of evidentiality was typical of the nineteenth-century climate in which religion, as John Caputo points out, '[f]ailing to meet the muster of "objective" proof and demonstration, . . . was lodged deep in the domain of subjectivity . . . [where] it was either considered safe and sheltered from the harsh lights of its critics . . . or it was written off by the heartless, hard-nosed scientifically minded as some kind of purely private buzz' (56). As Corelli sets out to offer such 'objective proof', she does not forget to denounce repeatedly the 'atheistic' tendencies of the age of unbelief that she inhabits. She condemns the way in which 'in this cultivated age a wall of scepticism and cynicism is gradually being built up by intellectual thinkers' (3). Then she embarks on a meticulous critique of the contemporary 'secularisation' discourse that challenged the possibility of religious miracles because of their basis in extra-evidentiary claims. She starts by defending the miraculous as germane to the very idea of faith and the fundamental experience of religion: 'There are no proofs as to why such things should be; but that they are, is indubitable' (4). Reminding us of scholars like John Caputo and Brag Gregory discussed in previous chapters, who explain that the religious is distinctive and meaningful in that it does not call upon the empirical and the evidential and in that it derives meaning precisely from a faith in the impossible, Corelli disparages the state of the nineteenth-century world with its scepticism towards the spiritual and the miraculous:

> Unbelief is nearly supreme in the world to-day. Were an angel to descend from heaven in the middle of a great square, the crowd would think he had got himself up on pulleys and wires, and would try to discover his apparatus. . . . Anything rather than believe in angels—the nineteenth century protests against the possibility of their existence. It sees no miracle—it pooh-poohs the very enthusiasm that might work them. (4)

The issue of miracles lay at the very heart of the nineteenth-century 'secularisation' discourse, bringing to a head the question of the truth-claims made by Christianity in particular and religion in general, and determining therefore the verity, viability and relevance of faith in the 'modern' rational world. It also figured prominently in the claims made by different religions in the nineteenth century, including those that were seen as threatening Christianity with their popularity. This is especially significant in light of the popularity of Buddhism in late-Victorian Britain and the constant evocation of the figure of the Buddha as a model comparable to the Christ. Franklin, in *The Lotus and the Lion*, shows us how the miraculous abilities of figures of religious authority was an intellectual and cultural issue that defined the reception of, and comparison between, various religions of late-Victorian England. In his essay 'The Life of the Buddha in Victorian England', Franklin insightfully studies the 'Buddhism steep'd nineties' of Victorian England and comments on the way the figure of the Buddha was presented in relation to that of the Christ, revolving around issues of the supernatural and the miraculous (941). Franklin explains the way a 'crisis of faith' forms the context into which Buddhism (and Comparative Religion) were contributing. He observes, 'Darwinian evolutionary theory, Comparative Religion, and the first major object of its study, Buddhism, entered British public consciousness at roughly the same time, contributing separately and conjointly to the ongoing crisis of faith in Christianity' (943). Franklin discusses how contemporary literary representations of Buddhism 'underwrote and helped create a popular understanding of Buddhism as the original protesting reformation', contributing to the appeal of Buddhism (951).[6] This literature was directed more at post-Darwinian readers and (in slightly varying degrees though undoubtedly) excluded the supernatural/miracles and presented a historical Buddha. Clearly, alternative colonial faiths that percolated into late-Victorian England were drawn into the conversation on religious supernaturalism and Christian miracles—issues that framed their presentation in contemporary literature and defined their appeal in Victorian culture. It is placed against this context that Corelli's commentary on the miraculous acquires importance. As noted by Ayres and Maier, 'during a period when Christianity was indicted as outdated and challenged by both science and new and alluring belief systems', Corelli advanced 'a unique type of syncretic theology' that combined elements of both of these perceived sources of 'secularising' threats (139).

As far as alternative colonial belief systems are concerned, Corelli addresses the threat that colonial religions, and in particular Buddhism, were supposed to embody. *Romance* seems, at one level, to be unsettled in its Christian faith by its relation to several competing faiths popular in the late-nineteenth-century West. Thus, the text shows how this hybrid 'electro-aesthetic Christianity' was influenced by these traditions, and especially by Buddhism. As Franklin explains, and as will become evident in the following section of my analysis, this novel 'simultaneously utilizes and attacks Buddhist concepts both directly and indirectly' (The Counter-Invasion of Britain by Buddhism 26). But for now it may suffice to note how the narrator encounters an assertion of the superiority of Christianity over competing faiths, and that of faith over scepticism, in Heliobas's treatise on his own religious creed. In this document titled 'Electric Principle of Christianity'—what Jill Galvan calls a 'religio-technological treatise' ('Christians, Infidels, and Women's Channeling in the Writings of Marie Corelli' 83)—Heliobas expatiates on Buddhism, remarking that though this religion has 'so many million followers', it 'lacks the supernatural element'. Furthermore, Heliobas's document presents the Buddha not as a divine figure but as a 'wise and ascetic' man who 'died a hermit at the age of eighty'. As opposed to this, Heliobas notes, '[t]he death and resurrection of Christ were widely different'. Finally, he concludes vehemently that '[a]nyone can be a Buddha again; anyone can NOT be a Christ', and while Buddhism offers a 'flattering picture', Christianity is the 'plain original'—that is, '[a]ll religions, as known to us, are *mere types* of Christianity', and Buddhism 'is itself *a type* of Christ's teaching' (105; emphasis added). Corelli clearly gestures towards a common set of anxieties surrounding the nineteenth-century 'crisis of faith' narrative when she burrows deeper into this question about the nature of Christ—a question that formed the heart of the contemporary debate on whether Christ was a historical personage or a divine entity. This embeddedness in the 'secularisation' debate becomes more obvious when one day, while playing at the organ, the narrator is unexpectedly assailed by a pang of religious doubt: 'Was Christ indeed Divine—or is it all a myth, a fable—an imposture?' Following this, she flees the scene in 'strange incomprehensible terror' (59), and the benign Heliobas chastises her for her '[u]nbelief,' rebuking her in a way that unsettles the quantificatory logic of modern 'secularisation' discourse: 'Unbelief is easily scared! . . . You have been led astray, my child, by the conflicting and vain opinions of mankind. You, like many others in the world, delight to question, to speculate, to weigh this, to measure that, with little or no profit to yourself or your fellow-creatures' (60).

Another remarkable feature of the novel's 'electric–aesthetic Christianity' and the narrative challenge that it represents to 'secularisation', is its hybrid incorporation of several predominant spiritual–technological tendencies of the fin-de-siècle that were typically seen as embodying threats to Western Christianity. The most visible of such narrative manoeuvres is the one where Corelli blends science and faith into her 'hybrid Christianity' in order to shrink what was seen as the ever-widening gap between these two polarities in the late nineteenth and early twentieth century (Franklin, 'The Counter-Invasion of Britain by Buddhism' 28).[7] As Scheider notes, 'After all the struggles of scholars and churchmen, ... Science and Religion are reconciled in a flash by Marie Corelli' (41). In particular, Stiles notes the way neuroscience figures prominently in Corelli, and how Corelli, unlike her contemporaries, 'was the only one who saw spiritual fulfillment as compatible with Victorian neuroscience' (24). Worth notes how scientific media such as the telegraph (and others like the telephone and the phonograph) find their way into *Romance*. Jill Galvan (*The Sympathetic Medium*) explains the contextual symbolic importance of this kind of communication media by noting that the figure of the female medium, embodied by the narrator in the novel, occupied a crucial place at the intersection of two possible types of remote communication that dominated the cultural imagination in the second half of the nineteenth century— scientific (telegraph, telephone, photography, film, typewriter) and mystical (paranormal phenomena like Spiritualism, hypnotism, automatic writing, telepathy). Thus, these scientific and religious modes of remote connectivity that, as Worth elucidates, were seen at the time as underlying the modern colonial regime, are used in *Romance* to bolster a united 'electric' Christian universe. As Franklin explains, '[i]f this novel can be said to be primarily "about" any one thing, it is about resurrecting Christianity as a modern scientific religion, which it calls the "Electric Principle of Christianity"' ('The Counter-Invasion of Britain by Buddhism' 27). Galvan notes how Corelli's postscript shows science as strengthening religion instead of testing it: 'The greater and wider the discoveries of Science, ... the nearer shall we feel the actual presence of God' (Galvan, 'Christians, Infidels, and Women's Channeling in the Writings of Marie Corelli' 87; quoting Corelli 356). In *Romance*, Christ himself is presented as 'an Embodied Electric Spirit', a body 'charged with electricity'—a capacity that scientifically enabled him to heal the sick 'by a touch or a look' and to walk on water through 'a purely electric effort' (106). Stiles also notes how the novel is influenced by 'heterodox spiritual traditions such as Rosicrucianism, Christian Science, and Victorian spiritualism', and by the approaches of the scientifically oriented 'Society for Psychical Research'—a wide range that combines assumptions drawn both from 'science' and 'religion' (163). Robyn Hallim similarly argues that 'electric-aesthetic Christianity', in a novel such as *Romance*, was designed to be a creed capable of defying materialism and reconciling science and religion. As I will also suggest in passing, the text draws on these contemporary tensions and overlaps, incorporating several of the predominant scientific advances of the times that were often seen as embodying threats to Western Christianity, and overturns the 'secularising' narrative by welding them into a larger spiritual–technological system.

My primary aim in the next two segments is to show how Corelli's *Romance* problematises the late-nineteenth-century cultural assumptions of 'secularisation' through the ways in which it juxtaposes claims of 'secularisation'—perceived as a crisis in morality—with a moral epiphany, an ethical conscientious awakening to imperialist wrongs and to the imperialist instrumentalisation of the idea of pain/suffering.

ELECTRIC-AESTHETIC CHRISTIANITY AND THE AWAKENING OF COLONIAL GUILT

Aaron Worth explores how 'the reality of British colonialism registers in *Romance*' in the 'context of a kind of cyberfantasy of female participation in the vicarious pleasures of imperialist expansion' (41). He explains that though in *Romance* 'explicit references to the political realities of the day are relatively scarce, and sometimes veiled (if very thinly)', the context for the novel is undeniably colonial (41): 'Corelli's ethereal fantasies of the spirit world, though ostensibly far removed from the cut and thrust of party politics in Westminster, or the sordidly practical problems of colonial administration in India or the recently (if unofficially) annexed Egypt, are . . . [unquestionably] *historically grounded in such real-world contexts*' (41; emphasis added). I would argue in this section that in *Romance*, Corelli offers a commentary about the Western involvement in imperialism and its burden of guilt. It is useful to begin by noting how this is worked out in the representation of the 'electric-aesthetic Christian' Heaven and Hell. In constructing the Heaven and Hell of this imagined techno-religious universe, the novel draws repeatedly on 'the key Buddhist (as well as Hindu) concepts of karma, reincarnation, and nirvana', while also significantly altering it (Franklin, 'The Counter-Invasion of Britain by Buddhism 26). Departing from a conventional Christian understanding, Heaven is depicted as an experience of 'spiritual progressivism' where 'spiritual progress occurs in stages, rather than being an all-or-nothing gambit at the end of one life' and it is in the 'process of spiritual awakening, [that] the protagonist takes a transmigratory journey up into the spirit-world' (29). The case of Hell is even more interesting and it is here that Corelli's narrative intervention becomes most significant. In Heliobas's manuscript, Hell is described as follows: 'It has been asked whether the Electric Theory of Christianity includes the doctrine of Hell, or a place of perpetual punishment. Eternal Punishment is merely a form of speech for what is really Eternal Retrogression. But there is one thing it can never escape from—MEMORY. And in that faculty is constituted Hell' (Corelli 108). Heliobas's manuscript describes the retrogression in terms of decreasing levels of humanity, such as in the case of a man who 'by choice, forces his soul DOWNWARD to inhabit hereafter the bodies of dogs, horses, and other like animals' (108), and explains that in Hell 'he does so at the cost of everything except Remembrance'. As the manuscript details, 'Eternal Retrogression means that the hopelessly tainted electric germ recoils further and further from the Pure Centre whence it sprang, ALWAYS BEARING WITHIN ITSELF the knowledge of WHAT IT WAS ONCE and WHAT IT MIGHT HAVE BEEN' (108). Thus, in Corelli's Hell as described in Heliobas's manuscript, all errant souls are reincarnated repeatedly, and through the entire experience, they remain saddled with memories of their past misdeeds. This endless recollection of their wrongs causes them agonising torment. In this Hell of Corelli's 'electric-aesthetic Christianity', we see a translation of the Christian Hell into 'the Buddhist law of karma and reincarnation, with the added, non-Buddhist torture of continuous memory as the karmic accounting book' (Franklin, 'The Counter-Invasion of Britain by Buddhism' 29–30).[8] Thus, for Corelli, the most defining and compelling dimension of her religious universe lies in the way the memory of one's retrogression lingers endlessly as punishment. Or, as I suggest, the typically Hellish nature of the experience derives from the way one's diminishing humanity/humaneness lingers as a conscientious burden, a guilty reminder of humaneness lost and wrongs committed.

Though Corelli does not specify the colonial dimension of this guilt, imperialism and its attendant pressures form the subtext for *Romance*. The image of the colonial voyage is evoked obliquely in describing the narrator's astronomical journey that leads to the discovery of the 'true religion'—Corelli's 'electric-aesthetic Christianity'. Heliobas exhorts the narrator ahead of her spiritual journey, telling her how she is about to 'soar into an unexplored wilderness of spheres', and adds that to do so 'weighted by [her] ... own doubts, would [make it] ... a fruitless journey' (79). Again, we see Heliobas talking about how he had let his disciple Cellini 'go on a voyage of discovery' from which he had '[come] back perfectly satisfied' (38). At a rudimentary level, these references to expectantly productive ('fruitful') journeys serve as images of imperial adventures into the 'darker' continents, and both Cellini and the narrator are shown to undertake such endeavours that function as imagistic parallels for exploratory imperialist voyages, travelling past the astronomical circles and spheres, discovering the Heavenly circle and the Hellish rings. The 'doubts' surrounding religion fade away as the traveller discovers the true meaning of spiritual progression and retrogression, or the 'electric-aesthetic Christian' Heaven and Hell—religious experiences that allay fears of unbelief and reinforce faith in Christ's supernatural power. Furthermore, the imperialist universe with all its attendant tensions comes tangibly alive in the description of the spectrum of colonial faiths, in particular Buddhism. As Franklin explains, *Romance* is 'saturated with Buddhism'— 'Buddhism is pervasive in the margins and in the background, as it was in late-century Europe' ('The Counter-Invasion of Britain by Buddhism' 26). Additionally, Easterners populate the text as though they are designed to 'rejuvenate the desiccated faith of Occidental characters and readers' (Galvan, 'Christians, Infidels, and Women's Channeling in the Writings of Marie Corelli' 88), including

Heliobas himself who is a Chaldean descendant of the wise men of the East spoken of in the Bible,[9] and his sister Zara who is a dedicated and superlative follower of the Gospel. These 'Easterners' are represented as anterior to the West in their acquaintance with, and grasp of, Christian tenets. As Ayers and Maier note, 'To Corelli the Orientals were more spiritual than the English; therefore, she created mystical characters from the East to proselytize the West' (164). Revealingly enough, by the logic of the novel, even the Christian Gospel needs supplementing through 'Oriental' wisdom. Appended to the novel, in the Appendix, we find Corelli's response to one of the letters written to her where she clarifies that Christ did not die as a sacrifice but out of His goodness, and then adds that if there is still confusion about the 'perfection of goodness depicted in Christ's own words', then one must turn to 'the terse Oriental maxim': '"Diving, and finding no pearls in the sea, Blame not the ocean, the fault is in THEE." AUTHOR' (150). This discursive strategy instals the East at the heart of the most privileged narratives of the West and, therefore, establishes the colony as intrinsic to the Western experience and imagination. As such, in a text like *Romance* that is so suffused with the presence and primacy of the East, quiet reminders about the burdens of imperial guilt hardly seem inconceivable or inconsequential. And memory—implicitly that of colonial exploitation and injustice—comes to represent the definitive feature of Corelli's Hell.

This is very different from the collective cultural memory that, according to Hervieu-Léger, is at the heart of all religion and that helps to define and buttress it. She explains the working of this kind of constructive memory: 'In Jewish and Christian traditions, the religious wresting of the past from history is given privileged significance by the core events being magnified in time' (124). According to Hervieu-Léger, this is the *normative* character of religious memory. This is vastly different from Corelli's understanding of memory as an ethical burden borne out of the West's conscientious recollection of colonial wrongs committed against the natives. This notion is distict from Hervieu-Léger's constructive understanding of religious memory where memory abstracts from history to institutionalise something as sacred.

Instead, in Corelli's deployment, memory *reinscribes* history within the astronomical 'electric-aesthetic Christian' Hell in the form of colonial guilt—disavowing/abjecting this shameful history instead of institutionalising it. A helpful way of understanding this 'hybrid Christian' Hell is to read its defining feature of undying memory, i.e., the impossibility of 'forgetting', in the context of Žižek's analysis of the foundational cultural moment of forgetting. Žižek explains how colonial ideology works by narrating the 'spectral fantasmatic history [which] tells the story of a traumatic event'—a traumatic event 'that "continues not to take place", that cannot be inscribed into the very symbolic space it brought about by its intervention, . . . [that] continues to haunt the living' (58). Žižek is talking about the foundational violent and traumatic act that sets up the order of the Law but that cannot itself be incorporated within the Symbolic realm it sets up because this realm *retroactively* renders such an act sinful/illegal/unethical, as a result of which the act must compulsorily be forgotten. As an archetypal example, Žižek cites the rise of Christianity and how it was accompanied by the 'excessively violent gesture of repressing the pagan universe and imposing the universal rule of the One of Law' (57). Speaking particularly of the Jewish repression (through Moses) of 'the pagan pre-monotheistic cosmo-religion of One Nature in which a multitude of deities can coexist' (57), Žižek explains that the '"repressed" of Jewish monotheism is *not* the wealth of pagan sacred orgies and deities but the disavowed excessive nature of *its own* fundamental gesture: that is – to use the standard terms – the crime that founds the rule of the Law itself, the violent gesture that brings about a regime which retroactively makes this gesture itself illegal/criminal' (57). Thus, what is 'disavowed' is the excessive, violent and founding 'cannibalistic' act implied in the adage that Žižek humorously quotes: '[T]here are no cannibals in our tribe, we ate the last one yesterday' (57). And this, suggests Žižek, is what becomes the 'obscene Other' of history, the '"*spectral*" *fantasmatic history* that effectively sustains the explicit symbolic tradition, but has to remain foreclosed if . . . [the symbolic history] is to be operative' (58). Žižek's explanation of the disavowed founding gesture of the symbolic order provides a helpful elucidation of colonial practices. Colonial regimes justified their reign by the civilisational logic, arguing that colonialism instituted in the colonies a process of noble, just and non-violent administration by those that were 'racially superior', all the while disavowing the initial excessive act of violence on which the colonial regime had been founded in the first place. Placed against this backdrop, Corelli's 'electric-aesthetic' Hell seems to be what her brand of religion offers as a symbolic ethical space that disallows the 'forgetting' (disavowal/repression) of colonial violence.

Interestingly, Corelli connects this experience of colonial guilt with a religious impulse and therefore with her critique of the 'secularisation' narrative itself. She observes that 'inner forebodings of *guilt*' are felt 'by the most careless, the most cynical' under the 'subtle influence and incontestable, though mysterious, authority exercised upon their lives by higher intelligences than their own— intelligences unseen, unknown, but felt' (3; emphasis added). Corelli notes that even in modern times these 'sudden appeals [that are] made without warning to that compass of a man's life, *Conscience*' by what are implicitly the higher spiritual realms finally lead us on, 'heedless of consequences, to the performance of great and noble deeds' and constitute for our world 'some *miracle* of a stupendous nature' (3; emphasis added). This ethical awakening is, for Corelli, the perfect instance of the modern *miracle*—a term echoing the complex debates surrounding modern unbelief and religious claims in a post-Enlightenment world. In Corelli's vision, the only 'miracle' of the unbelieving nineteenth-century universe is the triggering of such a conscientious guilt-ridden reminder of colonialist wrongs and materialistic evils perpetrated by the West. Corelli concludes, 'The miracles enacted now are silent ones, and are worked in the heart and mind of man alone' (4). This functions powerfully, on the one hand reinstating the religious possibility of the 'miracle' while dismantling the logic of 'secularisation', and on the other hand mandating an inner ethical transformation inside the 'heart and mind' of the modern individual. Without this, political rejuvenation, economic prosperity, or social health is impossible. As Heliobas sums up, many are 'being brought up without any faith in God or religion', the 'result [of which] will be an increase of vice and crime' (118). Ayres and Maier bolster such a reading by observing how Corelli created fictional worlds that allowed a critique of contemporary sociopolitical issues—that she 'envisioned utopias with harmony and freedom from gender constraints that, in their contrast, allowed her to criticize current *English politics*, marriage *and religion*' (164; emphases added). Such is the novel's critique of contemporary imperialist wrongs and modern 'secularisation' theories—all of it facilitated through a reimagined hybrid religious structure that accommodates both science and spirituality, and aims to redress both political wrongs and religious unbelief in its approximation of true ethicality.

In a meaningful continuum with these implicit critiques of imperialist injustices, Corelli shames the avaricious who propel crimes against humanity. Heliobas says agitatedly to an audience that includes, besides Zara and the narrator, other people from their social circle like Mrs Everard, Colonel Everard, the Challoners, their two daughters, and Father Paul: '[C]hildhood, I say, is being gradually stamped out under the cruel iron heel of the Period—a period not of wisdom, health, or beauty, but one of drunken delirium, in which the world rushes feverishly along, its eyes fixed on one hard, glittering, stony-featured idol—Gold' (118). This idolatrous pursuit of wealth that lies at the heart of colonial conquests is evoked and shamed for its inhumanity. In no uncertain terms, Heliobas condemns this world where 'wealth is a god, and the greed of gain a virtue' (82):

> Get on!—be successful! Trample on others, but push forward yourself! Money, money!—let its chink be your music; let its yellow shine be fairer than the eyes of love or friendship! Let its piles accumulate and ever accumulate! . . . There is poverty in many places, but why seek to relieve it? Why lessen the sparkling heaps of gold by so much as a coin? Accumulate and ever accumulate! Live so, and then—die! (118)

Earlier in the narrative, implying the spiritually bankrupt condition of the Western world, Heliobas's manuscript mentions that most people ignore the 'electric spark' within themselves and fail to cultivate it so that, not 'fanned into a fire', it escapes, and they are reduced to 'a mere lump of clay' (104). Consequently, they 'habitually deaden the voice of conscience and refuse to believe in the existence of a spiritual element within and around them' (104). This planet where 'faith is martyred, and unbelief elected sovereign monarch of the people', is where *'nation wars against nation'* (82, 83; emphasis added). Mired in this moral abyss of religious uncertainty and imperialist despotism, the Western incapacity for guilt and faith emerges as nineteenth-century modernity's unrelenting tragedy and unsurpassable threat. Azul, the narrator's spirit–guide, remarks that 'the sublime, unreachable mysteries of the Universe are haggled over by poor finite minds' (82–83) and Corelli herself laments in the final passages of the novel: 'Belief—belief in God— belief in all things noble, unworldly, lofty, and beautiful, is rapidly being crushed underfoot by—what? By mere lust of gain!' (145). In a final call to the readers, Corelli urges a careful reconsideration as she watches millions turn unbelivers: 'The end for all of you can be but death; and are you quite positive after all that there is NO Hereafter?' (145). To this conflicted religious question, Corelli attaches her wary, cautionary note against the materialism that underlies both exploitative colonisation and resolute unbelief: 'Be sure, good people, be very sure that you are RIGHT in denying God for the sake of man—in abjuring the spiritual for the material— before you rush recklessly onward' (145). Thus, through a strangely redesigned form of 'electric-aesthetic' hybrid Christianity, the text combines principles of both faith and science to offer significant political commentary and to trigger deeper moral awakening by the enlivening of colonial guilt and the debunking of the 'secularisation thesis' in a world largely perceived to be bereft of faith.

'ELECTRIC-AESTHETIC CHRISTIANITY' AND REDEFINITIONS OF PAIN

The novel's most overt preoccupation is with the problem of pain, often referred to as 'misery' or 'suffering'—an experiential format that it reads from a non-Western postsecular perspective to excavate alternative templates of agency. The narrator's primary complaint seems to be about a kind of physical pain which Heliobas attempts to soothe or alleviate by guiding her on a set of astronomical journeys.

Early in the text, the narrator recounts how she 'summoned all [her] . . . stock of will-power to beat back the insidious *physical and mental misery*' that 'threatened to sap the very spring of [her] . . . life' (5; emphasis added). Predictably, for a colonial age that was preoccupied with milking the global coffers for domestic consumption, the primary fear seems to be the loss of productivity and functionality resulting from a debilitating incursion of pain. The experience and threat of incapacitating pain is consequently represented in the text as the most insidious ailment in need of urgent treatment. This constant narrative attempt to eliminate pain for the sake of individual and imperialist productivity needs to be read alongside postsecular studies to which I have referred in earlier chapters that explain how a 'secularist' approach categorically devalues the experience of pain as disabling. Central to this body of work is Talal Asad's study of the cultural construction of pain down the ages. Asad notes that the 'secular' perception of pain—in which the individual undergoing pain is 'conceived as [an] object' in a 'state of passivity'—undermines and nullifies pain's agentive possibilities (84). Challenging the 'secular' 'assumption that the agent always seeks to overcome pain', Asad recuperates the alternative traditions and meanings of painful experience. Corelli's text stages at length the 'secular' devaluation of pain before meaningfully recuperating the agentive spiritual value of this experience in certain suggestive sections. Echoing assumptions of the redundancy of pain, the narrator recalls the horrors of her early life, explaining how she had been the 'victim of miserable dejection, pain, and stupor' (25). After Cellini uses the electric force to remedy the narrator's pain, she confesses her reflief: 'The heavy marks under my eyes, the lines of pain that had been for months deepening in my forehead, the plaintive droop of the mouth that had given me such an air of ill-health and anxiety—all were gone as if by magic' (17). Later, after Heliobas practises similar remedial techniques on the narrator, administering 'a different little phial of liquid' to her bath water everyday, she gratefully records her restored energies and revived functionality: 'I was free from all my customary aches and pains, and a delightful sense of vigour and elasticity pervaded my frame' (56, 43). While on her astral travels with her spirit-guide Azul, the narrator receives assurances from him about how the electric force will cure her of her pains and restore her ability to work: 'Sin, sorrow, *pain*, disease and death thou shalt know no more. Thou shalt be able to remember happiness, to possess it, and to look forward to it. Thou shalt have full and pleasant *occupation without fatigue*' (88; emphases added). Looking into a mirror later, the narrator congratulates herself on the transformation effected by the electric force: 'The face that looked back at me from the glass was a perfectly happy one, ready to dimple into glad mirth or bright laughter. *No shadow of pain* or care remained upon it to remind me of past suffering, and I murmured half aloud: "Thank God!"' (114; emphasis added). Sufficiently buttressed to deliver her full productive potential in an imperialist, industrialised and commercialised economy, the narrator announces, '[E]very hour I grew better, brighter, and stronger . . . and every hour I grew better, brighter, because all my senses seemed to be sharpened and invigorated and braced up to the keenest delight' (56). Located in the fin-de-siècle that was visibly defined by imperialist and industrial hierarchies, the text consistently emphasises the need for an individual's physical functionality and productivity. The urgency to have people contribute to the commercial churn of the world is underscored by the sagacious Cellini who explains to the narrator how she and everyone else who have a spiritual spark inside them must keep the physical body healthy in order to be able to accomplish its potential. Cellini even admonishes the narrator for failing this task: '[Y]ou have sacrificed your body so utterly to your spirit that *the flesh rebels and suffers. This will not do. You have work before you in the world, and you cannot perform it unless you have bodily health* as well as spiritual desire' (25–26; emphasis added). Speaking of his own treatment under the care of Heliobas, Cellini says that Heliobas's 'remedies, external and internal' ultimately 'had a marvellous effect in renovating and invigorating [his] . . . system', so that, after the course of treatment, he 'was strong and well—a sound and sane man' and his 'brain was fresh and eager *for work*' (32; emphasis added). This secular devaluation of pain and the curating of fit individuals for what are implicitly imperialist regimes of functionality finds its historical unpacking in Asad's anthropological work where he observes how the Empire distinguished between the 'unnecessary' pains valued by colonies and the 'necessary' pains required for imperialist consolidation. As Asad explains, this distinction was applied by the West in the colonies to discredit as 'unnecessary' forms of pain that the colonial natives found meaningful, often spiritually, and to legitimise as 'necessary' those forms of pain/suffering to which they were subjected during the Western imposition of 'secular' imperialist profit-driven structures.[10] Replaying this distinction and echoing the contemporary imperialist hierarchies, Corelli's work not only stages the curative benefits of expelling the unproductive pains suffered by Cellini and the narrator but also inscribes the hierarchical understanding of pain wherein the calculated therapeutic pains imposed upon them by the powerful Heliobas are welcomed as necessary for their entry into the productive economy. Thus, prior to Heliobas's electric treatment of the narrator, Zara asks her in cautious undertones if she really understood the full (and implicitly demanding and painful) nature of the process on which she was about to embark. Invoking the unequal power dynamic between Heliobas and the narrator, and explaining how he would impose a pain of his own making upon her in order to eliminate hers, Zara enquires if she was 'quite resolved . . . to let Casimir [Heliobas] *exert his force*' upon her (64; emphasis added). Issuing further suggestive warnings about Heliobas's purportedly benign force, and with her 'eyes . . . darker and deeper in the gravity of . . . intense meditation', she asks the narrator guardedly: 'And you have no fear . . . You understand the nature of an electric shock?' (64). Zara then delineates the potentially fatal nature of Heliobas's electric force:

> Well, there are different kinds of electric shocks—some that are remedial, some that are fatal. There are cures performed by a careful use of the electric battery—again, people are struck dead by lightning, which is the fatal result of electric force. But all this is EXTERNAL electricity; now what Casimir will use on you will be INTERNAL electricity. (64)

Zara's description of Heliobas's therapeutic invasion exposes his hierarchical power privilege that allows him to disregard the intensely painful effect of his curative force and to assume its inevitability in a productive economy: 'Casimir has more [internal electricity] . . . and *he will exert his force over your force, the greater over the lesser*' (64; emphasis added). Zara explains that consequently, the narrator's body will undergo pain, 'experience[ing] an INTERNAL electric shock, which, like a sword, will separate in twain body and spirit' (64). What will result from this is a functional body, a productive individual, and a lucrative (mechanistic) industrialised economy because, as Zara concludes, the life of the narrator will return to her inert body after the electric treatment is complete to '*put its machinery in motion* once more' (64; emphasis added).

However, despite this dramatisation of the 'secular' imperialist devaluation of pain, the value of religious suffering is resuscitated indirectly in the text through discussions surrounding Corelli's 'electric-aesthetic Christianity'. Exploring what 'electric-aesthetic Christianity' regards as the meaning of Christ's crucifixion, and specifying that in *this* axiom lay 'the main difference between the Electric Theory of Christianity and other theories', Corelli explains: 'CHRIST DID NOT DIE BECAUSE GOD NEEDED A SACRIFICE. . . . Christ's death was not a sacrifice; . . . A sinless Spirit *suffered to show us how to suffer*' (105–06; emphasis added). Not only does the text reinforce this spiritual value of pain, it portrays the narrator's own surrender to pain and suffering as Christ-like. Claiming the 'crown of thorns' emblematic of the saviour on the cross, the narrator remarks: '[I suffered from] the insidious physical and mental misery that threatened to sap the very spring of my life; . . . But it was at night that the terrors of my condition manifested themselves. Then sleep forsook my eyes; a dull throbbing *weight of pain* encircled my head like *a crown of thorns*' (Corelli 5; emphases added). As such, the text recuperates premodern traditions that privileged religious pain within Christianity before the onset of 'secularist' Enlightenment modernity. Asad, for example, draws on Judith Perkins's *The Suffering Self* to explain how the 'early Christian martyrologies "refuse[d] to read the martyrs' broken bodies as defeat, but reverse[d] the reading, insisting on interpreting them as symbols of victory over society's power"' (Perkins 117; qtd in Asad 85). In this tradition of thought, '[l]ike Christ's passion on the cross, the martyrs' passivity was an act of triumph' and this 'openness to pain was precisely part of the structure of their agency as Christians' (85). The text not only explicates the centrality of pain to the Christian meaning of crucifixion—locating this tennet at the heart of its 'electric-aesthetic Christianity'—but also offers colonial religion as a foil against which the significance of this Christian premise is established. Thus, Heliobas categorically argues that Buddha was only a 'wise and ascetic' man who 'died a hermit at the age of eighty', while the 'death and resurrection of Christ were widely different' (105).

Drawing on Corelli's postulation of a 'hybrid Christianity'—one that combines traditional Protestant Christianity, colonial religions (Buddhism) and science—the text both accommodates and overcomes the fin-de-siècle threat of 'secularisation' that was understood to arise from a combination of precisely these elements of science and colonial faiths. The text also facilitates a quiet but effective critique of the Western imperialist machinery by activating colonial guilt and moral introspection at a time interpreted as one of religious and implicitly moral 'crisis'. Imbricated in the 'secular' paradigms emerging within post-Enlightenment rationality, while also critical of modern West-centric understandings of pain and suffering, the text resorts to the spiritual wellsprings of premodern Christianity and Eastern religiosity (represented by the Chaldean Heliobas and by the Buddhist tropes), to reinstate the spiritual superiority of 'Electric Christianity' in particular, and Christianity in general—powerfully debunking the myth of modern unbelief. The novel ends with the glorious achievement of the narrator's noble aim that she articulates hesitantly to Heliobas early in the novel before he sets her off on her first extensive astral journey: 'I desire to know why this world, this universe exists; and also wish to prove, if possible, the truth and necessity of religion. And I think I would give my life, if it were worth anything, to be certain of the truth of Christianity' (79). Produced during an age inundated with troubling 'crisis'-narratives, Corelli's novel leaves the reader in no doubt about the spiritual truth or the politico-moral necessity of religion as a whole and 'electric-aesthetic Christianity' in particular.

NOTES

1. The narrator's travels through space have an evident parallel in the late-nineteenth-century occult concept of astral travel, a staple in the realm of ritual magic practised by organisations such as the Golden Dawn. It required the adepts to explore higher realms of their consciousness through their magical practices, and spatialise these introspections by representing them as routes of astral travel in the cosmic realms. After progressing to the Second Order, Golden Dawn adepts were taught to produce 'an intense sense of a personal double, a materialized replica of an embodied self, which left the temporal body of the occultist and journeyed at length in astral realms' (Owen, *Place of Enchantment* 128). The adepts formulated their own 'Sphere of Astral Light', which would replicate their person, and then travelled in the 'astral light' using 'astral currents'. The novel consistently describes the narrator's journeys through space as occult astral travel.

2. In describing 'electric Christianity', Corelli also denounces the churches, and 'the old Jewish doctrine of original sin and necessary sacrifice', in her July 1887 introduction to the novel ('Introduction to the New Edition', *Romance* 10).

3. The first element of Corelli's creed, explained primarily through Heliobas's manuscript entitled the 'Electric Principle of Christianity', is its core of powerful electric force both at the individual and the cosmic level. Franklin identifies and analyses the second element, i.e. the 'aesthetic spiritualism' of Corelli's Christianity, noting how '[o]ne strand of Corelli's renewed Christianity is an aestheticism' and how materialism is a threat to spirituality because 'it is particularly antithetical to artistic freedom' or the aesthetic spirit (28). The novel posits this idea of the artistic as a conduit to the sacred through the figures of Cellini, Zara and the narrator. Cellini approximates the divine through his act of painting, Zara does so through her gifted sculpting, and the narrator's abilities as a pianist improve after her astral travels that allow her to hear the 'music of the spheres' ('The Counter-Invasion of Britain by Buddhism' 27, 28).

4. Martin Hipsky quotes one of Corelli's biographers, Helen Rappaport, to claim the opposite. He says that the 'religious openness' of Corelli may in fact explain Queen Victoria's attraction to Corelli's works. Rappaport explains that the Queen

herself exhibited an 'idiosyncratic brand of Christianity, which was an eclectic and contradictory amalgam of both High and Low Church ritual', 'with an emphasis on the devotional element rather than the traditional fear of God's punishment' (an aspect that is repeatedly emphasized in *Romance*), 'coupled with a strong belief in the afterlife—a belief that fuelled a considerable interest in the paranormal' (Hipsky 273; quoting Rappaport 312).

5. Anne Stiles quotes from Marie Corelli's letter to George Bentley (Stiles 196): Marie Corelli to George Bentley, November 15, 1886, Corelli Collection (Cat. No. GEN MSS 332), Yale University, Beinecke Rare Book and Manuscript Library.

6. In 'The Life of the Buddha in Victorian England', Franklin bases his analysis majorly on the two most important late-nineteenth-century literary texts that portray Buddhism and embody its fascination in late-nineteenth-century Britain—Edwin Arnold's *The Light of Asia* (1879) and Richard Phillips's *The Story of Gautama Buddha and His Creed: An Epic* (1871).

7. It may be useful to understand this conflation of science and religion by examining Marjorie Wheeler-Barclay's historical–biographical study where she studies the newly emergent late-nineteenth-century scholarly enterprise in Britain called the 'science of religion'. This was a 'distinct field of discourse dedicated to the scientific study of religious practices and belief systems as human institutions meeting definite social and psychological needs' (1). This field treated religion 'purely as an element in human cultures' and included works from several areas like 'anthropology, sociology, classics, and Oriental studies' (2). Wheeler-Barclay remarks that we should not see this new field as a cause of 'secularisation' as is traditionally understood, but must understand it as 'both a response to and a reflection of the sense of religious crisis that troubled so many Victorians' (2). In her narrative of the rise of the discipline of sociology in twentieth-century France, Hervieu-Léger highlights the perceived conflict between science and religion that leads to the inherent nineteenth-century contradiction of a *sociology* (implying scientific critique) of religion (implying faith in the institution) (17). Wheeler-Barclay, however, explains that 'science of religion' between 1860 and 1915 defused this contradiction. As a field, 'science of religion' made it obvious how its Victorian audience 'respected the authority of science, but . . . also hoped for the affirmation of religious values

and meanings' (6)—an insight which has prompted many scholars to rethink flattening assumptions of Victorian 'secularisation'.

8. Martin Hipsky studies this aspect as well, noting that Corelli's early romances of the 1880s and 90s attempt to 'reconcile Christianity with reincarnation, karma, astral projection, and other Buddhist, Hindu, and mystical topoi' (69). Stiles similarly observes how Corelli '[e]schew[s] the traditional idea of Hell' and imports foreign concepts into her brand of Christianity by drawing on 'elements of theosophy and late-Victorian popular understandings of Buddhism' (162).

9. To the heroine's query, 'You are a Chaldean?', Heliobas responds, 'Exactly so. I am descended directly from one of those "wise men of the East" . . . who, being wide awake, happened to notice the birthstar of Christ on the horizon before the rest of the world's inhabitants had so much as rubbed their sleepy eyes' (*Romance* 67–68; ch. 5).

10. Asad explains that the imperialist structures of administration were premised on the secularist understanding of pain as disabling, and that they attempted to administratively eliminate colonial forms of pain through reforms while naturalising other forms of what they considered 'necessary' pains that were an integral part of the imposition of Western colonial rule. The thinking of the colonialists was not dominated, however, by their 'concern with indigenous suffering' but by 'the desire to impose what they considered civilized standards of justice and humanity on a subject population—that is, the desire to create new human subjects' (110). Essential to this process was the definition, categorisation, and prohibition of certain kinds of pain that the colony found (often spiritually) meaningful, while imposing other forms of pain that were essential to the stabilisation of the Western imperialist rule.

REFERENCES

Achebe, Chinua. *Morning Yet on Creation Day: Essays*. Anchor Press, 1975.

Asad, Talal. *Formations of the Secular: Christianity, Islam, Modernity*. Stanford UP, 2003.

Ayres, Brenda, and Sarah E. Maier, editors. *Reinventing Marie Corelli for the Twenty-First Century*. Anthem Press, 2019.

Bhattacharya, Prodosh. 'The Reception of Marie Corelli in India.' *New Readings in the Literature of British India, c. 1780–1947*. Edited by Shafquat Towheed, Studies in English Literatures Series, Volume 9. Ibidem, 2007. pp. 219–44.

Caputo, John. *On Religion*. Routledge, 2001.

Corelli, Marie. *A Romance of Two Worlds*. 1886. Okitoks Press, 2017.

---. 'Introduction to the New Edition.' *A Romance of Two Worlds*. W. M. L. Allison Company, 1887, pp. 3–14.

Cox, Jeffrey. *The English Churches in a Secular Society*. Oxford UP, 1982.

Crozier-De Rosa, Sharon. 'Shame, Marie Corelli, and the "New Woman" in Fin-de-Siècle Britain.' *Emotions and Social Change: Historical and Sociological Perspectives*. Edited by Ann Brooks and David Lemmings. Taylor and Francis, 2014, pp. 252–68.

Federico, Annette R. *Idol of Suburbia: Marie Corelli and Late-Victorian Literary Culture*. UP of Virginia, 2000.

Franklin, J. Jeffrey. 'The Counter-Invasion of Britain by Buddhism in Marie Corelli's *A Romance of Two Worlds* and H. Rider Haggard's *Ayesha: The Return of She*.' *Victorian Literature and Culture*, vol. 31, no. 1, 2003, pp.19–42. *JSTOR*, www.jstor.org/stable/i25058609

---. 'The Life of the Buddha in Victorian England.' *ELH*, vol. 72, no. 4, 2005, pp. 941–74. *Project MUSE*, doi:10.1353/elh.2005.0033.

---. *The Lotus and the Lion: Buddhism and the British Empire*. Cornell UP, 2008.

Fraser, Robert. *Book History through Postcolonial Eyes: Rewriting the Script*. Routledge, 2008.

Galvan, Jill Nicole. 'Christians, Infidels, and Women's Channeling in the Writings of Marie Corelli.' *Victorian Literature and Culture*. Issue on 'Victorian Religion' vol. 31, no. 1, 2003, pp. 83–97. *JSTOR*, www.jstor.org/stable/25058615.

---. *The Sympathetic Medium: Feminine Channeling, the Occult, and Communication Technologies, 1859–1919*. Cornel UP, 2010.

Gregory, Brad S. *The Unintended Reformation: How a Religious Revolution Secularized Society*. Belknap Press of Harvard UP, 2015.

Hallim, Robyn. 'Marie Corelli's Best-selling Electric Creed.' *Writing. Issue on 'Marie Corelli'*, vol. 13, no. 2, 2006, pp. 267–83. doi: 10.1080/09699080500527428

Hartnell, Elaine M. 'Morals and Metaphysics: Marie Corelli, Religion and the Gothic.' *Women's Writing. Issue on 'Marie Corelli'*, vol. 13, no. 2, 2006, pp. 284–303. doi: 10.1080/09699080500527436

Hervieu-Léger, Danièle. *Religion as a Chain of Memory*. Rutgers UP, 1993.

Hipsky, Martin. *Modernism and the Women's Popular Romance in Britain, 1885–1925*. Ohio UP, 2011.

Ives, Maura, and Ann R. Hawkins, editors. *Women Writers and the Artifacts of Celebrity in the Long Nineteenth Century*. Routledge, 2016.

Masters, Brian. *Now Barabbas Was a Rotter: The Extraordinary Life of Marie Corelli*. H. Hamilton, 1978.

Owen, Alex. *The Place of Enchantment: British Occultism and the Culture of the Modern*. U of Chicago P, 2004.

Perkins, Judith. *The Suffering Self: Pain and Narrative Representation in the Early Christian Era*. Routledge, 1995.

Rappaport, Helen. *Queen Victoria: A Biographical Companion*. ABC-CLIO, 2003.

Scheider, R. M. 'Loss and Gain? The Theme of Conversion in Late Victorian Fiction.' *Victorian Studies*, vol. 9, no. 1, 1965, pp. 29–44. *JSTOR*, www.jstor.org/stable/3825366

Stiles, Anne. *Popular Fiction and Brain Science in the Late Nineteenth Century*. Cambridge UP, 2012.

Wheeler-Barclay, Marjorie. *The Science of Religion in Britain, 1860–1915*. U of Virginia P, 2010.

Worth, Aaron. *Imperial Media: Colonial Networks and Information Technologies in the British Literary Imagination, 1857–1918*. Ohio State UP, 2016.

Žižek, Slavoj. *The Fragile Absolute: Or, Why is the Christian Legacy Worth Fighting For?* Verso, 2009.

Chapter Nine

The Perils of 'Home' and Paradoxes of the Hijab

REVISITING REBELLION AND LIBERAL AGENCY IN SATRAPI'S *PERSEPOLIS*

In the world that we inhabit, fascination with the hijab is ubiquitous.[1] On the one hand, Mona Eltahawy writes in her *New York Times* column (2009) that '[a]s a Muslim woman and as a feminist,' she would 'ban the burqa,' and that she agrees with the otherwise disagreeable French President Sarkozy on his assertion that the burqa is not a religious sign but a sign of the subjugation and submission of women. On the other hand, the twelve-year-old finalist in the 2019 'BBC Young Reporter Competition,' Fatima, declares that her hijab 'is a sign of freedom not oppression' ('My hijab is a sign of freedom not oppression'). As Reina Lewis summarises, the veil is a garment 'whose meaning cannot be contained' for it is 'fought over by adherents and opponents, many of whom claim that their understanding of the veil's significance is the one and true meaning' (Lewis 10).

The sheer range of the garment's cultural representations is truly bewildering. At one end is the strange exoticisation of the figure of the mysterious hijab-clad Middle Easterner in *Sex and the City 2* (2010). Disorientingly, the film builds towards a climax where New York City women realise that the veiled and seemingly distant Abu Dhabi women were in fact desperate lovers of (Western) fashion and lipsticks—a shared passion that finally unites privileged women from across hemispheres despite their irreducible cultural differences. Dariush Mehrjui's *Sara* (1992), an Iranian adaptation of Ibsen's *A Doll's House*, is another of the many cultural texts that harness the complex charge of the hijab's undecipherability. The film transplants the patriarchal hierarchy of the Torvald–Nora relationship from Ibsen's play into the Iranian landscape where the conflict is played out between the husband, Hessam, and the wife, Sara. Barely three minutes into the film, we encounter an elaborate shot of Sara meticulously dressing to visit her ailing husband at the hospital who she will eventually save by secretly borrowing money from one of his colleagues (Goshtasb, Krogstad's counterpart in the film). The camera rests on her arms and head in turns, focusing on the elaborate and practised process of a Muslim woman dressing herself in multiple layers of traditional clothing—a long jacket, hijab, and chador—slipping the jacket onto her shoulders, rolling back the scarf and fixing it as the hijab over her head, and finally draping the looser chador over the whole body. Instead of capturing the entirety of her frame from a distance, the camera steadies itself over individual parts of her body as Sara drapes them one by one as part of a rehearsed regimen before stepping out into the public domain, offering a commentary on the way her very individuality seems to be structured through these sartorial layers. Her protest against her husband takes much longer to unravel in the film, and when it does it is emblematised through her financially empowering journey of becoming a professional tailor, and her secret and laborious sewing of an alternative kind of clothing through the night and into the wee hours of the morning.

The disturbing cultural and semantic context in which the hijab functions is nowhere more evident than in the use of this garment in a notorious subgenre of pornography, recently discussed by Mia Khalifa, the famous adult film actor, in her 2019 interview with Stephen Sackus on *BBC Hard Talk*. Evidently regretful of her professional choices that she suggests were less than voluntary, Khalifa explains her unwitting entry into the field, admits that she was terrified and traumatised when the production team asked her to wear the hijab during the first shoot, and recounts how she kept panicking and thinking that this would surely get her killed. Khalifa's polemical disclosure focused the global spotlight on the arguably sexist and offensive use of the hijab in the adult film industry wherein the male viewer's voyeuristic gaze is captured and his sexual pleasure triggered by a garment that simultaneously embodies female docility, mystery, and submission—both interpersonal and sexual.

This diverse set of meanings surrounding the hijab—its representation as mysterious and exotic, or regressive and violent, and its embedment in a fusillade of questions—is protested by Mona Hayder, a Syrian-American rapper, in her highly stylised song, 'Hijabi'. Hayder is among several pop cultural artists who proudly sport the hijab, another very visible instance being the Indonesian girl band *Voice of Baceprot*. Hayder's 'fashionable' protest is a powerful riposte to a Western audience bubbling with curious questions: 'You only see oriental / . . . [I'm] Not your exotic vacation / I'm bored with your fascination'. Rupturing the garment's persistent associations with mystery and regressive traditionalism, Hayder tethers it to the modern and fashionably subversive musical form of rap. With the inescapable pun on the words 'rap'/'wrap', she sings her powerful refrain, 'I still wrap my hijab,' that mutates into the disruptive—'I still *rap* my hijab.' The cultural iconicity of the garment is harnessed in Indian films such as *Lipstick Under My Burqa* (2016) and *Secret Superstar* (2017). In the case of the former which had to pass through a grueling battle with the Indian Censor Board, the exotic and consequently delimiting associations of the hijab are categorically dismantled, and the garment is converted into a subversive carrier of female sexuality.

If we look beyond cultural representations, we see how the hijab has proved to be an incendiary issue in the political landscape. Several European countries have sparked uncontainable protests by attempting to eliminate the hijab from the public sphere. France has gone from banning the wearing of the veil by school students in 2004, to banning the use of headscarves by mothers who accompany their children on school field trips in the May 2019 Senate vote. Even as I write, Bengaluru has erupted with student unrest, and educational institutions have had to be shut down over the right-wing opposition to Muslim students wearing the headscarf, a development that has directed focus onto the bravery of Muskan Khan (who refused to remove her hijab when accosted by a group of right-wing men sporting saffron scarves, and yelled 'Allahu Akbar' in reply), and the censure by Malala Yousafzai (Mogul et al.). At the same time, there are exceptional sidenotes such as UK's first hijab-clad Mayor (Councillor Rakhia Ismail), the first veiled American Congresswoman (Ilhan Omar), and the first veiled American national television news anchor (Noor Tagouri, also featured on the October 2016 *Vogue* cover). Countless battles continue with some fortunate victories. For instance, there was the fight to get the International Basketball Federation to lift their ban on the hijab which had disqualified the Qatar team in the 2014 Asian Games, or the struggle to reverse the international hijab ban for the boxing community that once held back Safiyya Syeed, or the battle against the US Army's hostility towards veiled servicewomen that was fought by Cesilia Valdovinos. In a world that is so scared and baffled that its police personnel compel women to remove their headgear on the beaches of France or dramatically ban their use of burkinis in the aftermath of terrorist attacks, what remains lamentably obvious is the rampant Islamophobia and a nagging discomfort with the hijab. As Reina Lewis concludes, the hijab remains 'an item of clothing dramatically overburdened with competing symbolism' and one that occupies a whole range of meanings between the 'individual experiences of veiling and its complex and contested status in a variety of public arenas' (Lewis 10).

Leila Ahmed provides a useful historical antidote to these recurrent politico-cultural anxieties by contextualising the origins of the hijab. She notes that beginning in the late nineteenth century, the meaning that the hijab acquired was the result of a Western colonialist construction of the East as primitive and backward. The hijab, or colonial styles of dressing, were associated with this cultural backwardness which as a whole was taken to justify colonial rule. Ahmed notes that these new colonial meanings of the hijab were very different from 'precolonialist Middle Eastern notions of the meaning of the veil, notions rooted in Islamic, Christian, and Jewish local meanings'—notions that were therefore not unique to Islam at all and that were the common inheritance of the Semitic faiths. Ahmed explains that gradually the 'local meanings of the veil' were 'superseded by Westerners' view of the veil as a sign of the inferiority of Islam and Muslim societies and peoples, as well as of Islam's "degradation" of women' (44). The new perception was that Eastern societies proved themselves either advanced or backward by the extent to which they emulated the West and abandoned their native practices such as the donning of the veil. Thus, several countries such as Egypt, Turkey, Syria, Jordan, Lebanon and Iraq proceeded on the path of 'modernisation' by unveiling. Ignorant of this complex history, the large majority today unproblematically accepts the association of the veiled woman with disempowerment. As Reina Lewis notes, the veil is often seen 'as proof of the oppression of Muslim women or as a marker of cultural difference in need of "toleration"' (10). But it is crucial to understand that, unlike our contemporary moment, the Muslim countries that embarked on the path of unveiling in the early twentieth century did not perceive of unveiling as an act contrary to the principles of Islam at all, but only as a metaphor for Westernisation and modernisation on both public and personal levels. Ahmed explains that after the age of unveiling (1900–1920s), came a time (1920s–1960s) when going bareheaded was the norm. There were generations who came of age during the latter phase and who therefore did not know of a time when women had veiled. On the whole, during the long period of unveiling (1900s–1960s) the masses did not associate the wearing of the hijab with religious conduct or the removal of it with 'secularisation'. However, a major shift set in with the Islamic resurgence of the 1970s—characterised by the rise of the Muslim Brotherhood and of Islamist currents backed by Saudi Arabia—which resulted in the reappearance of the veil in the mid-1970s, first among small groups of female university students and then in society at large. It was only at this much later stage that the act of unveiling acquired connotations of religious profanity or Western 'secularity' for the first time. Thus, as Ahmed shows, the hijab's adoption has not been historically and uniquely associated with Islam, or its rejection with modern Western 'secularisation'. In conclusion, Reina Lewis observes the shifting set of assumptions surrounding the hijab: '[T]he heterogeneous use of veiling, as dress act and visual trope, is endlessly repositioned by changing world events and constantly reframed by the nuanced shifting responses of veiling communities' (10).

Questioning the assumptions that have congealed around the image of the veil in recent times, Fatima Mernissi contests the culturally predominant idea that Islam as a religion is fundamentally opposed to women's rights or that the Western public sphere (in its 'daily activities', its 'creative thinking', and its 'approach to the world around' [vi–vii]) is in any way intrinsically 'secular' and free of Judaeo-Christian mythology and assumptions. Instead, Mernissi concludes succinctly that religion in general 'can be [and has been] used by all kinds of organizations in the modern world to promote money-making projects', and that this kind of instrumentalisation is not unique to Islam. Consequently, she clarifies, since 'Islam is no more repressive than Judaism or Christianity', those that make Islam and women's rights (or human rights) seem mutually exclusive are essentially driven by their covert profit-driven agendas and only mobilise religious rhetoric to disguise these mercenary interests, 'camouflag[ing] their self-interest' and 'dip[ing their] . . . spurious rationale' in religious logic 'to give it a glow of authenticity' (vii).

There are several examples of literary and popular cultural works which question the unproblematic association that is set up between Western 'secular'–liberal democracies and justice on the one hand, and Islamic structures/states and repression on the other. One of the most significant is the case of Mohsin Hamid's *The Reluctant Fundamentalist* that I studied at length in chapter two. Another passing exanple is from *Designated Survivor* (2018–19), a Netflix show where one of the episodes ('Slippery Slope') shows the American President (Kirkman) immersed in a complex conversation with the Saudi Arabian ambassador on the topic of Saudi Arabia's child marriage situation. The conversation begins with the ambassador shaming the American President for expressing a stereotypical view of an Islamic state as regressive. Kirkman tries reminding her that not only were Saudi nationals culpable and involved in the 9/11 attacks, but that her state itself had a long history of repressively enforcing the burqa, killing the free press, persecuting religious minorities and female activists, and murdering protesting journalists. However, Kirkman is stumped by her citation of the many cases of human rights violations that are systemically supported by the American state. With quiet condescension against Kirkman's 'righteous indignation', the ambassador observes scathingly that his country was founded as 'a slave state', and that it was infamous for its high incarceration rate, soaring murder rates, high levels of civilian gun ownership, and rampant homelessness. Admitting the baselessness of Islam-vs-West power binaries—whether charted as faith versus knowledge or religious fanaticism versus 'secular' liberalism—and the futility of the resultant violence, Kirkman concedes in words reminiscent of Christ's injunction (John 8:7): 'Let he who is without sin cast the first stone. Point taken.'

In this chapter I examine Marjane Satrapi's *Persepolis* that was published in its original French version between 2000 and 2003, to understand how the text problematises the typically naturalised relationship between 'secularism' and women's rights. *Persepolis* is a graphic autobiography that depicts Satrapi's childhood in Iran during and after the Islamic Revolution, her subsequent adult attempt to embrace Western 'secularity' in Vienna, her emotional return to Iran in search of a home, and her final exit from her country at the end of the narrative. In this bildungsroman, we watch as the protagonist Marjane (or Marji) tenderly connects with her grandmother, learns how to challenge fundamentalist patriarchy from her parents, participates in civil protests, parties with her friends in defiance of the Islamist regime, escapes to the Western world in search of liberation, succumbs to drugs in this foreign land, returning to Iran to rebel against unjust laws within the country, and heartbrokenly abandons her family and country at the end. What the text also offers alongside is a detailed politico-cultural history of the Iranian nation through disturbing images of war, violence, repression and torture. I examine the way the novel casts its net wide, critiquing West-centric models that define individual agency as a derivative of rebellion, and posit the subordination–rebellion power nexus as the site for subjectivity-formation. I discuss how *Persepolis* repeatedly reminds us of the hypocrisies, inequalities, and injustices that underlie this culturally mandated template of revolt. Finally, I end by demonstrating how the representation of the hijab in the novel attempts to break free of both alternatives in the pre-set anthropological/geopolitical 'religious Islam-vs-"secular" West' binary and instead hopes to understand the full and complex ambivalence of human actions in their pragmatic everyday contexts where they represent compulsion as much as resolution, and compromise as much as idealism.

DISMANTLING REPRESSION, VOICING RAGE

As Samuli Schielke observes, a predominant direction in the recent anthropological analyses of Islam is associated with 'the study of piety, ethics and tradition', carried out most prominently by Saba Mahmood and Charles Hirschkind, and in different variations by Michael Lambek, Heiko Henkel, Lara Deeb and Stefania Pandolfo. A significant premise of much of this anthropological work is that Muslim lives must be understood as being determined by (the practice of) Islam and that this requires a restructuring of existing global assumptions and hierarchies that are determined by the domination of the West. However, as I discussed at length in chapter two, critics like Sadia Abbas, Matt Waggoner, Bharat Ranganathan, and Sindre Bangstad among others have since highlighted the problematic moral relativism underlying such anthropological approaches, and especially that of Saba Mahmood, observing how such a scholarly approach on the one hand makes it impossible to engage cross-culturally with gender issues being faced by Muslim women from other contexts (such as from within the Egyptian mosque/piety movement) and on the other hand, often makes a justificatory argument in favour of violent political groups based on the logic of self-referential meanings. Lila Abu-Lughod summarises that the 'significant political-ethical problem the burqa [and Islam] raises [within anthropology] is how to deal with cultural "others"', how 'are we to deal with difference without accepting the passivity implied by the cultural relativism for which anthropologists are justly famous—a relativism that says it's their culture and it's not my business to judge or interfere, only to try to understand' (786). Abu-Lughod notes that while cultural relativism is 'certainly an improvement on ethnocentrism and the racism, cultural imperialism, and imperiousness that underlie it' the *'problem is that it is too late not to interfere'* (786; emphasis added). Inserting itself within this scholarly conversation, Satrapi's literary masterpiece recognises this urgency and exposes the spectre of Iranian patriarchal repression after the Islamic Revolution.

One very early example appears when Marji's parents smuggle back from their Istanbul vacation several foreign items for their daughter—a denim jacket, chocolates, a pair of Nike sneakers, and posters of Kim Wilde and Iron Maiden that were banned in Iran during the Islamic Revolution (131–32). A jubilant Marji proudly struts around in these new clothes when she is stopped and harassed by members of the women's branch of the 'Guardians of the Revolution' for dressing wrongly and for wearing a Michael Jackson pin that one of the women calls a 'symbol of decadence' (133). The chapter ends impactfully with an iconic illustration of Marji in a gesture of angry protest within the privacy of her room. Another example is Satrapi's indignant portrayal of Islamist segregation and repression in Iranian educational institutions at the time. We are shown how in Marji's own university girls are compelled to drape a hijab, take a different set of staircases than the boys, and sketch a veiled woman for an art class on 'nudes', for the sake of propriety. In protest against these systemic wrongs, Marji emerges as an uncontainable firebrand. She vociferously opposes segregation and veiling, demolishing the institutional rationale that longer veils helped ensure that men do not get sexually excited. Consequently, the university is forced to concede partially and assigns her the task of designing women's uniforms (trousers and head-scarf) in a way that would balance the conservative requirements of the administration which prescribed concealment with the practical needs of female students who required mobility (298–300). During this phase, Marji assumes leadership of the popular opposition to statewide repression, retorting furiously when she is blamed for breaking 'the moral code' by staring at the male model whom she is painting in her art class and when she is asked to refrain from running while catching a bus because it made her posterior engage in 'obscene' movements. (302, 303). As Gilmore and Marshall observe, '[o]n one level, then, *Persepolis* . . . affirms ideologies associated with Western neoliberalism, such as an individual's right to freedom of expression and "choice,"' which they say 'explains in part the popularity of the text and its use by conservatives and liberals alike' (681). Studying the pedagogical transaction of the text, Botshon and Plastas also note that Satrapi's 'feisty protagonist is particularly compelling' to American students because in her they 'find models of liberation' (6). Matching up to this admiration, the rebellious and perceptive Marji—filled with resolve and insight— registers her summative protest against a fundamentalist Iran that she is determined to battle—noting that the regime had understood that if a person left her house asking herself if her trousers were the right length, or if her veil was in place, or if she could get whipped by the police, then she would no longer demand her fundamental rights or ask political questions (304).

However, besides critiquing Islamist repression by measuring it against a (Western) 'secular' democratic template, Satrapi's larger agenda—as I will show in the following section—is also to problematise the Western frameworks that prescribe the 'religious Islam-vs-"secular" West' formula globally and that announce the latter's unquestioned politico-cultural superiority.

FIGHTING PROTEST, FRAMING FREEDOM

A closer reading of *Persepolis* reveals how Satrapi not only exposes the historical inequalities that structurally define Western templates of freedom/agency/justice but also challenges the Western domination of other territories that these templates are used to justify and facilitate. Interestingly, in her anthropological work, Abu-Lughod emphasises that even while not giving in to the 'danger' of cultural relativism by endorsing (non-Western) culturally-specific gender injustice, one can still attempt to recuperate alternative perspectives rooted in these diverse contexts. Following from such insight, it becomes crucial to see how texts fracture the larger Western narratives of cultural and 'secular'-liberal superiority. Studying the case of Afghan women under the Taliban regime, Abu-Lughod digs deeper and declares that in addition to feminist freedom from the repressive (Taliban) regime, Muslim (Afghan) women might want a more fundamental restructuring—

> a global redistribution of wealth . . . [and] the [universal human] right to freedom from the ravages of war, the everyday rights of having enough to eat, having homes for their families in which to live and thrive, having ways to make decent livings so their children can grow, . . . and having the strength and security to work out . . . how to live a good life, which might very well include changing the ways those communities are organized. (787)

As Gilmore and Marshall's analysis of Satrapi's text clarifies, *Persepolis* echoes this demand by attempting to 'dislocate [the West] as a privileged site of knowledge' (679). This, therefore, is the more complex and interesting work performed by Satrapi's text.

At a basic level, Satrapi contests the Western stereotypes of Middle Eastern lives by showing in part how an Iranian upbringing was very similar to a Western one. Her portrayal of Marji's childhood with her love for Western popular cultural icons such as Iron Maiden, Kim Wilde and Michael Jackson is meant less as an approximation of Western models of cultural fashion and more as a reminder of how similar some of Marji's cultural preferences were to that of Western girls, lamentably characterised however by the lack of freedom to pursue them. Satrapi corroborates this interpretation when she notes elsewhere about *Persepolis* that she meant for this memoir of hers to be read by others unfamiliar with Iran so they would realise that she 'grew up just like other children' ('On Writing Persepolis'). The heavier onus the text bears, however, is that of contesting the assumptions surrounding religious oppression and its target victims that were especially crucial in the post–9/11 world in which the novel was published—a world which, as Gilmore and Marshall explain, was exemplified by Laura Bush's radio address on 17 November 2001. In this address, Bush spoke about terrorism's toll on the women and girls of Afghanistan, as a way to justify 'military aggression and human rights violations [thereafter] initiated by the US government' within Afghan territory (Gilmore and Marshall 680). This novel therefore 'seeks to educate Western readers about [the misrepresentations of] Iran and

Islam' (679), and determinedly 'interrupt[s] monolithic discourses [that portray] . . . all Muslim girls as subjects in need of rescue' (680). As Satrapi begins by asserting in her preface, the nation of Iran should not be defined by the actions of a few extremist elements in its society. *Persepolis* problematises Western anxieties surrounding Islamist fundamentalism and 'fanaticism', and systematically dismantles the pre-existing ethical hierarchies and ruling sociopolitical assumptions that undergird the moral claims of West-led 'secular'-liberal democracies. As a result, the very ideas of liberal ethics, democratic values, just protest, and radical rebellion are muddied through Satrapi's narratorial exposition of systemic inequities and hypocrisies. Lisa Botshon and Melinda Plastas observe how the Western modes of empowerment and rebellion acquire greater complexity in the context of the fraught Iranian conditions that the novel represents. They critique, for instance, Marji's unthinking adoption of 'classic twentieth-century middle-class Western rites of passage'—the wearing of a jacket, slim-fit jeans and a Michael Jackson pin gifted by her parents—noting that while 'American readers may appreciate Marji's rebellion, they also must realize the great danger in which she places herself by wearing her jacket and Michael Jackson pin on the streets of Tehran' (7). However, *Persepolis* goes a step further, not merely staging the reinterpretation of Western modes of rebellion in the Middle East, but also dramatising their complete irrelevance and ludicrousness in this context. Therefore, the text emphasises the need to re-examine borrowed Western narratives of rebellion, templates of identity and definitions of agency/liberty.

In *Politics of Piety*, Saba Mahmood undertakes an anthropological study of the mosque movement that emerged in Egypt in the 1970s 'in response to the perception that religious knowledge, as a means of organizing daily conduct, had become increasingly marginalized under modern structures of secular governance'— the impact of which upon Egyptian society was usually described by the participants of the movement as '"secularization" . . . or "westernization"'. The participants contended that this development had 'reduced Islamic knowledge (both as a mode of conduct and a set of principles) to an abstract system of beliefs that has no direct bearing on the practicalities of daily living' (4). As discussed in earlier chapters, this reduction/transformation of religion into a set of abstract principles is a template that grew out of developments internal to Christianity (originating out of medieval Christianity, passing through the Reformation, leading into the Enlightenment) and that, according to Mahmood, other religions constantly feel compelled to emulate. Mahmood admits that the 'pious subjects of the mosque movement', who practise daily forms of 'pious' living like donning the hijab, occupy an ambiguous position in feminist scholarship because they 'pursue practices and ideals embedded within a tradition that has historically accorded women a subordinate status' (4–5). These templates of action, in a post–9/11 world, have therefore come to bear a naturalised association with 'terms such as fundamentalism, the subjugation of women, social conservatism, reactionary atavism, [and] cultural backwardness'—associations that are now often treated as '"facts" that do not require further analysis' (5). In opposition to these modes of behaviour, modernity enshrines the ethic of 'freedom'—a politically charged concept around which West-led 'secular'-liberal democracies rally and define themselves. Abu-Lughod suggests that while examining the situation of women in Afghanistan, for example, we need to 'accept that there might be different ideas about justice and that different women might want, or choose, different futures from what we envision as best' (787–88). David Harvey famously critiques this enthronement of 'freedom' as the underlying basis and justificatory rationale of neoliberal political and economic systems that ultimately seek to institutionalise and perpetuate a profit-driven exploitative global market. In a chapter titled 'Freedom's Just Another Word . . .', Harvey shows how the 'founding figures of neoliberal thought' built a 'conceptual apparatus' based on the 'political ideals of human dignity and individual freedom'—'compelling and seductive ideals' guaranteed to appeal 'to our intuitions and instincts, to our values and our desires'—that they posited as 'fundamental' to a political system (5). Neoliberal thought then propounded the cardinal assumption that *'individual freedoms are guaranteed by freedom of the market and of trade'* (7; emphasis added), and therefore ultimately sought to impose—especially as reflected in US foreign policy approaches in Iraq or Afghanistan in a post–9/11 world—'a state apparatus whose fundamental mission was to facilitate conditions for profitable capital accumulation on the part of both domestic and foreign capital' (7). In the current global imagination, this rightful system of individual freedoms encounters its evil antithesis in fanatic and regressive [Islamist] religious governments. Satrapi's *Persepolis* participates in this conversation, highlighting—as we have already seen—the injustices of a dictatorial religious order, but also exposing the inequalities underlying the promises of the neoliberal order.

As part of this intervention, Satrapi questions some of the most crucial premises of Western 'secular' feminism. To understand Satrapi's critical manoeuvre, it is useful to refer to Saba Mahmood and Lila Abu-Lughod who explore the complex issue of (un)freedom at the conjunction of gender and Islam. Abu-Lughod, for instance, reminds us that even if 'we object to state imposition of th[e] form [of the veil], as in Iran or with the Taliban'—an objection voiced vociferously in *Persepolis*—we must 'work against the reductive interpretation of veiling as the quitessential sign of women's unfreedom' (786). Writing before Abu-Lughod, Mahmood delivers a more fundamental blow through her ethnographic analysis of the women who started to practise piety as part of Egypt's mosque movement. Instead of attempting to recuperate 'latent liberatory potentials' from within a movement that is widely regarded as nonliberal, Mahmood informs us about the very different templates of agency and subjectivity that the movement's prescribed religious conduct makes available to its participants. She declares that 'the concept of agency should be delinked from the goals of progressive politics' because this 'tethering . . . has often led to the incarceration of the notion of agency within the trope of resistance against oppressive and dominating operations of power' (34). Within the modern 'secular'–liberal imaginary, and based on the otherwise welcome interventions of poststructuralist feminist scholarship, agency is conceptualised 'in terms of subversion or resignification of social norms' and 'within those operations that resist the dominating and subjectivating modes of power' (14). However, the Egyptian mosque movement reveals modalities of human action that do not 'map onto the logic of repression and resistance' (14) because there is a whole spectrum of human life in which agentival capacity derives not only from 'those acts that resist norms but also in the multiple ways in which one *inhabits* norms' (15). As Abu-Lughod asks, '[I]s liberation even a goal for which all women or people strive? Are emancipation, equality, and rights part of a universal language we must use?' (788). Rejecting templates offered by poststructuralist feminist theory in which the subject 'often remains a liberatory one, whose agency is conceptualized on the binary model of subordination and subversion', Mahmood welcomes the inroads made by the mosque movement in reimagining individual agency (Mahmood 14).

Persepolis exemplifies this politico-philosophical intervention by barraging the very notion of subversion/rebellion—questioning its desirability, exposing its hypocrisies, critiquing its underlying inequalities, ridiculing its claims, depicting its inescapable binary closed-endedness, and ironising the very notion of liberty/freedom that is understood to be its teleological culmination. The text begins by showing an innocent and lovable Marji, puny and big-eyed, inhabiting an organic and meaningful relationship with a God of her imagination who frequently visits her thoughts and dreams. Her inner spiritual ruminations cease at exactly the point when she and her friends begin to adopt the fanciful foreign rhetoric of revolution, christening themselves Fidel, Che Guevara and Trotsky, and swearing by the call to rebel.[2] Marji now immerses herself into an extensive study of all texts of the Western canon that theorise or espouse the idea of rebellion, from Descartes to Marx, to the extent that she replaces her worship of God with a devotee-like reverence of Marx—thus transferring her allegiance from a personal God to a notional rebellion. Satrapi communicates this pictorially by showing Marx and God face-to-face as though engaged in combat; while Marji observes that it was quite amusing that God and Marx resembled each other (17). At the end of this chapter, she returns to find the God of her inner imagination gone, unyielding to her tearful and distressed entreaty, 'God, where are you?' (21). The presumed naturalness of this transition in the eyes of contemporary global modernity is replayed when an older Marji decides to shift from Iran to Austria—having decided to 'leav[e] a *religious Iran* for an *open and secular Europe*' (157; emphasis added). Marji's search for political resolution into a utopian 'secularity' is accompanied by her simultaneous emotional expectation that her 'mother's best friend' (Zozo) would love her 'like her own daughter' in the foreign land (157). With Zozo's increasing indifference towards Marji and the unravelling of her emotional expectations, Marji's hopes of a clear and reassuring politico-cultural binary with a promised Western 'secular' salvation, are also summarily demolished. Interestingly therefore, Marji embarks on a categorical critique of the rootless and 'free' modern existence typically romanticised in West-centric 'secular'-liberal political imaginaries.

Reminding us of Saba Mahmood's observation that 'the idea of freedom and liberty as the political ideal is relatively new in modern history' (14), the text expresses Marji's jaded longing for other forms of subjectivity that she finds more honestly self-fulfilling. In the chapter titled 'The Vegetable', Marji writes about the peer pressure she faces in Vienna's 'liberal' foreign climate where she has to fit in as a cultural outsider from the Middle East. She rejects the apparent 'liberty' that comes with the foreign and fashionable modes of conduct, only *pretending* to smoke every time she is offered a joint by her friends because her parents had once discussed how doping turns one into 'a vegetable' (194). Depressed and agonised, she confides in the reader through an image that shows her trying to straddle vast distances in an uncomfortably long single stride, confessing that the harder she tried to assimilate to the new culture, the more she felt as though she was betraying her parents and origins, distancing herself from her own culture, and 'playing a game by somebody else's rules' (121, 196). This desperate attempt to belong to the freeing western 'secular' space, away from fundamentalist Iran, becomes most visible when she pretends to be French among her acquaintances in Vienna, because 'at the time, Iran was the epitome of evil and to be Iranian was a heavy burden to bear' (198). However, she starts to deeply resent this choice in her quieter moments when she thinks back to how her grandmother had exhorted her to always keep her 'dignity' and to 'be true' to herself (198). Her initial unthinking emulation of the foreign, and her shame at this expression of her 'cowardice' and 'betrayal' (133), climaxes in her enraged outburst only a few pages later when she overhears a demeaning conversation about herself and her parents in the cafeteria and erupts, 'I am Iranian and proud of it' (200). Thus, Marji redefines the 'rules' and discovers her attachment towards her religiously complex and disturbed homeland. As such, she demonstrates the problematic aspects of cultural assimilation and questions, as does Mahmood, the very 'entelechy of liberatory politics' that underlies the modern 'secular' imaginary and Western feminist understanding (Mahmood 14).

The text problematises the simplistic binary between the 'secular'-liberal West and the 'repressive' Middle East by exposing the frivolity and ignorance of the former's claims to superiority. As Marji befriends another Iranian girl (Shirin) in Vienna, she is shocked to discover that this girl—located in the heart of Western cosmopolitan privilege—is callously unaware of the gruesome wars, Islamist fundamentalism and political mayhem that grip Iran. Not suspecting this at first, Marji begins her conversation with a candid reference to the domestic Iranian oppression that she herself had experienced, hoping to find in Shirin an empathetic fellow-sufferer, and expressing her relief in being able to go to school without the hijab (158). To this, the ignorant Shirin responds nonchalantly by babbling about her ear muffs, her 'raspberry-scented pen', and her 'pearly pink' lipstick. Marji angrily concludes that Shirin was a 'traitor' because she had no empathy for those suffering back in their country. The horror of Shirin's insouciance pales in comparison to the uncomprehending patronisation that Marji receives from her teacher, an educated man eager to learn but unable to grasp Iran's grim reality. Marji talks to him about her experiences—about war and bombings, the assassination of her uncle, and about how she would always be worried about her parents' safety back home (217). In response, however, she senses that he did not believe her and probably thought she was 'exaggerating' (217). In the face of the unapologetic indifference towards ground realities manifested by Shirin and the teacher, the binary of a restrictive 'religious Iran' and a free 'open and secular Europe' begins to crack and weaken, rendering the meaning and value of West-centric cosmopolitan 'freedoms' dubious (157). What makes the West's claims of empowerment even more ambiguous is the way it stereotypically straitjackets Marji as a suffering 'third-worlder' as the price for granting her visibility as a global citizen (169). It is in this capacity that she finds acceptance within her gang of friends in Vienna—Julie, Momo, Thierry and Olivier (169). Julie introduces Marji to Momo by underscoring her fetching quality of having experienced war as an Iranian—a revelation to which Momo responds awestruck ('War?'), with the facile question about whether she had already seen a lot of dead bodies (168). Later a group of students whisper about Marji, unaware that she can hear them, blaming her for having made a false claim just to 'make herself seem interesting' (199). The West's fashionable privileging of an exotic Iranian experience, bereft of any real concern for or engagement with the starkness of this reality, reveals the contrived conditions for a life in 'open and secular Europe' and the doubtfulness of its superiority over more visibly repressive regimes (157). Another exposition of the privileged and frivolous definitions of 'freedom' in the Global North—removed from any real understanding of its nature or necessity—emerges during the discussion about the philosophy of anarchism. Anarchism, the anti-authoritarian political philosophy that aimed to destabilise sociopolitical hierarchies and had radical nineteenth-century beginnings in Bakunin, is adopted by Marji's new group of friends in Vienna. The text, however, demonstrates their facetious understanding and practice of this philosophy. Momo belittles the political weight and urgency of anarchism when he says that according to the true vision of anarchism, vacations should be mandatory because 'man isn't made for work', and follows this up by advising Marji to 'relax' and holiday (175). Marji bubbles with rage to see how the Western agents deploy anarchism to justify the elite privilege of restful vacations, and in the process malign its historically rebellious impulse against inequality. The disillusionment reaches a peak when Marji's 'half-Austrian, half-Spanish' boyfriend, Enrique, takes her to 'an anarchist party'. At first, Marji is thrilled while thinking ahead to what the party might look like, and imagines a politically engaged demonstration of like-minded anarchists with sloganeering against the bourgeoisie or in praise of Bakunin (210–11). Dreaming about this excitedly—in a panel strikingly free of dark shades and therefore suggestive of the enormity, optimism and naivety of her hopes—she mulls over the idealistic battles of her childhood in Iran, and hopes that the party will give her an insight into Bakunin's ideas (211). Though fired up by this philosophy and possibility of a real sociopolitical change that would also connect to her revolts in Iran, she is disappointed to discover that the anarchists' party is literally a game of hide-and-seek in the middle of the forest. The page in the novel that depicts this is a sprawling mass of darkness with small puppet-like figures yelling childlike cries from behind what appear to be trees in the forest—their literal and symbolic immersion in darkness indicative of their insouciance, pettiness, and irrelevance. Witnessing this frivolous game in the Western enclave just as Iran was plummeting in the throes of war and oppression, Marji laments its half-baked, hypocritical, and unegalitarian implementation of notions of rebellion and liberty, and feels 'disgust and profound contempt' (212).

The narratorial pursuit of justice and 'liberal' human rights in the text is rendered blurry even within Iran when Marji is shown to realise her elite privilege that allows her own social group to engage in certain templates of 'secular' rebellion against fundamentalist oppression that are not only inaccessible to the underprivileged constituencies but also meaningless for them. Botshon and Plastas note how *Persepolis* shows that 'power circulates differently depending on one's location, including national origin, religion, gender, or class', and eventually even Marji realises that 'her position', as 'dangerous as it might be, pales in comparison to other Iranians who may not have the same class advantages' (Botshon and Plastas 7). At the very beginning of *Persepolis*, we find Marji feeling guilty for the class privileges she has been born into. She self-consciously notes that her father owned a Cadillac, or bemoans social injustices by saying that their maid did not eat with them (6). This is made explicit when she wonders why her family endorses the system of unequal 'social classes' by employing a girl her own age (Mehri) as domestic help whose poverty had compelled her to work for them. Marji bitterly observes as her otherwise revolutionary father unhesitatingly disowns Mehri when she is suspected of being in a relationship with the neighbour's boy—justifying it later to Marji by remarking that in Iran one must stay in one's own social class (37, 41). To this hypocritical rift between political faith and personal implementation, Marji responds with bewilderment and frustration, 'But is it her fault that she was born where she was born??? Dad, are you for or against social classes?' (41).

A mordant critique of 'secular' and 'liberal' democratic assumptions surfaces when the text juxtaposes what is a fate of little choice for the poor Iranian youth—getting blown up on the battlefield in the name of defending the nation—with the heady euphoria of the rich Iranian youth who advocate for a democratic Iran and demonstrate against the ongoing war by arranging illegal mixed-gender parties infused with alcohol, music and dance. On the one hand, the text strongly critiques the Islamist indoctrination of the poorest and most vulnerable Iranian youth that is meant to recruit them as soldiers in the 'pure carnage' of the ongoing war with Iraq (105). This is the case with Mrs Nasrine's son who is inducted into the army along with other poor boys like him with the prospect of a gory death on the battlefield and the lure of a lavish afterlife in a rich heaven full of women. Marji's cousin, Shahab, confirms this strategic exploitation of the poor through the mobilisation of Islamic rhetoric, remarking that a large number of boys who had been '[en]trance[d]' with songs of the regime designed to 'hypnotize ... and ... toss them into battle' and beguiled with the promise of an 'afterlife ... even better than disneyland', arrived from economically disadvantaged areas in numerous buses to join the battle (105). On the other hand, the text makes it evident that the privileged and 'secular' detachment of the West-inspired 'liberal' sections who party raucously to establish their protest is not ethically justified either. So when Marji plans and enjoys her 'first party', with her edgy social circle dressed in the subversive sartorial form of the 'punk rock', parallel panels show the violent deaths of poor children on the battlefield—a juxtaposition that highlights the meaninglessness of Marji's facile 'secular' rebellion and her class inability to comprehend or care about the strategic violence against the poor (106). Satrapi's illustration stages the contrast between the self-serving alcoholic abandon of Marji's class and the choiceless and tragic explosion of poor Iranian boys on the battlefield, forcing us to confront the selfish and privileged indifference underlying the Western claims of liberalism and democracy that Marji's social circle advocates and models.

The text also foregrounds the hypocritical and elitist presumption underlying the choice of the party as the revolutionary medium of protest. While Marji's group continues to resolutely party, the narrative margins are populated with distressing news of bomb blasts and the grim flogging of innocents by the 'Guardians of the Revolution' (105–06). In one instance, while Marji's family and friends immerse themselves in music and dance, and one of her uncles builds a 'wine-making lab in his basement', the poor Mrs Nasrine is condemned to crushing grapes in the bathtub even as the rich claim empowerment through convivial wine-infused celebration. In another chapter where Marji is arrested for partying and has to be bailed out for her to revel in the rebelliousness of her conduct, she reflects quietly on systemic inequalities, 'Our parents paid and we were released . . . until the next time. *To be able to party, you had to have means*' (309; emphasis added). In one such party that ends tragically when Marji's friend (Farzad) is chased down and killed by the state police, the text offers a grim critique of such prescribed imitative codes of 'secular'/'libertarian' conduct. The voiceless panels showing the horror of Farzad's final fatal chase, and the mindlessness of the surviving friends' group who offer homage to their departed friend through the deluded daze of another such party, highlights the disturbing complexity of adoptive foreign templates—a problem portended very early in the text when young Marji had vented her rage against Iranian repressive dress codes by dancing furiously to Kim Wilde's 'We're the Kids in America Whoao' in her closed room (134).

Satrapi's text also repeatedly suggests the ridiculousness of attributing any kind of real emancipatory potential to forms of conduct considered fashionably assertive in popular cosmopolitan representations. Marji begins by downplaying the facile association of smoking with empowerment,[3] and then launches an offensive against templates of Western feminism. She makes a reductive reference to Western feminism, drawing a puerile interpretation of Simone de Beauvoir and attempting a kind of gender empowerment by trying to urinate standing up that she thinks Beauvoir advised. Having failingly attempted this cumbersome manoeuvre, Marji expresses her dejection and indignation, 'So I tried. It ran lightly down my left leg. It was a little disgusting'. In the next panel, there is a tone of resignation as she pees sitting down and confesses that it is much more comfortable. She realises that 'before learning to urinate like a man, I needed to learn to become a liberated and emancipated woman' (177). Albeit through a caricatured interpretation, Marji holds up for judgment ideals such as 'liberty' and 'emancipation' that are typically enshrined in Western 'secular' feminist discourse. These ideals are more seriously questioned in a chapter appropriately titled 'The Pill' where Marji challenges the desirability of the 'sexual revolution' that emerged as a movement primarily in the US and the developed world in 1960s, overlapping with the second wave of feminism, fuelled by the development of the contraceptive pill among other factors, and focused on the exploration of sex outside the framework of marriage as a template for liberation (in the form of extramarital sex, premarital sex, homosexuality). Describing this historical juncture, the text shows Marji raising serious doubts about these Western formulae for empowerment as paraded by Julie in Vienna. Marji is scandalised when she attends one of Julie's get-togethers that overflow with drugs and sexual intimacy. She wakes up in the middle of the night following the party, startled by the orgasmic sounds coming from Julie's bedroom, and is tortured at the sight of Julie and her partner in an intimate state of undress. Realising soon after that this man was not even Julie's current boyfriend (Ernst) of whom she had heard, but was in fact a casual encounter (Wolfy), she concludes the chapter with a grim and sarcastic realisation about the contrived and meaningless templates of Western 'rebellion' against (religious) conservatism: 'That night, I really understood the meaning of "The Sexual Revolution".... It was my first big step toward assimilating into western culture' (190).

It is important to note at this point that understanding the text entirely in these terms—that is, through this oppositional 'juxtaposition of the Islamic and the "secular"-liberal'—needs reconsideration according to some critics. Samuli Schielke remarks, for example, that this approach may be 'flawed and may need to be revised in favour of an approach that is more perceptive of the situational, pragmatic and incomplete nature of discursive power' (Schielke, 'Second Thoughts about the Anthropology of Islam' 3). Schielke objects to what is 'the most influential and productive research programme in the anthropology of Islam at the moment: the study of piety, ethics and tradition', which as I noted earlier is most promiently associated with Mahmood and Hirschkind and was developed in different ways by Lambek, Henkel, Deeb, and Pandolfo. According to Schielke, this anthropological turn to Islam has 'too much Islam' in the sense that there is 'a lack of balance between the emphasis on religious commitment and a not always sufficient account of the lives of which it is a part' (Schielke, 'Second Thoughts about the Anthropology of Islam' 2). Firstly, the emphasis on 'moral and pious subjectivity' privileges 'pious pursuits in isolation from wider paths of life', gauging lives 'based more on what people argue for and less on how they actually live' (6). Secondly, while the 'wider master narrative' that juxtaposes 'the Muslim tradition of ethics, affect, devotion and debate . . . [against the] liberal and secular notions about the state, law, self and so on' is useful in its own way, it is ultimately problematic (6). It is helpful because it performs 'a political self-critique of liberalism and secularism' by 'revealing how the alleged superiority and universality of Western traditions of enlightenment actually conceal mechanisms of coercion, silencing, and exclusion,' and how they establish 'culturally and historically specific notions that cannot be taken to be valid for all of humanity' and because it therefore argues that 'we have to recognise the humanity of Muslims (and anyone else) as they see themselves and not reduce them to the ideological patterns of Western liberalism' (6). But the problem with this narrative is that it 'carries the risk that we will find it too easy to point our finger at the usual suspects, with the result that our enquiries may fail to account for what is really at stake for the people involved' and 'we may once again fail to seriously recognise the humanity of people on their own terms' (6). With this critique in mind, we need to take a final look at the text's representation of the hijab and its surrounding politics to understand how it offers a useful template for discursive intervention without the endorsement of these pre-set anthropological and geopolitical binaries.

THE HIJAB AND ITS ANXIETIES: DISCOMFORT AND DEBATE

As I began this chapter by observing, the site of the hijab has registered endless charged discussions and conflicting positions. It is challenging to represent the whole range of opinions and explorations that has been offered by legal experts (Lisa M. La Fornara, Urfan Khaliq, Hera Hashmi, Kathleen Miller), psychologists (Nina Bosankić), journalists (Adam Taylor, Kavitha Surana), or anthropologists (Talal Asad, Saba Mahmood, Charles Hirschkind, Lila Abu-Lughod, Christine M. Jacobsen, Anjum Alvi, Sertaç Sehlikoglu, Samuli Schielke, Michael Lambek, Heiko Henkel, Lara Deeb, Stefania Pandolfo), and my focused literary intervention that is not located in the domains of ethnography or theology benefits most not from any exhaustive account of this discursive field but from the mining of some key conceptual interventions as diveboards for textual analysis. It is useful to start by looking at what Margot Badran identifies as the two different templates for feminist expression that evolved from within the constituency of Muslim women and that can roughly be called secular and Islamic feminisms. Badran observes that these two traditions 'have never been hermetic entities' and points to how Talal Asad and Saba Mahmood have shown them to be interconnected categories (Badran 2). She explains that secular feminisms among Muslim communities first arose in various emergent nation states in Africa and Asia from the late nineteenth century through the first half of the twentieth century, during 'processes of modernization, nationalist anti-colonial struggle, dynastic decline, and independent state building' (2–3). Secular feminism is thus understood to signify a model of feminism that is 'located within the context of a secular territorial nation-state composed of equal citizens, irrespective of religious affiliation'—'a state protective of religion while not officially organized around religion' (3). Islamic feminism, however, emerged in the global Muslim community in the late twentieth century, simultaneously in the East and West, during the 'late postcolonial moment' when an 'Islamist movement, or movement of political Islam' was accelerating (and in the case of Iran or, later, Sudan, following the installation of an Islamic regime), as well as when a widespread Islamic religious cultural revival was taking place in many 'Muslim-majority secular states and minority societies' (3). In *Persepolis*, there is a crucial concurrence of these forces and the text draws on both 'secular' and religious notions of feminist freedom subtextually, encouraging us to understand how, as Mahmood or Abu-Lughod indicate, a (feminist) experience of faith that is empowering for women can also be conceptualised without grievously and irrevocably injuring the possibility and promise of equal human rights.

In her ethnographic work Mahmood notes that in comparison with other currents within the Islamic Revival, the mosque movement[4] is unique in the immense 'pedagogical emphasis it places on outward markers of religiosity—ritual practices, styles of comporting oneself, dress, and so on'—and that it therefore involves extensive 'training in this kind of ascetic [bodily] practice' (31). What is crucial about those who insist on the importance of donning the veil is how they argue that 'the veil is a necessary component of the virtue of modesty because the veil both expresses "true modesty" and is the means through which modesty is acquired' (23). That is, they establish an indispensable relationship between 'the norm (modesty) and the bodily form it takes (the veil) such that the veiled body becomes the necessary means through which the virtue of modesty is both created *and* expressed' (23; emphasis added). So we look at the bodily action, such as the wearing of the veil, as something that does not just express/represent who the individual is but that fundamentally *brings that individual into being*. Popular representations in the West tend to stereotype and privilege certain kinds of sartorial choices as more empowering and more truly 'feminist', with variations across time and place as to how this liberatory potential is defined and with what kind of clothing it is associated.[5] Typically, the hijab emerges in popular perception, and in widely influential geopolital and cultural discourses, as symbolic of patriarchal repression and fettered individuality, while its renunciation is perceived to be emancipatory.[6] Mahmood's aim, as one of the classic and defining approaches in the anthropological turn to Islam, is to critique the mainstream Western understanding of Muslim communities and the hijab, and to extract this garment's interpretation from the usual bind of liberal Western feminism. However, as I noted at the end of the previous section, a key problem here as summed up by Samuli Schielke is that this anthropological focus on Islam is 'part of a history of exceptionalism in the study of cultures and societies in which Islam is the dominant religious tradition'—a move that perversely carries an Orientalist heritage (Schielke, 'Second Thoughts about the Anthropology of Islam' 5). In this approach, '[i]nstead of being the backward other of European modernity', Islam is '[e]levated to . . . a position of significant alterity' as 'the pious other of secularism, the resisting other of neo-colonialism or the methodological other of comparative social science' (5). As a result, in this anthropological approach, while 'the religious traditions of Muslims gain particular brilliance and importance for the sake of highlighting their particularity through their difference', 'the faith and lives of Muslims in their own uniqueness, their specificity in their own right – and not just comparatively – become opaque, reduced to their Islamic-ness' so that while engaging in 'sophisticated theoretical debates' on Islam, we also easily 'overlook the ways Islam actually matters in the lives of people who adhere to it' (5). In the kind of 'political meta-narrative' that anthropologists like Mahmood offer, there is an 'insistence on framing . . . [the issue] as a quasi-systemic difference between the Islamic and the secular/liberal' (8). In Schielke's view, this generic critique of modern power ignores the 'complexity, richness and ambivalence' of human responses/actions with all their 'existential concerns and . . . pragmatic considerations' that do not fit neatly into either side of this binary (9, 12). Instead of this 'reductioninst' analytical framework, Schielke advises that 'populism may do much better' as an interpretive approach because of how it recognises the everyday nature of human lives, the ambiguity of human actions, the opportunistic cultivation of available emotions, and the prevailing moral unease (8). Taking into account the confusion, uncertainty, ambiguity, and greyness of human choices/actions, Schielke's anthropological approach to Muslim communities not only overturns the easy distinction between liberal 'secularism' and religious devotion but also destabilises the opportunistic geopolitical interpretations that dovetail with this binary. Thus, even as cultural and autobiographical discourse on the history of a Muslim community, *Persepolis* contributes significantly to this conversation by portraying the reality of everyday Iranian lives which defy such purposive reductionism.

Satrapi's text ridicules the facile structured neatness of the binary ('religious Islam-vs-"secular" West') by highlighting the complex ambiguity of all human action that blurs such binaries. In several parts of the text, Marji graphically represents the various kinds of hijab—with differing degrees of visible hairline or of varying length/coverages—and ironically mentions the corresponding levels of successful modernisation and feminist emancipation that they were supposed to represent in the contemporary cultural climate and that they continue to represent in reductioninst anthropological/political discourse.[7] In the very first chapter Marji inaugurates this discussion with the declaration that she had a dual identity—'deep down [she] . . . was very religious' but she came from a family that was 'very modern and avant-garde' (10). Satrapi depicts the absurdity of this neat binary through diagrammatical arithmetic symmetry, showing Marji's figure split accurately down the vertical middle—one side of her draped by the veil and framed by oriental designs, and the other side short-haired, covered in 'westernwear', and wallpapered with scientific motifs (instruments, tools, and geometric patterns). In a later chapter, Marji once again etches an orderly binary, this time between 'The Fundamentalist Woman' and 'The Modern Woman', both defined and differentiated through their clothing. The former is shown draped in a hijab that elides her bodily contours and covers all her hair, while the latter wears a three-pieced body-hugging Islamic dress, her form covered but silhouetted—with a head scarf that exposes a fringe of hair, a calf-length shirt (*kurta*), and a pair of figure-outlining pants. Marji reveals the absurdity and meaninglessness of this plotted binary by noting underneath

'The Modern Woman' illustration: 'You showed your opposition to the regime by letting a few strands of hair show' (10).[8] A similar pictorial commentary is offered through the contrast between 'The Fundamentalist Man', with a beard and untucked shirt, and 'The Progressive Man', clean-shaven and tucked-in. With an ironic undertone, Marji declares how 'wearing the veil was a real science', how it had to be worn so tufts of hair showed from the front but none at all from the sides, and how political progress in achieving the rights of women is reflected in the fact that 'year by year, women were winning an eighth of an inch of hair and losing an eighth of an inch of veil' (296). In the next extended panel, Marji lays out her critique of this approach even more clearly when she shows the profiles of three women draped in hijabs, and then shows each of them through a transparent hijab-outline so their bodily contours can be guessed. Once again, her illustration highlights the irrelevance and ludicrousness of such grid-like binaries into which everyday identities had to be artificially plotted in order for the usual anthropological and geopolitical slots to make sense: 'With practice, even though they were covered from head to foot, you got to the point where you could guess their shape, the way they wore their hair and even their political opinions' (297). Summing up the simplistic theoretical bifurcation of global discourse and the resulting reductive interpretation of human (Muslim) lives with disdain, Marji summarises scoffingly: 'Obviously, the more a woman showed, the more progressive and modern she was' (297). This mordant critique climaxes when, resonating Schielke's insight, the text stages the ambiguities of everyday existence in Muslim communities that confuse and defy the clear-cut boundaries of the 'religious Islam-vs-"secular" West' binary. While fleeing Iran for the first time amidst rising domestic tensions, Marji laments visibly, voicing her evident discomfort both with national religious sentiment and with the global lure of 'secular' liberty. Heartbroken and longing for a home, however messily and uncertainly poised that may be between the two sides of the binary, Marji confesses, 'Nothing's worse than saying goodbye. It's a little like dying' (153). And later, while preparing for her return from Vienna to Iran after a turbulent stay away from home, she admits candidly: 'I needed so badly to go home' (177). Donning the hijab once again after a long time in order to regain entry into Iran, Marji is seen in a pensive mood. Representing this forced choice of wearing the hijab in all its complexity, the illustration depicts her—resolutely, albeit contemplatively, gazing at herself in the mirror—pondering the impossibility of absolute or clear positions in the otherwise polarised geopolitical landscape: '[S]o much for my individual and social liberties' (199). At the very end of the novel when Marji departs from Iran the second and final time, she watches her woebegone and disconsolate grandmother say goodbye at the airport and utters the final reflective words of the novel that once again express her practical confusion in choosing between the oppositionally charted options of Western freedom and Iranian rootedness: 'Freedom had a price' (183).

Thus, subjected to a postsecular analytical lens, Satrapi's novel, produced from the margins, ends by having accomplished a meaningful intervention both into the scholarly studies and the politico-cultural narratives surrounding the 'other' religion. Significantly qualifying the existing discourse on the non-normative/non-Western religion—the faith of the 'other'—Satrapi attacks its force of fundamentalist repression where necessary, reinstates its religious alterity that defies politicised hierarchies, and redirects attention to its actual everyday pragmatics that are premised on confusion and compromise rather than commitment and resolve.

NOTES

1. I will be using the term 'hijab' as a metonymical stand-in to refer to the various kinds of Islamic clothing adopted by women across many different geographical and historical contexts. As Lisa M. La Fornara or Adam Taylor among many others note, the Quran lists three types of dress (*hijab*, *jilbab*, *khimar*) and the vast variety of names and types that are sweeped under common references to the 'hijab' includes the *burqa*, *niqab*, *chador*, *al-amira* and *shayla*.
2. For the purposes of this novel, Satrapi characterises the Marxist notion of rebellion as Western in so far as it derives cultural centrality from its inclusion in the Western theoretical canon and

is understood as a socio-political system that derecognises or devalues religious modes of subjectivity/meaning.

3. Describing the connection between a repressive structure—in this case her mother's dominance over her in the household—and the defiant act of smoking as a mark of protest, Marji remarks that 'the regime became more repressive' (111) and that she rebelled by smoking. This undeterred resolve to revolt, however, is very soon tempered by her violent coughing and the tearful grudging admission of how awful the experience has been, alongside a forced show of revolutionary conviction: 'But this was not the moment to give in' (117).

4. The continuing relevance and even resurgence of this 1970s movement in Egypt, and therefore its prevailing importance for our discussion, becomes evident in several journalistic pieces such as the 2004 reckoning offered by Lisa Anderson.

5. While this is a vast and multi-disciplinary area of scholarship, two quick references will highlight the Western feminist theorisations of this relationship. In the first, Elizabeth Groeneveld analyses the 2006 fashion issue of *BUST* magazine, a 'third-wave publication' that announced on its cover, 'Be a feminist or just dress like one' and presented looks inspired by 'six of feminism's so-called "fashionable feminists"' (179). Groeneveld remarks that the *BUST* fashion spread is 'symptomatic of a set of larger trends within third-wave feminist praxis' which include 'the reclamation of feminism as stylish and sexy' and therefore cast 'feminism in a positive light, as fashionable and desirable, a position clearly contrary to most mainstream media representations of feminist movements', but which also risk 'inscribing feminism solely in terms of personal style' (179). From a fashion history perspective, Keila Tyner and Jennifer Paff Ogle study the *Ms.* Magazine to understand the 'emergence and evolution of dress and the body as topics presented within the modern feminist movement', focusing on two overarching themes—the expression of 'experiences of oppression through dress' and 'experiences of empowerment and self-realization through dress' (74). They analyse the various waves of feminism and approaches to body theorisation to understand the way 'feminist authors have framed the topics of dress and the body as issues germane to the larger women's liberation movement' (75).

6. One only has to look cursorily at recent significant world developments to understand the global currency of these views. A few of the numerous instances include the 2012 Olympic ban of the Iranian women's hijab-clad national soccer team, Angela Merkel's declaration that the full facial veil should be banned wherever legally possible, Marion Anne Perrine's ('Marine' Le Pen) refusal to wear the headscarf for meeting with Lebanon's Grand Mufti, Tony Blair's denunciation of the hijab as a 'mark of separation', French criticism of the Council of Europe's social media campaign on promoting respect for the hijab, and the European Court of Justice's 2021 ruling that made it legal for European Union companies to ban their employees' use of the headscarf under certain conditions.

7. The current endorsement of this correlation between dressing (in its many small variations) and empowerment is played out repeatedly on the global platform. Thus, multiple countries (France, Austria, Switzerland, Netherlands, Belgium, Bulgaria) make a distinction between the *hijab* (head-scarf) and the *burqa/ niqab* (full-face veil with covered or exposed eyes), often banning/ restricting the latter but not the former. Again, in the controversy in Karnataka where veiled Muslim students have been banned from attending classes by certain educational institutions and have been harassed by saffron-clad men, senior advocate Devadatt Kamat challenged Udupi Women's PU College's ban in Karnataka High Court on behalf of his petitioner who had been refused entry into college for wearing a hijab by stating that his client's concern was regarding the *hijab*, which is different from a *burqa* or full-body veil (Sinha).

8. My aim here, and in what I suggest elsewhere in the chapter, is not to discredit what may be the lived reality for many women who seek to garner a semblance of agency when trapped within oppressive patriarchal structures by choosing to make slight variations in dressing patterns that happen to carry subjective meaning for them. Marji gestures towards such realities when she indicates the conscious choice many Iranian women made to use a lipstick or wear a short-length dress in order to feel agentive. However, my analytical energies are invested into discussing how secondary scholarship, anthropological intervention, and Satrapi's work reveals the way external binaries are discursively imposed upon everyday actions performed by (non-Western/Muslim)

people and how these pre-set templates align with the geopolitical agenda to install the domination of the Global North over the rest of the world.

REFERENCES

Abbas, Sadia. 'The Echo Chamber of Freedom: The Muslim Woman and the Pretext of Agency.' *At Freedom's Limit: Islam and the Postcolonial Predicament*. Fordham UP, 2014, pp. 41–71.

Abu-Lughod, Lila. 'Do Muslim Women Really Need Saving? Anthropological Reflections on Cultural Relativism and Its Others.' *American Anthropologist*, vol. 104, no. 3, 2002, pp. 783–90. https://www.jstor.org/stable/3567256.

Ahmed, Leila. *Women and Gender in Islam: Historical Roots of a Modern Debate*. Yale UP, 1993.

Alvi, Anjum. 'Concealment and Revealment: The Muslim Veil in Context.' *Current Anthropology*, vol. 54, no. 2, 2013. https://www.journals.uchicago.edu/doi/full/10.1086/669732

Anderson, Lisa. 'Egypt's Cultural Shift Reflects Islam's Pull.' *Chicago Tribune*, 21 March 2004. https://www.chicagotribune.com/news/chi-0403210513mar21-story.html

Badran, Margot. *Feminism in Islam: Secular and Religious Convergences* (2009). Oneworld Publications, 2013.

Bangstad, Sindre. 'Saba Mahmood and Anthropological Feminism After Virtue.' *Theory, Culture and Society*, vol. 28, no. 3, 2011, pp. 28–54.

Beauvoir, Simone de. *The Second Sex*. 1949. Translated by Constance Borde and Sheila Malovany-Chevallier. Vintage Classics, 2015.

Bosankić, Nina. *Psychosocial Aspects of Niqab Wearing: Religion, Nationalism and Identity in Bosnia and Herzegovina*. Palgrave Macmillan, 2014.

Botshon, Lisa, and Plastas Melinda. 'Homeland In/Security: A Discussion and Workshop on Teaching Marjane Satrapi's *Persepolis*.' *Feminist Teacher*, vol. 20, no. 1, 2009, pp. 1–14. *JSTOR*, www.jstor.org/stable/10.5406/femteacher.20.1.0001.

Darda, Joseph. 'Graphic Ethics: Theorizing the Face in Marjane Satrapi's *Persepolis*.' *College Literature*, vol. 40, no. 2, 2013, pp. 31–51. *JSTOR*, https://www.jstor.org/stable/24543168.

Deeb, Lara. 'Piety Politics and the Role of a Transnational Feminist Analysis.' *Journal of the Royal Anthropological Institute*, vol. 15, 2009, pp. S112–26.

Eltahawy, Mona. 'Ban the Burqa.' *New York Times*, 2 Jul. 2009, https://www.nytimes.com/2009/07/03/opinion/03iht-edeltahawy.html.

Gilmore, Liegh, and Elizabeth Marshall. 'Girls in Crisis: Rescue and Transnational Feminist Autobiographical Resistance.' *Feminist Studies*. Issue on 'Sex and Surveillance', vol. 36, no. 3, 2010, pp. 667–90. *JSTOR*, www.jstor.org/stable/pdf/27919128.pdf.

Groeneveld, Elizabeth. '"Be a Feminist or Just Dress Like One": BUST, Fashion and Feminism as Lifestyle.' *Journal of Gender Studies*, vol. 18, no. 2, 2009, pp. 179–90.

Hamid, Mohsin. *The Reluctant Fundamentalist*. Penguin, 2007.

Harvey, David. *A Brief History of Neoliberalism*. Oxford UP, 2005.

Hashmi, Hera. 'Too Much to Bare?: A Comparative Analysis of the Headscarf in France, Turkey, and the United States.' *University of Maryland Law Journal of Race, Religion, Gender & Class*, vol. 409, 2010. https://digitalcommons.law.umaryland.edu/rrgc/vol10/iss2/8.

Hayder, Mona. 'Hijabi.' *Hijabi*, Tunde Olaniran, 2017, https://www.youtube.com/watch?v=XOX9O_kVPeo.

Henkel, Heiko. 'Between Belief and Unbelief Lies the Performance of Salat: Meaning and Efficacy of a Muslim Ritual.' *Journal of the Royal Anthropological Institute*, vol. 11, 2005, pp. 487–507.

Hirschkind, Charles. *The Ethical Soundscape: Cassette Sermons and Islamic Counterpublics*. Columbia UP, 2006.

Jacobsen, Christine M. 'Troublesome Threesome: Feminism, Anthropology and Muslim Women's Piety.' *Feminist Review*, no. 98, 2011, pp. 65–82. https://doi.org/10.1057/fr.2011.10.

Khalifa, Mia. 'BBC Hard Talk.' Interview by Stephen Sackur. 27 August 2019. https://www.bbc.com/news/av/entertainment-arts-49453376/mia-khalifa-why-i-m-speaking-out-about-the-porn-industry.

Khaliq, Urfan. 'Beyond the Veil?: An Analysis of the Provisions of the Women's Convention in the Law as Stipulated in Shari'ah.' *Buffalo Journal of International Law*, vol. 2, no. 1, 1995.

La Fornara, Lisa M. 'Islam's (In)compatibility with the West?: Dress Code Restrictions in the Age of Feminism.' *Indiana Journal of Global Legal Studies*, vol. 25, no. 1, 2018, pp. 463–94.

Lambek, Michael. 'The Anthropology of Religion and the Quarrel between Poetry and Philosophy.' *Current Anthropology*, vol. 41, 2000, pp. 309–20.

Leservot, Typhaine. 'Occidentalism: Rewriting the West in Marjane Satrapi's *Persépolis*.' *French Forum*, vol. 36, no. 1, 2011, pp. 115–30. JSTOR, https://www.jstor.org/stable/41306680.

Lewis, Reina. Preface. *Veil: Veiling, Representation, and Contemporary Art*. Edited by David A. Bailey and Gilane Tawadros, Institute of International Visual Arts, 2003.

Lipstick Under My Burqa. Directed by Alankrita Shrivastava, performances by Ratna Pathak, Konkana Sen Sharma, Aahana Kumra and, Plabita Borthakur. Prakash Jha Productions, 2017.

Mahmood, Saba. *Politics of Piety: The Islamic Revival and the Feminist Subject*. Princeton UP, 2012.

Mernissi, Fatima. *The Veil and the Male Elite: A Feminist Interpretation of Women's Rights in Islam*. Translated by Mary Jo Lakeland. Addison-Wesley Publications, 1992.

Miller, Kathleen. 'The Other Side of the Coin: A Look at Islamic Law as Compared to Anglo-American Law—Do Muslim Women Really Have Fewer Rights than American Women?' *New York International Law Review*, vol. 16, 2003, pp. 65.

Mogul, Rhea, Manveena Suri, and Swati Gupta. 'Hijab Protests Spread in India as Girls Refuse to be Told What Not to Wear.' *CNN World*. 11 February 2022. https://edition.cnn.com/2022/02/10/india/hijab-karnataka-india-protest-intl-hnk/index.html.

'My hijab is a sign of freedom not oppression.' *BBC News*, 25 April 2019, www.bbc.co.uk/news/av/uk-england-47886842/my-hijab-is-a-sign-of-freedom-not-oppression.

Pandolfo, Stefania. 'The Burning: Finitude and the Politico-Theological Imagination of Illegal Migration.' *Anthropological Theory*, vol. 7, no. 3, 2007, pp. 329–63.

Ranganathan, Bharat. 'Mahmood, Liberalism, and Agency.' *Soundings: An Interdisciplinary Journal*. vol. 99, no. 3, 2016, pp. 246–66.

Sara. Directed by Dariush Mehrjui, performances by Niki Karimi, Amin Tarokh, Khosro Shakibai and Yassamin Maleknasr. Produced by Hashem Seifi, Dariush Mehrjui, and Farabi Cinema Foundation, 1993.

Satrapi, Marjane. *Persepolis: The Story of a Childhood and the Story of a Return*. Vintage, 2008.

---. 'On Writing Persepolis.' *Penguin Random House*. https://www.penguinrandomhouse.com/authors/43801/marjane-satrapi/.

Schielke, Samuli. 'Ambivalent Commitments: Troubles of Morality, Religiosity and Aspiration among Young Egyptians.' *Journal of Religion in Africa*, vol. 39, no. 2, 2009, pp. 158–85.

Schielke, Samuli. 'Second Thoughts about the Anthropology of Islam, or How to Make Sense of Grand Schemes in Everyday Life.' *ZMO Working Papers*, no. 2, 2010. https://d-nb.info/1019243724/34.

Secret Superstar. Directed by Advait Chandan, performances by Zaira Wasim, Meher Vij, and Raj Arjun. Amir Khan Productions, 2017.

Sehlikoglu, Sertaç. 'Revisited: Muslim Women's Agency and Feminist Anthropology of the Middle East.' *Contemporary Islam*, vol. 12, 2018, pp. 73–92. https://link.springer.com/article/10.1007/s11562-017-0404-8

Sex and the City 2. Directed by Michael Patrick King, performances by Sarah Jessica Parker, Kim Cattrall, Kristin Davis and Cynthia Nixon. Produced by New Line Cinema, HBO, and Village Roadshow Pictures, 2010.

Sinha, Bhadra. 'Hijab Case in Karnataka HC.' *The Print*. 9 Feb 2022. https://theprint.in/judiciary/hijab-case-in-karnataka-hc-petitioner-says-its-essential-to-islam-protected-by-constitution/825031/

'Slippery Slope.' *Designated Survivor*, created by David Guggenhiem, season 3, episode 2, ABC Television Network, 7 June 2019.

Surana, Kavitha. 'Update: Conflicting Reports Over Whether ISIS Banned Face Veils in Iraq.' *Foreign Policy*. 6 September 2016. https://foreignpolicy.com/2016/09/06/even-in-isis-territory-a-backlash-for-burqas/.

Taylor, Adam. 'Germany's Potential Burqa Ban has a Problem: Where are the Burqas?' *Washington Post*. 6 December 2016. https://www.washingtonpost.com/news/worldviews/wp/2016/08/19/germanys-potential-burqa-ban-has-a-problem-where-are-the-burqas/.

Tyner, Keila, and Jennifer Paff Ogle. 'Feminist Perspectives on Dress and the Body: An Analysis of Ms. Magazine, 1972 to 2002.' *Clothing & Textiles Research Journal*, vol. 25, no. 1, 2007, pp. 74–105.

Waggoner, Matt. 'Irony, Embodiment, and the "Critical Attitude": Engaging Saba Mahmood's Critique of Secular Modernity.' *Culture and Religion: An Interdisciplinary Journal*, vol. 6, no. 2, 2005, pp. 237–61.

Wilde, Kim. 'We're the Kids in America.' *Never Say Never*, Ricky Wilde and Uwe Fahrenkrog-Petersen, 2006, https://www.youtube.com/watch?v=UqMcevcUmqg.

Other books in the series

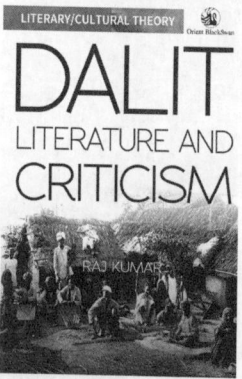

For more information, visit www.orientblackswan.com

Other books in the series

For more information, visit www.orientblackswan.com